Gotham Court

JACOB A. RIIS

HOW THE OTHER HALF LIVES

STUDIES AMONG THE TENEMENTS OF NEW YORK

EDITED BY SAM BASS WARNER, JR.

INTRODUCTION BY ALAN TRACHTENBERG

JOHN
HARVARD
LIBRARY

THE BELKNAP PRESS OF HARVARD UNIVERSITY PRESS

Cambridge, Massachusetts, and London, England   2010

Library of Congress Cataloging-in-Publication Data

Riis, Jacob A. (Jacob August), 1849–1914.
How the other half lives : studies among the tenements of New York /
Jacob A. Riis ; edited by Sam Bass Warner ; introduction by Alan Trachtenberg.
p. cm.
Originally published by same publisher in 1970, with the addition of
an introduction, chronology of Riis's life, and a selected bibliography.
Wherever possible, the engravings based on the Riis's originals that were
included in the 1970 ed. are replaced by Riis's original photographs.
Includes bibliographical references and index.
ISBN 978-0-674-04932-1 (pbk.)
1. Tenement houses—New York (State)—New York.
2. Poor—New York (State)—New York.   I. Title.
HV4046.N6R55   2010
305.5'69097471—dc22   2009043594

Contents

v

Illustrations

Introduction

L OOKING BACK IN 1901 at the runaway success of his first book, published in 1890, Jacob Riis confessed that it had caught him by surprise. "For myself," he wrote a bit coyly, "I have never been able to satisfactorily explain the great run *How the Other Half Lives* had. It is a curiously popular book even today."[1] Why "*curiously* popular?" Was it the lucky coincidence of the publication the same year of William Booth's account of dangers in London slums in *In Darkest England* and of Ward McAllister's gossip about the New York upper elite in *Society as I Have Found It?* Together, though from opposite sides, the two books opened a space perfectly shaped for Riis's New York tenement exposé. Perhaps it was the book's sheer verbal force. "I had it in me so long," he wrote, "that it burst out at last with a rush that caught on." But what does "in me" mean?

Riis implies that the book had possessed him to the degree that he lost control over it; it "burst out," as if on its own accord, "with a rush."

Was it, as Harriet Beecher Stowe said of *Uncle Tom's Cabin*, really out of his hands? Stowe famously confessed that her book came by dictation from above; she merely took it down, a faithful amanuensis. More modest, or ironic, Riis said only that the title "had a deal to do with it" and that "it [book and title] came of itself. Like Topsy, it growed" (*Making*, 309). This not-so-sly reference to *Uncle Tom's Cabin* cleverly clears Riis of suspicion that he shares Mrs. Stowe's hubristic claim of divine intervention; just "growed," like Topsy, is a sassy little joke he shares with readers likely to catch the allusion and its wit. But even ironic, his identification with the author of *Uncle Tom's Cabin* confirms the evangelical element in Riis's view of himself and his work.

Similarly, Riis's mention of the book's title is more than a throwaway line. Far from coming "of itself," the title came ultimately from Rabelais's *Pantagruel,* where the narrator, having just discovered an entire land complete with cities and farms inside the mouth of the giant Pantagruel, remarks that "one half of the world knoweth not how the other half liveth; considering that no one has yet written of that Country." The relation between what is known and what is written goes unstated in Riis's appropriation but the implication remains. Just as Rabelais's narrator claims to have written a "great book" on the history of the Gorgians, inhabitants of Pantagruel's gorge, Riis will bring the realm of the tenement, with its dark gorge-like lineaments, within compass of the known by means of a book.

The title came to Riis, as he explained in his autobiography, in another Stowe-like moment. Covering a meeting in 1888 of New York ministers "concerned about the losing fight the Church was waging among the masses," he heard a speaker cry out, "How are these men and women to understand the love of God you speak of, when they see only the greed of man?" Riis wanted to jump and yell "Amen." "I had my text" (*Making*, 248). Later that winter he scribbled out a title page and had it copyrighted. It opens with unacknowledged homage to Rabelais: "One Half the World does not know how the other Half Lives"; then, the title of a lecture already given: "The Other Half, How it lives and Dies in New York"; and below: "With one hundred illustrations, photographs from real life, of the haunts of poverty and vice in the great city." Next follows his name and who he was: "police reporter of the New York Tribune and the Associated Press at Police Headquarters."[2]

Riis acted prudently in registering the copyright, recognizing a good idea for a book when he saw it. Apart from the glimpse of Riis's entrepreneurial side, the mock-up reveals an opportune concept of a book on the order of popular "city mysteries" with titles such as "Secrets of the Great City," "Sunshine and Shadow," "The Nether Side," "Mysteries and Miseries of America's Great Cities"—titles that promise titillation among the forbidden sights of the big city. A typical blurb announced, "Few living in the great city have any idea of the terrible romance and the hard reality of the lives of two thirds of the inhabitants." Half, two-thirds, or the three-quarters Riis himself claims in his book—the exact number matters less than there being any number at all to clutch. Riis's revelations speak little of "vice" and crime; he writes not to tease or titillate but to arouse moral conscience and outrage at social injustice. Borrowing from sensationalist devices of the "city mystery" genre—"unmasking social evils"—Riis has other ends in view, though his use of the conventions and rhetoric of the genre (the guided tour, for example) sometimes colors perception in lurid hues. On the whole, the new life he breathed into the popular genre lay in the realism of actual observation, including the poorly reproduced photographs, and his fresh use of pedagogy, sermon, and sentiment.

Older versions of the city mystery proffered the safety of vicarious experience in the form of verbal spectacles. Another blurb promises that "[the reader's] curiosity can be satisfied in these pages, without incurring the danger attending an effort to see it." Seeing in the flesh runs real risks in the territory of the "other half." Spectacle keeps the viewer/reader at a safe distance. But the camera complicates the matter. As Riis's narrative shows, the camera has its own dangers—the flash powder can, and on occasion did, ignite fires and injure the photographer's face. But printed on a page side-by-side with text, the camera image offers a secure way of encountering the real city without bodily harm. It would not be until the 1970s that the public would have a chance to see photographs and text together on a page the way Riis imagined it. Coincidentally the 1970s also witnessed radical reappraisals of Riis's classic book.[3] Revised estimates of the book together with restored accessibility of the photographs and better understanding of their origins and functions have resulted in a text whose history of changing interpretations makes it an even more enticing and revealing work.

That he planned to include a hundred photographs in the first edition reveals how important the camera became to him as an adjunct to the pen. He had learned of flash photography in 1887 and persuaded friends to help him make photographs exposing evidence of overcrowding and squalor in dark places.[4] Eventually he took up the camera himself—he called himself "a photographer, after a fashion" —and experimented in conjoining reform and journalism into a composite mode of picturing and writing. The camera provided irrefutable proof; "my negatives, still dripping from the darkroom," could not be gainsaid (*Making*, 273). Copied as glass slides and projected onto a screen, these images created an extraordinary illusion of being at the scene of the picture. Their immediacy was overwhelming.

Neither Riis nor anyone else took his photography as a permanent part of his identity; it was only for the sake of the irrefutable that he took up the camera in the first place, and after a few years he put it down again, pictures and negatives shoved into a closet and lost for some forty years. Their recovery in the 1940s marked a new era in the understanding of Jacob Riis, now revealed as an extraordinary pioneer of social realism in photography. For about three years before the book appeared and for many years subsequently, Riis presented his photographs with commentary in his "magic lantern" slide lectures. The importance of this mode cannot be stressed enough. Projection of photographs printed on glass slides gave an even brighter and more brilliant experience than later "fine" printing. For readers of the book who had attended the lectures, the flat halftone reproductions must have been a letdown, whatever other rewards the printed text offered. Even in their less-than-luminous state in the original edition, the photographs make it all the more apparent how personal a book this is, how much it tells of the author's own experience, how much the author's eye represented by the photographs works in tandem with his voice, image and words together casting him as the ever-present narrator in an artfully composed story.[5]

The photographs are a major achievement, stunning encounters with a reality never before seen in American visual art. Riis's pictures give the concept of "the other half" a vital presence, a material and a human reality not only irrefutable, but, once seen, never to be forgotten. Pictures like "Bandit's Roost," "In the Home of an Italian Rag-Picker," "A Black-and-Tan Dive in 'Africa,'" and "Hunting River Thieves" are icons of social realism in American photography, the tradition called "documentary." In retrospect they lay out an agenda for later documentary work, depicting material living conditions in underclass regions of the city: interiors where people live and work in the same grimy, dingy spaces; alleys like narrow valleys formed by overhanging tenement blocks; marketplaces dense with pushcarts and dense with people; random patterns of walkers in the streets;

children, "street Arabs," shooting craps, sleeping in doorways; drunks splayed against sidewalks; "lodgers" scattered like lifeless bundles on police-station floors. Like Riis's prose, the pictures evoke noise and stench, the whole physical and psychological condition of poverty: squalor, degradation, humiliation in the face of the camera's often violent—the burst of the flash—intrusion. The pictures also allude to an entire repertoire of newspaper drawings and engravings of "lower order" types and scenes, rendering the conventional newly vivid and credible and "real" as photographs.

With traces of spontaneity visible in their composition, the pictures project an illusion that we are there at the making of the exposure. This is often an effect of the flash, or rather, an effect of the expression on the face of the person disclosed as if just jolted from sleep or puzzled by the disturbance. The pictures usually show the point of interest in the center of the frame; sometimes groups of people are dispersed across the frontal plane of the image. The pictures give an overwhelming sense of a material world on the edge of decay, a world about to collapse into clutter and detritus. The photographs are not exactly parallel texts to the writing; they are presented in the book, and presumably were presented in the slide lectures as well, as illustrations, pictures of the way the world looks as if through an open window, not as subjects or artifacts or creative expressions in their own right. They themselves, as crafted visual objects, are not what is discussed but adjuncts to the discussion. This may be a clue to why Riis gave up photography so soon. Perhaps he never practiced it as an artist conscious of having pictorial intentions appropriate to the medium. Still, his pictures mark an incandescent moment in American visual art.

"Full of life and color," wrote one reviewer about the text of the book; disheartening but "extremely profitable reading." Riis's pictures, wrote another reviewer, "dark and ominous in line and color, ought to stir in the prosperous, the happy, and the indolent a sense of the misery of a large part of their fellow beings, and stimulate them to practical action." And another, typifying the tenor of reviews of the first edition of the book: "*How the Other Half Lives* is a department of knowledge which modern society must master if it would preserve itself."[6] An anatomy of squalor brought home to readers from somewhere else, a place other than where likely readers were presumed to live, the book captivated even the most genteel of readers. James Russell Lowell, who had earlier granted permission for use of his poem "With Gates of Silver and Gates of Gold" as an epigraph, wrote to Riis after reading the book: "I felt as Dante must when he looked over the edge of the abyss at the bottom of which Gorgon lay in ambush. I had but a vague idea of these horrors before you brought them so feelingly home to me" (*Making*, 308). Lowell caught the essential fact of the "other half," that it's an abyss on the edge of which we stand, looking down. A dangerous perch: the Gorgon defending the gates of the City of Dis in Dante's *Inferno* might choose to turn us to stone. The frisson of dread serves Riis's purpose to awaken the will to reform out of self-interest as much as benevolence. "I cannot conceive," Lowell added in his letter, "how such a book should fail of doing great good, if it moves other people as it has moved me." The final words of *How the Other Half Lives* come again from Lowell, making America's premier "polite" poet a collaborator of sorts: "—Think ye that building shall endure / Which shelters the noble and crushes the poor?"[7]

When *How the Other Half Lives* appeared, Jacob Riis held a conspicuous place in the overlapping worlds of journalism and reform. He was forty-one years old, a star police reporter for the *New York Tribune,* and a lecturer in churches on the "evils" of the tenement-house—a journalist and an evangel for reform. A growing number of middle-class and upper-class philanthropic, civic, and church groups had emerged in response to the deepening misery of the urban poor of the 1880s he had taken up the cause of reform and the mantle of crusader, his writing rang with the timbre of a distinctive voice.

Riis felt great affection for his birthplace in Denmark, Ribe, and credited it for his love of nature, family, and home. He also took special pride in his Danish heritage of Vikings and crusaders. "When I put on the old crusader's cross which King Christian sent me," he wrote, "and think of the valiant knights who wore it, I feel glad and proud that, however far behind, I may ride in their train" (*Making*, 291). He wore the cross "gladly," he wrote; "for the knighthood it confers pledges to the defense of women and of little children, and if I cannot wield lance and sword as the king's men of old, I can wield the pen" (*Making*, 430). Of course Riis was no royalist but a solid Republican of the party of Lincoln and of abolition, though to the annoyance of party bosses he was known to support an occasional Democratic office-seeker. Neither was he foolishly quixotic. The term crusader served as a practical perspective, a figure of speech that endowed his pen with the power of lance and sword, stalwart weapon in a good fight.

Riis himself had known hard times during his early years in America. He had come not to flee persecution or the trap of grinding poverty, like the masses that filled city slums, but to escape the adolescent smart of a rejection by the daughter of the richest man in town. When she relented and became his wife, the sentimental plot of the life story with which he often began his church lectures came full circle, a happy American ending. A new immigrant in the early 1870s, he had knocked around for about three years, an itinerant laborer looking for work, something to eat, a place to rest at night, "some sheltering ash-bin or doorway." "I joined the great army of tramps" (*Making*, 66). This was not an impersonation or disguise for romantic adventure, not what one critic has called "class transvestism."[8] Riis first discovered America from the underside, distinctly the "other half." His foreign accent earned him the nickname "the Dutchman." His years as an outsider on the skids taught him what it was like on the other side. After a few years of scratching out his survival by wit, luck, and the down-and-outer's bag of tricks, his fortune changed, there came a break, and he settled into his life-long vocation as a police reporter and crusader for the good.

Lincoln Steffens, fellow reporter and friend on the police beat at the Mulberry Street headquarters on the Lower East Side, recalled Riis in the early 1890s as someone who "not only got the news but cared about the news." And Riis "could write." He wrote the news "as stories, with heart, humor, and understanding."

> He hated passionately all tyrannies, abuses, miseries, and he fought them. He was a "terror" to the officials and landlords responsible, as he saw it, for the desperate condition of the tenements where the poor lived. He had "exposed" them in articles, books, and public speeches, and with results.[9]

Riis had a story of his own to tell, the plot of which is encapsulated in the title of his autobiography, *The Making of an American*. The story of his rise from outcast immigrant to respected public figure, contented family man, and secure owner of a home in the suburbs adjoins and implicitly informs his story of the "other half."

Passion for fame along with security for his family also fed his drive for success. What Riis strived for, a middling worldly success along with prestige, was the inverse of the condition he found among the dwellers of the tenements. While his own story might be taken as an implicit reproach to feckless and despondent tenement-house people, their story, the story he wrote of them, gave powerful negative support to his own. Riis does not make this reciprocal-if-inverted relation to his subject explicit in *How the Other Half Lives*, though it runs between the lines. Riis's perspective on tenement-house culture is inevitably influenced by his own experience as what he called a self-made American.

Riis's interest in the tenements evolved in the mid-1880s. It was inspired in part by Felix Adler, founder of the Society for Ethical Culture, who in 1884 gave an influential series of public lectures on "the Tenement House Question." Riis covered the lectures, as well as meetings of the Tenement House Commission, which was established the same year by the New York state legislature spurred by Adler's lectures. Riis was attracted to Adler's fusion of moral fervor and practical proposals for combining private and public enterprises.[10] Adler's moralism stopped short of blaming slum dwellers for slum conditions. "It is not the squalid people that make the squalid homes," he wrote, "but the squalid homes that make the squalid people." Riis adopted the same view, an environmental determinism or sociological outlook. He deliberately eschewed social theory, preferring to worry over practical solutions rather than conceptual formulations. Riis's ethical instincts together with his journalist's training turned him toward individual lives, to what it meant to be poor, what it looked like, how it felt. "Squalid," Riis agreed with Adler, referred to a way of life, not to the people living that way by necessity. Riis was the first American writer to carry such questions into actual investigations; at the turn of the century and later there came a host of younger impassioned writers like Jack London, Stephen Crane, Walter Wyckoff, Bessie and Marie Van Vorst, and Theodore Dreiser, former newspaperman, who traced the descent of Hurstwood from flop house to flop house with rigorous yet empathic detachment in *Sister Carrie* (1900). Mike Gold's *Jews without Money* (1930), a passionately vivid account of growing up in a Lower East Side tenement at the turn of the century, and James Agee and Walker Evans's *Let Us Now Praise Famous Men* (1841), the most compelling American documentary excursion across the poverty line, also belong among Riis's distinguished progeny.

Riis raised the tenement into a looming symbol of intransigent social difference. As if quarantined to the narrow, cramped streets and alleys of lower Manhattan, including "the most densely populated district in the world" (*Other Half*, 10), the tenements stood as grim reminders of class conflict; like ancient fortresses or cliff-dwellings encrusted with dirt and grime, they were terrible to look at and fearful to contemplate. Yet there was a certain frisson in the subject; portrayed as markers of absolute difference—not only social and economic but ethnic and cultural—the tenements were fascinating in their terribleness.

What sort of book is *How the Other Half Lives?* Its status as pioneer social reportage is unchallenged. As an account of what was there to be seen in these particular places, *How the Other Half Lives* has no peers. It is also a remarkable piece of writing, a work of non-fiction crafted by a master journalist who has been to school with master novelists like Charles Dickens. An artful mingling of genres—reportage, storytelling, history, statistical description, sermon, picture book—the book is best understood as a personal narrative, a narrative of discovery told in the first person. The opening sentence of the preface announces this primary fact about the book: "The belief that every man's experience ought to be worth something to the community from which he drew it, no matter what that experience may be, so long as it was obtained in the line of some decent, honest work, made me begin this book" (*Other Half*, xix). By "experience" Riis means the content of the book itself, the results of the narrator's "decent, honest work" of observing and witnessing. By "community from which he drew it," Riis means both the tenements and the community known as "the public," the divided community of separate halves. The book gives itself back as something of *worth*, worth earned by the honest labor it represents, and worth measured by the good it might do. Also, the reference to "every man's experience" expands the range of worth to embrace even poor slum dwellers, the *worthy* poor whose honesty and perseverance provide a model of worth itself. The reciprocity intimated here suggests an important idea of equality, linking the narrator's experience with that of "every man," but the book does not always live up to this opening egalitarian gesture.

In thinking about the kind of book this is, it's useful to keep in mind the intertwining of a voice that speaks of physical places and statistical facts, and a voice that speaks of people, the human component of the "other half." In the introduction Riis cites a report after the "great riot" of 1863—the Draft Riots—that refers to tenements as "nurseries of crime" where inhabitants have "lost connection with home life." Tenements destroy "the ordinary wholesome influences of home and family" (*Other Half*, 2). Material places have determinative powers: in Riis's words, "the dark bedroom, prolific of untold depravities" (*Other Half*, 8). Or, this passage quoted from a report by the Society for the Improvement of the Condition of the Poor:

> Crazy old buildings, crowded rear tenements in filthy yards, dark, damp basements, leaking garrets, shops, outhouses, and stables converted into dwellings, though scarcely fit to shelter brutes, are habitations of thousands of our fellow-beings in this wealthy, Christian city. (*Other Half,* 14)

The physical detail in this passage and the irony of "this wealthy, Christian city" set the stage for the major action of the book—its discourse on the poor, their miseries, their drudgery, their creative and even hopeful shifts for survival. It's a stage, we soon learn, on which not "half" but a statistical "three-fourths" of New York's population dwells in some thirty-seven thousand tenements, up from fifteen thousand a generation earlier. The book opens upon a gloomy picture of worsening conditions, while uncaring landlords garner profits of between 15 and 30 percent. Although they have not yet appeared in the early pages of the book, the tenants are introduced proleptically as victims of an oppressive physical environment and a system of exploitation they are helpless to overcome.

It's indicative that Riis often refers to the role of perception in the telling of the tale. "It all depends on the angle from which one sees it which is right," he writes, appropriately for a photographer. At stake in this instance is how to identify "overcrowding," at best a relative term. To the professional or official sanitarian, there's one set of numbers, for the "unsalaried agitator" or reformer, another. What one sees depends on how one sees, from what set of interests and values.

> Under the pressure of the Italian influx the standard of breathing space required for an adult by the health officers has been cut down from six to four hundred cubic feet. The "needs of the situation" is their plea, and no more perfect argument could be advanced for the reformer's position. (*Other Half,* 67)

In many ways the entire book is an account of conflicting perspectives derived from conflicting values. There is always "another story to tell"; for example, the huge counter story only hinted at: "A story of thousands of devoted lives, laboring earnestly to make the most of their scant opportunities for good; of heroic men and women striving patiently against odds and by their courage coming off victor in the battle with the tenement" (*Other Half,* 161).

The preface speaks of a definitive conflict between "a purely economic point of view" and "the outlook from a Christian standpoint." The expediency of the sanitarians earns Riis's acerbic sarcasm, a device he used frequently to underscore differences of point of view and affirm his own. Apart from public controversies between reformers and officialdom, Riis pursues the viewpoints of the tenants themselves. Statistics that indicate worsening conditions and details of the grim environment represent his broad sociological outlook, an outlook that includes historical genealogy of the tenement as a housing form and its decline into the dissolute slum dwelling. Rather than contradicting the sociological, the standpoint he calls Christian supplements it with concern for the day-to-day conditions of the poor. Riis wants to know and to tell what it's like to live on the edge, besieged by hunger, disease, noise, fetid air, unsafe water, constant darkness in cellar quarters or rooms without windows. Despair, despondency, and desolation instantly assault the senses, yet Riis looks for signs of life. His report, hardly cheerful but not utterly hopeless, survives as a major expression of a white Anglo-Saxon American middle-class effort to imagine social difference and ethnic otherness. It's in his response to the class beneath his own—professional, suburban, propertied—and to racial and ethnic difference that Riis reveals his conflicted and contradictory bourgeois character: compassionate yet given to fear, confident yet insecure, quick to judge but also to forgive, moralistic yet accepting, at ease with power yet a sentimental democrat.

Among the mostly positive reviews of How the Other Half Lives, one struck a dissonant note that has since resonated. "There is a lack of broad and penetrative vision," the reviewer complained, "a singularly warped sense of justice at times, and a roughness amounting almost to brutality. The 'Heathen Chinee' and the Russian Jew fleeing from persecution in his own land, find no mercy in Mr. Riis's book."[11] Such merciless comments abound in the book: the "imperturbable cheerfulness" of "the negro" (Other Half, 153); "the Italian is gay, light-hearted . . . inoffensive as a child" (Other Half, 53); the Chinese "serve no useful purpose here" (Other Half, 102); as for Jews, "money is their God" (Other Half, 107). The presence of unambiguous ethnic and racial stereotypes and slurs is a major stumbling block for readers of the book. Some readers excuse the offensive terms as a reflex of Riis's times, less terrible than, say, Henry Adams's anti-Semitism or Henry James's ethnic stereotypes (Jews as monkeys) in *The American Scene* (11907); moreover, except for the Chinese, whom he shamelessly defames, he usually finds something praiseworthy to say along with the scurrilous. About Negroes, he is sensitive to the burdens of discrimination they face (*Other Half*, 139–140), and he admires Jewish "native combativeness" that has survived "oppression, persecution" (*Other Half*, 109).

But the bias of the book is unmistakably in favor of what Riis calls "a distinctively American community" (*Other Half*, 21). He means native-born whites. In the chapter called "The Mixed Crowd," he ticks off its members: "One may find for the asking an Italian, a German, a French, African, Spanish, Bohemian, Russian, Scandinavian, Jewish, and Chinese colony. Even the Arab" (*Other Half*, 21). Who then is the American? You need to speak English, to begin, in order to qualify, and then, as his own *The Making of an American* will try to show, you need to *make* yourself into a good property-owning citizen. But the issue is murky even in his autobiography, as it was and is in reality. From the point of view of ethnicity, race, and nationality, "American" remains a problematic identity: open to everyone in principle, yet still exclusionary in some minds on grounds of cultural difference.

"Mixed crowd" versus "a distinctively American community" points to the deepest contradiction in Riis's undertaking: the effort to "know" the other half as both poor and of mixed origins. He well understands that "poor" names a class position, not an inherent but an imposed condition. He has great clarity about the class situation of the tenement poor. "The necessities of the poor," he writes, "become the opportunity of their wealthier neighbors" (*Other Half*, 8). To be generous to Riis, we might speculate that his shameful recourse to ethnic and racial stereotypes seems less a reflexive act of absolute prejudice than a mistaken attempt to understand the poor by their shared ethnic *culture* rather than their shared poverty, their solidarity as *poor*. At one point a recognition breaks through:

> The readiness of the poor to share what little they have with those who have even less is one of the few moral virtues of the tenements. Their enormous crowds touch elbows in closeness of sympathy that is scarcely to be understood out of them, and has no parallel except among the unfortunate women whom the world scorns as outcasts. (*Other Half,* 172)

Beyond ethnicity! A fascinating passage in which Riis seems to surpass himself in recognizing that the tenement poor themselves, even the "unfortunate women" he identifies with the euphemism "outcasts," provide the model of selfless sympathy, charity, and good acts he seeks to awaken in his readers. There's perhaps a hint of recognition here that ethnicity may be a self-protective garment worn by immigrants who naturally cluster together and try to maintain common ways in a strange and unwelcoming land.

A superb police reporter, Riis is less trustworthy as an ethnographer. What he seems to mean by culture is little more than stereotypes, the baggage of prejudices that come along with having made himself into that figure of cultural myth, "the American." Riis must be credited with a genuine wish to know and to understand the poor, but chastised for confusing stereotype with reality. In pursuit of the inner life or phenomenology of poverty, he stumbled over received prejudices, though not without memorable flashes of how things are.

The narrator offers himself as cicerone on the descending stairs of hell; he tells of hearing the father of an infant just dead from measles say to his wife, "need we complain—such as we?"

> Such as we! What if the words ring in your ears as we grope our way up the stairs and down from floor to floor, listening to the sounds behind closed doors—some of quarrelling, some of coarse songs, more of profanity. They are true. (*Other Half,* 44)

This is persuasive writing. It's the true sounds, the true sights of these nether regions that Riis contracts with his reader to reproduce and to interpret. But not sounds and sights alone. Riis wants to grasp the inner life, the mentality of human life under these conditions. "What sort of an answer, think you, would come from these tenements to the question 'Is life worth living?'" *Worth* again. Riis poses the question after telling the story of a mother who had thrown herself out a window. "No doubt she was wrong in not taking life philosophically, as did the four families a city missionary found housekeeping in the four corners of one room. They got along well enough together until one of the families took a boarder and made trouble" (*Other Half*, 47).

Riis in fact guided distinguished visitors through the tenements, most famously the then commissioner of police Theodore Roosevelt, with whom he developed a close lifetime friendship. But in the book, addressing his readers' imagination, he urges that they make the visit themselves: "You shall come away agreeing with me that, humanly speaking, life there does not seem worth the living" (*Other Half*, 162). "Humanly speaking"! The alternative to answering the question with a "nay" is a hard-nosed stoicism—or, with cynical realism, "the saloon, always handy, as the refuge from every trouble." Tenement dwellers are seen as victims of degrading circumstances rather than as persons capable of shaping their own lives and their environment. But it is exactly this existential deadening of love of life, the birthright of all people, that Riis charges as the worst crime of the tenements: theft of the desire to live. Riis means this to be an optimistic book. "We can dimly discern behind it all that good is somehow working out of even this slough of despond" (*Other Half*, 281). But it's the existential question that Riis leaves us to ponder. "Tenement houses have no aesthetic resources" (*Other Half*, 163). The question is not whether poverty can be made bearable, but whether, humanly speaking, the rest of society can live in peace with itself while hearing its "other" ask, "Is life worth living?"

How the Other Half Lives rises above its worst moments because its best moments remain so good. Riis cares about the way environment can block or stimulate, can deprive or nourish human well-being. It's a book of exceptional witnessing: "I am satisfied from my own observation that hundreds of men, women, and children are every day slowly starving to death in the tenements" (Other Half, 170–171). The book is still capable of making us feel we are seeing certain things for the first time. For although these particular tenements are gone, and, in a familiar irony of revived districts of inner cities, swanky residences now stand in their place, we know that the circumstances pictured in How the Other Half Lives have counterparts today, that injustices and inequalities in living conditions remain, and that vast regions of the space we share with others remain out of sight, still hidden in darkness.

Notes

1. Jacob A. Riis, *The Making of an American* (New York: The Macmillan Company, 1901), 309. Page numbers in the text refer to this edition.

2. Quoted in Bonnie Yochelson and Daniel Czitrom, *Rediscovering Jacob Riis: Exposure Journalism and Photography in Turn-of-the-Century New York* (New York: The New Press, 2007), 146–147.

3. The strongest example is Sally Stein, "Making Connections with the Camera: Photography and Social Mobility in the Career of Jacob Riis," *Afterimage* 10, no. 10 (May 1983): 9–16.

4. On his flashlight tenement excursions starting in 1887 Riis was joined principally by Dr. John T. Nagel of the health department and two members of the New York Society of Amateur Photographers, Dr. Henry G. Piffard, a surgeon, and Richard Hoe Lawrence, a banker. For fuller discussion of the authorship of the photographs, see Maren Stange, *Symbols of Ideal Life: Social Documentary Photography in America, 1890–1950* (New York: Cambridge University Press, 1989), 1–29.

5. On the "magic lantern" slide lectures, see Ferenc M. Szasz and Ralph F. Bogardus, "The Camera and the American Social Conscience: The Documentary Photography of Jacob A. Riis," *New York History* 55, no. 4 (October 1974): 409–436.

6. Louise Ware, *Jacob A. Riis: Police Reporter, Reformer, Useful Citizen* (New York: D. Appleton-Century Co., 1938), 74.

7. Jacob A. Riis, *How the Other Half Lives* (New York: Charles Scribner's Sons, 1890), 297. Page numbers in the text refer to this edition.

8. Eric Schocket, "Undercover Explorations of the 'Other Half,' Or the Writer as Class Transvestite," *Representations* 64 (Fall 1998): 109–133.

9. Lincoln Steffens, *The Autobiography of Lincoln Steffens* (New York: The Literary Guild, 1931), 203–204.

10. Yochelson and Czitrom, *Rediscovering Jacob Riis,* 60–61.

11. Quoted in Ware, *Jacob A. Riis,* 75.

Note on the Text

How the Other Half Lives has been in print since its original publication in 1890, except for the period 1947–1957. The John Harvard Library edition is an exact reprinting of the first edition of November 1890 (text and appendix), except for the modernization of spelling and punctuation. There is no evidence the text was altered in a second edition of March 1891 or subsequent printings.

Modern explanatory notes and citations for material quoted by Riis were prepared for a 1970 John Harvard Library edition by Sam Bass Warner, Jr., and are reprinted here with few changes. Explanatory notes gloss names, places, and terms no longer familiar to readers. Regarding citations, Sam Bass Warner, Jr., writes, "it seemed worthwhile to make it possible for the modern reader to note Riis's sources. Accordingly, most of the citations of the text have been tracked down, and Riis's references have been amplified into modern notes. An occasional glance at these [endnotes] will thus reveal to the reader the genealogy of Riis's information."

The line engravings that appeared in the first edition of *How the Other Half Lives* were based chiefly on Riis's own photographs. Here, where possible, these engravings are replaced by Riis's always more interesting and vivid photography. For the John Harvard Library edition, prints have been made from the original photographs in the Jacob A. Riis Collection at the Museum of the City of New York. Several line engravings have been retained from the first edition and appear in their original placement in the text.

The Jacob A. Riis Collection at the Museum of the City of New York comprises the most complete compilation of Riis's pioneering works of photojournalism, including 415 original negatives, 326 glass lantern slides, and 191 vintage prints made by Riis in the 1880s and 1890s. After his death in 1914, Riis's collection was transferred to his family, where it remained largely undiscovered in an attic on Long Island. In 1946 the photographer's son, Roger William Riis, donated Riis's photographic works to the Museum of the City of New York. Although Riis considered himself a social reformer and not a photographer, today his works are valued by social and photographic historians alike.

Chronology of Jacob A. Riis's Life

1849   Born on May 3 in Ribe, in Jutland, Denmark, to Niels Riis, schoolteacher in the Ribe Latin School and part-time editor of the local paper, and Caroline Riis, homemaker and gifted storyteller. Third in a family of fourteen children and one foster child; ten siblings would die untimely deaths. Reads English as a child, favorite authors Charles Dickens and James Fenimore Cooper, along with Hans Christian Andersen. Helps his father in the editing of news, including reading proof.

1860   On July 6 his nine-year-old brother drowns in the Ribe River, a severe loss for his mother, who keeps the boy's chair at the dining table for years; Riis haunted by the experience.

1862   Often-mentioned episode: at age twelve Riis gives away his Christmas money to a needy family in Ribe.

1864   Performs poorly in grade school and is often troubled by disciplinary problems, to his father's disapproval. Decides on vocational training and starts apprenticeship as carpenter. Tries to enlist during war with Germany, rejected because only fifteen years old at the time. Falls in love with twelve-year-old Eliza-

1864   beth Dorothea Nielsen, adopted daughter of leading Ribe industrialist.

1865–1869   Continues apprenticeship with master builder in Copenhagen for four years. Proposes to Elizabeth, but is rejected by her father. Full-fledged member of the Carpenter's Guild but unable to find a job; without work or wife in Denmark, decides to leave for America.

1870–1873   Departs Ribe May 1, via Copenhagen and Glasgow, arrives at New York's Castle Garden June 5. Often unemployed and homeless during these years of "working and wandering," part of "the great army of tramps"; travels to upstate New York, New Jersey, western Pennsylvania, Ohio, Chicago, working as a miner, a brickyard and shipyard worker, lumberjack, farm hand, a salesman of flat irons and of subscriptions to novels by Charles Dickens. Tries unsuccessfully to enlist on the French side of the Franco-German war. Learns of Elizabeth's betrothal.

1873–1874   Panic of 1873, high unemployment. Henry George's *Progress and Poverty: An Inquiry into the Cause of Industrial Depression and of Increase of Want with Increase of Wealth* published. Riis finds job as reporter with New York News Association, then with *South Brooklyn News* (small local paper); soon promoted to editor; purchases the paper for $650—$75 from savings, the rest borrowed. Elizabeth's fiancé dies.

1875–1876   Pays off debt, then resells the paper at 500 percent profit. Elizabeth accepts his renewed offer of marriage. They marry in March 1876 in Ribe cathedral and set up housekeeping in rooms near Prospect Park, Brooklyn. Riis resumes reporting for the *News*, writes series of articles exposing high prices for small rooms of boardinghouses.

1877   Resigns from the *News* over political disagreements with owners—Democratic Party politicians unhappy with Riis's support of a Republican candidate. Son George Edward Valdemar born on February 22. Riis buys magic lantern slide projector and goes into business using slides to advertise farm-supply stores. In Elmira during nationwide railroad strike, he and his partner are caught between strikers and militia, forced to leave town; in Scranton they are attacked by strikers and abandon the business. Later Riis describes strikers as lawless troublemakers.

Hired on trial basis by the *New York Tribune,* soon made police reporter, covers police headquarters on Mulberry Street on Lower East Side, begins career as investigative journalist.

1878–1883 From press room on Mulberry Street covers stories of crime, fires, gangs, street life, epidemic disease. Becomes friends with Health Department officials, including Dr. Roger S. Tracy and Dr. John T. Nagel, whom he often accompanies on regular inspections of the tenements. Becomes known as "the Dutchman" or "Jake." Daughter Clara born 1880. Son John born 1882.

1884 Covers hearings of the Tenement House Commission chaired by Dr. Felix Adler and appointed by the state legislature to inquire into housing conditions in New York City. Grows increasingly interested in "the Tenement House Question."

1885 Becomes American citizen.

1886 Eager for a place in the country distant from the slums, moves with family into newly built house in Richmond Hill, Long Island; site and house bought with help of friends. Becomes increasingly involved with New York reform groups such as Charity Organization Society, Childrens' Aid Society, Society for the Prevention of Cruelty to Children, and others. Son Stephen born, dies within a year.

1887 Interest in photographs as evidence begins when he reads about recently developed flash powder for use with camera in darkness. First photographic excursions or "invasions" into tenements at night with friends from sanitation police and New York Society of Amateur Photographers; Riis begins preparing slides of the results for magic lantern lectures.

1888 Teaches himself to use a camera. First lecture with slides based on tenement photographs made with flash, "The Other Half: How It Lives and Dies in New York," January 25 for the New York Society of Amateur Photographers; later given at other venues. On February 12, publishes article in the *New York Sun,* "Flashes from the Slums: Pictures Taken in Dark Places by the Lightning Process." In March Riis secures copyright for title page for "The Other Half: How It Lives and Dies in New York." In May, two-part article on "the Tenement Question" appears in the *Christian Union* magazine. Supported by prominent churchmen Dr. Josiah Strong and Dr. Adolph Stauffer, Riis is invited

1888   to lecture at the Broadway Tabernacle, launching a phenomenal career as church lecturer; also helped by prominent Christian crusader against corruption and vice Charles Parkhurst.

1889   "How the Other Half Lives" appears in December *Scribner's* magazine as article with nineteen engraved copies of photographs; Riis urged by editor of *The Critic* to expand it into a book for Charles Scribner's Sons. Becomes involved in settlement house movement and with King's Daughters, a Christian service group.

1890   Begins book manuscript in January, completes it in ten months. *How the Other Half Lives* published in November, becomes a best seller. Theodore Roosevelt, then president of New York city police board, leaves card with message: "I have read your book, and I have come to help." Warm friendship ensues. Riis resigns from New York News Association, moves from *New York Tribune* to *New York Sun*.

1891   Max Frischel starts work at the *Sun* as Riis's news gatherer. Riis breaks story about sewage in the Croton water supply.

1892   *The Children of the Poor* published, sequel to *How the Other Half Lives*. Helen Campbell's *Darkness and Daylight: Or Lights and Shadows of New York Life* published, including several uncredited reproductions of Riis photographs.

1894   Plans to demolish Mulberry Bend set in motion. Riis increasingly active in "good government" and other reform clubs. Son Roger Williams born on March 4.

1895   Riis leads Roosevelt, now police commissioner of New York, on midnight-to-dawn tour of Lower East Side police posts and of police lodging rooms that Riis battled against.

1896   Roosevelt closes police lodging rooms in February.

1897   Small Park Act passed, as recommended by Tenement Commission. Most of the tenements identified as the worst are demolished. Mulberry Bend Park (now Columbus Park) opens June 15.

1898   Campaigns for Roosevelt for Governor of New York. *Out of Mulberry Street* published.

1900   *A Ten Years' War* published. Roosevelt declares "Jacob Riis is New York's most useful citizen" and also calls him "the best

American I ever knew." Overworked and often exhausted, Riis develops angina and shortness of breath; enlarged heart is diagnosed.

HOW THE OTHER HALF LIVES

Preface

THE BELIEF THAT every man's experience ought to be worth something to the community from which he drew it, no matter what that experience may be, so long as it was gleaned along the line of some decent, honest work, made me begin this book. With the result before him, the reader can judge for himself now whether or not I was right. Right or wrong, the many and exacting duties of a newspaper man's life would hardly have allowed me to bring it to an end but for frequent friendly lifts given me by willing hands. To the President of the Board of Health, Mr. Charles G. Wilson, and to Chief Inspector Byrnes of the Police Force I am indebted for much kindness. The patient friendship of Dr. Roger S. Tracy,[1] the Registrar of Vital Statistics, has done for me what I never could have done for myself; for I know nothing of tables, statistics and percentages, while there is nothing about them that he does not know. Most of all, I owe in this, as in all things else, to the womanly sympathy and the loving companionship of my dear wife, ever my chief helper, my wisest counsellor, and my gentlest critic.   *J. A. R.*

"With gates of silver and bars of gold
Ye have fenced my sheep from their father's fold;
I have heard the dropping of their tears
In heaven these eighteen hundred years."

"O Lord and Master, not ours the guilt,
We build but as our fathers built;
Behold thine images, how they stand,
Sovereign and sole, through all our land."

Then Christ sought out an artisan,
A low-browed, stunted, haggard man,
And a motherless girl, whose fingers thin
Pushed from her faintly want and sin.

These set he in the midst of them,
And as they drew back their garment-hem,
For fear of defilement, "Lo, here," said he,
"The *images* ye have made of me!"

James Russell Lowell[1]

Introduction

LONG AGO IT WAS said that "one half of the world does not know how the other half lives."[1] That was true then. It did not know because it did not care. The half that was on top cared little for the struggles, and less for the fate of those who were underneath, so long as it was able to hold them there and keep its own seat. There came a time when the discomfort and crowding below were so great, and the consequent upheavals so violent, that it was no longer an easy thing to do, and then the upper half fell to inquiring what was the matter. Information on the subject has been accumulating rapidly since, and the whole world has had its hands full answering for its old ignorance.

In New York, the youngest of the world's great cities, that time came later than elsewhere, because the crowding had not been so great. There were those who believed that it would never come; but their hopes were vain. Greed and reckless selfishness wrought like results here as in the cities of older lands. "When the great riot occurred in 1863," so reads the testimony of the Secretary of the Prison Association of New York before a legislative committee appointed to investigate causes of the increase of crime in the State twenty-five years ago, "every hiding place and nursery of crime discovered itself by immediate and active participation in the operations of the mob. Those very places and domiciles, and all that are like them, are today nurseries of crime, and of the vices and disorderly courses which lead to crime. By far the largest part—eighty percent at least—of crimes against property and against the person are perpetrated by individuals who have either lost connection with home life, or never had any, or whose *homes had ceased to be sufficiently separate, decent, and desirable to afford what are regarded as ordinary wholesome influences of home and family* . . . The younger criminals seem to come almost exclusively from the worst tenement house districts, that is, when traced back to the very places where they had their homes in the city here."[2] Of one thing New York made sure at that early stage of the inquiry: the boundary line of the Other Half lies through the tenements.

It is ten years and over, now, since that line divided New York's population evenly. Today three-fourths of its people live in the tenements, and the nineteenth century drift of the population to the cities is sending ever-increasing multitudes to crowd them. The fifteen thousand tenant houses that were the despair of the sanitarian in the past generation have swelled into thirty-seven thousand, and more than twelve hundred thousand persons call them home.[3] The one way out he saw—rapid transit to the suburbs—has brought no relief.[4] We know now that there is no way out; that the "system" that was the evil offspring of public neglect and private greed has come to stay, a storm center forever of our civilization. Nothing is left but to make the best of a bad bargain.

What the tenements are and how they grow to what they are, we shall see hereafter. The story is dark enough, drawn from the plain public records, to send a chill to any heart. If it shall appear that the sufferings and the sins of the "other half," and the evil they breed, are but as a just punishment upon the community that gave it no other choice, it will be because that is the truth. The boundary line lies there because, while the forces for good on one side vastly outweigh the bad—it were not well otherwise—in the tenements all the influences make for evil; because they are the hotbeds of the epidemics that carry death to rich and poor alike; the nurseries of pauperism and crime that fill our jails and police courts; that throw off a scum of forty thousand human wrecks to the island asylums and workhouses year by year; that turned out in the last eight years a round half million beggars to prey upon our charities; that maintain a standing army of ten thousand tramps with all that that implies; because, above all, they touch the family life with deadly moral contagion. This is their worst crime, inseparable from the system. That we have to own it the child of our own wrong does not excuse it, even though it gives it claim upon our utmost patience and tenderest charity.

What are you going to do about it? is the question of today. It was asked once of our city in taunting defiance by a band of political cutthroats, the legitimate outgrowth of life on the tenement house level.* [5] Law and order found the answer then and prevailed. With our enormously swelling population held in this galling bondage, will that answer always be given? It will depend on how fully the situation that prompted the challenge is grasped. Forty percent of the distress among the poor, said a recent official report, is due to drunkenness. [6] But the first legislative committee ever appointed to probe this sore went deeper down and uncovered its roots. The "conclusion forced itself upon it that certain conditions and associations of human life and habitation are the prolific parents of corresponding habits and morals," and it recommended "the prevention of drunkenness by providing for every man a clean and comfortable home." [7] Years after,

---

* Tweed was born and bred in a Fourth Ward tenement.

a sanitary inquiry brought to light the fact that "more than one-half of the tenements with two-thirds of their population were held by owners who made the keeping of them a business, *generally a speculation.* The owner was seeking a certain percentage on his outlay, and that percentage very rarely fell below fifteen percent, and frequently exceeded thirty.* [8] . . . The complaint was universal among the tenants that they were entirely uncared for, and that the only answer to their requests to have the place put in order by repairs and necessary improvements was that they must pay their rent or leave. The agent's instructions were simple but emphatic: 'Collect the rent in advance, or, failing, eject the occupants.'" Upon such a stock grew this upas tree. Small wonder the fruit is bitter. The remedy that shall be an effective answer to the coming appeal for justice must proceed from the public conscience. Neither legislation nor charity can cover the ground. The greed of capital that wrought the evil must itself undo it, as far as it can now be undone. Homes must be built for the working masses by those who employ their labor; but tenements must cease to be "good property" in the old, heartless sense. "Philanthropy and five percent" is the penance exacted.

If this is true from a purely economic point of view, what then of the outlook from the Christian standpoint? Not long ago a great meeting was held in this city, of all denominations of religious faith, to discuss the question how to lay hold of these teeming masses in the tenements with Christian influences, to which they are now too often strangers. Might not the conference have found in the warning of one Brooklyn builder, who has invested his capital on this plan and made it pay more than a money interest, a hint worth heeding: "How shall the love of God be understood by those who have been nurtured in sight only of the greed of man?"[9]

---

* Forty percent was declared by witnesses before a senate committee to be a fair average interest on tenement property. Instances were given of its being one hundred percent and over.

I

Genesis of the Tenement

THE FIRST TENEMENT New York knew bore the mark of Cain from its birth, though a generation passed before the writing was deciphered. It was the "rear house," infamous ever after in our city's history. There had been tenant houses before, but they were not built for the purpose. Nothing would probably have shocked their original owners more than the idea of their harboring a promiscuous crowd; for they were the decorous homes of the old Knickerbockers, the proud aristocracy of Manhattan in the early days.

It was the stir and bustle of trade, together with the tremendous immigration that followed upon the war of 1812 that dislodged them. In thirty-five years the city of less than a hundred thousand came to harbor half a million souls, for whom homes had to be found. Within the memory of men not yet in their prime, Washington had moved from his house on Cherry Hill as too far out of town to be easily reached.[1] Now the old residents followed his example; but they moved in a different direction and for a different reason. Their comfortable dwellings in the once fashionable streets along the East River front fell into the hands of real estate agents and boardinghouse keepers; and here, says the report to the legislature of 1857, when the evils engendered had excited just alarm, "in its beginning, the tenant house became a real blessing to that class of industrious poor whose small earnings limited their expenses, and whose employment in workshops, stores, or about the warehouses and thoroughfares, render a near residence of much importance."[2] Not for long, however. As business increased, and the city grew with rapid strides, the necessities of the poor became the opportunity of their wealthier neighbors, and the stamp was set upon the old houses, suddenly become valuable, which the best thought and effort of a later age has vainly struggled to efface. Their "*large* rooms were partitioned into *several smaller ones,* without regard to light or ventilation, the rate of rent being lower in proportion to space or height from the street; and they soon became filled from cellar to garret with a class of tenantry living from hand to mouth, loose in morals, improvident in habits, degraded, and squalid as beggary itself." It was thus the dark bedroom, prolific of untold depravities, came into the world. It was destined to survive the old houses. In their new role, says the old report, eloquent in its indignant denunciation of "evils more destructive than wars," "they were not intended to last. Rents were fixed high enough to cover damage and abuse from this class, from whom nothing was expected, and the most was made of them while they lasted. Neatness, order, cleanliness, were never dreamed of in connection with the tenant-house system, as it spread its localities from year to year; while reckless slovenliness, discontent, privation, and ignorance were left to work out their invariable results, until the entire premises reached the level of tenant-house dilapidation, containing, but sheltering not, the miserable hordes that crowded beneath smouldering, water-rotted roofs or the tenants died at the rate of one hundred and ninety-five to the thousand of population; which forced the general mortality of the city up from 1 in 41.83 in 1815, to 1 in 27.33 in 1855, a year of unusual freedom from epidemic disease, and which wrung from the early organizers of the Health Department this wail: "There are numerous examples of tenement houses in which are lodged several hundred people that have a *pro rata* allotment of ground area scarcely equal to two square yards upon the city lot, courtyards and all included." The tenement house population had swelled to half a million souls by that time, and on the East Side, in what is still the most densely populated district in all the world, China not excluded, it was packed at the rate of 290,000 to the square mile, a state of affairs wholly unexampled. The utmost cupidity of other lands and other days had never contrived to herd much more than half that number within the same space. The greatest crowding of Old London was at the rate of 175,816. Swine roamed the streets and gutters as their principal scavengers.* The death of a child in a tenement was registered at the Bureau of Vital Statistics as "plainly due to suffocation in the foul air of an unventilated apartment," and the Senators, who had come down from Albany to find out what was the matter with New York, reported that "there are annually cut off from the population by disease and death enough human beings to people a city, and enough human labor to sustain it." And yet experts had testified that, as compared with uptown, rents were from twenty-five to thirty percent higher in the worst slums of the lower wards, with such accommodations as were enjoyed, for instance, by a "family with boarders" in Cedar Street, who fed hogs in the cellar that contained eight or ten loads of manure; or "one room 12 × 12 with five families living in it, comprising

---

* It was not until the winter of 1867 that owners of swine were prohibited by ordinance from letting them run at large in the built-up portions of the city.

twenty persons of both sexes and all ages, with only two beds, without partition, screen, chair, or table." The rate of rent has been successfully maintained to the present day, though the hog at least has been eliminated.

Lest anybody flatter himself with the notion that these were evils of a day that is happily past and may safely be forgotten, let me mention here three very recent instances of tenement house life that came under my notice. One was the burning of a rear house in Mott Street, from appearances one of the original tenant houses that made their owners rich. The fire made homeless ten families, who had paid an average of $5 a month for their mean little cubbyholes. The owner himself told me that it was *fully* insured for $800, though it brought him in $600 a year rent. He evidently considered himself especially entitled to be pitied for losing such valuable property. Another was the case of a hardworking family of man and wife, young people from the old country, who took poison together in a Crosby Street tenement because they were "tired." There was no other explanation, and none was needed when I stood in the room in which they had lived. It was in the attic with sloping ceiling and a single window so far out on the roof that it seemed not to belong to the place at all. With scarcely room enough to turn around in they had been compelled to pay five dollars and a half a month in advance. There were four such rooms in that attic, and together they brought in as much as many a handsome little cottage in a pleasant part of Brooklyn. The third instance was that of a colored family of husband, wife, and baby in a wretched rear rookery in West Third Street. Their rent was eight dollars and a half for a single room on the top story, so small that I was unable to get a photograph of it even by placing the camera outside the open door. Three short steps across either way would have measured its full extent.

Tenement of 1863 for Twelve Families on Each Flat. D, dark; L, light; H, halls.

This "unventilated and fever-breeding structure" the year after it was built was picked out by the Council of Hygiene, then just organized, and presented to the Citizens' Association of New York as a specimen "multiple domicile" in a desirable street, with the following comment: "Here are twelve living-rooms and twenty-one bedrooms, and only six of the latter have any provision or possibility for the admission of light and air, excepting through the family sitting- and living-room; being utterly dark, close, and unventilated. The living-rooms are but 10 × 12 feet; the bedrooms 6½ × 7 feet."

EDITOR'S NOTE: Plan and explanatory footnote taken from Citizens' Association of New York, *Report of the Council of Hygiene and Public Health upon the Sanitary Condition of the City* (New York, 1865), pp. lxxxi–lxxxii.

There was just one excuse for the early tenement house builders, and their successors may plead it with nearly as good right for what it is worth. "Such," says an official report, "is the lack of houseroom in the city that any kind of tenement can be immediately crowded with lodgers, if there is space offered." Thousands were living in cellars. There were three hundred underground lodging houses in the city when the Health Department was organized. Some fifteen years before that the old Baptist Church in Mulberry Street, just off Chatham Street, had been sold, and the rear half of the frame structure had

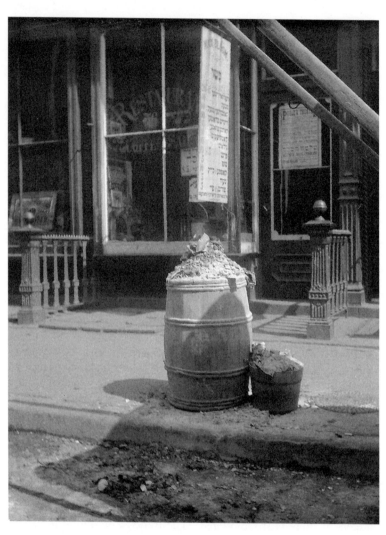

Ash Barrel of Old

been converted into tenements that with their swarming population became the scandal even of that reckless age. The wretched pile harbored no less than forty families, and the annual rate of deaths to the population was officially stated to be 75 in 1,000. These tenements were an extreme type of very many, for the big barracks had by this time spread east and west and far up the island into the sparsely settled wards. Whether or not the title was clear to the land upon which they were built was of less account than that the rents were collected. If there were damages to pay, the tenant had to foot them. Cases were "very frequent when property was in litigation, and two or three different parties were collecting rents." Of course under such circumstances "no repairs were ever made."

The climax had been reached. The situation was summed up by the Society for the Improvement of the Condition of the Poor in these words: "Crazy old buildings, crowded rear tenements in filthy yards, dark, damp basements, leaking garrets, shops, outhouses, and stables* converted into dwellings, though scarcely fit to shelter brutes, are habitations of thousands of our fellow-beings in this wealthy, Christian city."[3] "The city," says its historian, Mrs. Martha Lamb, commenting on the era of aqueduct building between 1835 and 1845, "was a general asylum for vagrants."[4] Young vagabonds, the natural offspring of such "home" conditions, overran the streets. Juvenile crime increased fearfully year by year. The Children's Aid Society and kindred philanthropic organizations were yet unborn, but in the city directory was to be found the address of the "American Society for the Promotion of Education in Africa."

---

* "A lot 50 × 60, contained twenty stables, rented for dwellings at $15 a year each; cost of the whole $600."

II

The Awakening

THE DREAD OF ADVANCING CHOLERA, with the guilty knowledge of the harvest field that awaited the plague in New York's slums, pricked the conscience of the community into action soon after the close of the war. A citizens' movement resulted in the organization of a Board of Health and the adoption of the "Tenement-House Act" of 1867, the first step toward remedial legislation.[1] A thorough canvass of the tenements had been begun already in the previous year; but the cholera first, and next a scourge of smallpox, delayed the work, while emphasizing the need of it, so that it was 1869 before it got fairly under way and began to tell. The dark bedroom fell under the ban first. In that year the Board ordered the cutting of more than forty-six thousand windows in interior rooms, chiefly for ventilation—for little or no light was to be had from the dark hallways. Air shafts were unknown. The saw had a job all that summer; by early fall nearly all the orders had been carried out. Not without opposition;

obstacles were thrown in the way of the officials on the one side by the owners of the tenements, who saw in every order to repair or clean up only an item of added expense to diminish their income from the rent; on the other side by the tenants themselves, who had sunk, after a generation of unavailing protest, to the level of their surroundings, and were at last content to remain there. The tenements had bred their nemesis, a proletariat ready and able to avenge the wrongs of their crowds. Already it taxed the city heavily for the support of its jails and charities. The basis of opposition, curiously enough, was the same at both extremes; owner and tenant alike considered official interference an infringement of personal rights, and a hardship. It took long years of weary labor to make good the claim of the sunlight to such corners of the dens as it could reach at all. Not until five years after did the department succeed at last in ousting the "cave dwellers" and closing some five hundred and fifty cellars south of Houston Street, many of them below tidewater, that had been used as living apartments. In many instances the police had to drag the tenants out by force.

The work went on; but the need of it only grew with the effort. The Sanitarians were following up an evil that grew faster than they went; like a fire, it could only be headed off, not chased, with success. Official reports, read in the churches in 1879,[2] characterized the younger criminals as victims of low social conditions of life and unhealthy, overcrowded lodgings, brought up in "an atmosphere of actual darkness, moral and physical." This after the saw had been busy in the dark corners ten years! "If we could see the air breathed by these poor creatures in their tenements," said a well-known physician, "it would show itself to be fouler than the mud of the gutters." Little improvement was apparent despite all that had been done. "The new tenements, that have been recently built, have been usually as badly planned as the old, with dark and unhealthy rooms, often over wet cellars, where extreme overcrowding is permitted," was the verdict of one authority. These are the houses that today perpetuate the worst traditions of the past, and they are counted by thousands. The Five Points had been cleansed, as far as the immediate neighborhood was concerned, but the Mulberry Street Bend was fast outdoing it in foulness not a stone's throw away, and new centers of corruption were continually springing up and getting the upper hand whenever vigilance was relaxed for ever so short a time. It is one of the curses of the tenement house system that the worst houses exercise a levelling influence upon all the rest, just as one bad boy in a schoolroom will spoil the whole class. It is one of the ways the evil that was "the result

Tenement of the Old Style.
Birth of the Air Shaft.

of forgetfulness of the poor," as the Council of Hygiene mildly put it, has of avenging itself.[3]

The determined effort to head it off by laying a strong hand upon the tenement-builders that has been the chief business of the Health Board of recent years, dates from this period. The era of the air shaft has not solved the problem of housing the poor, but it has made good use of limited opportunities. Over the new houses sanitary law exercises full control. But the old remain. They cannot be summarily torn down, though in extreme cases the authorities can order them cleared. The outrageous overcrowding, too, remains. It is characteristic of the tenements. Poverty, their badge and typical condition, invites—compels it.

All efforts to abate it result only in temporary relief. As long as they exist it will exist with them. And the tenements will exist in New York forever.

Today, what is a tenement? The law defines it as a house "occupied by three or more families, living independently and doing their cooking on the premises; or by more than two families on a floor, so living and cooking and having a common right in the halls, stairways, yards, etc." That is the legal meaning, and includes flats and apartment houses, with which we have nothing to do.[4] In its narrower sense the typical tenement was thus described when last arraigned before the bar of public justice: "It is generally a brick building from four to six stories high on the street, frequently with a store on the first floor which, when used for the sale of liquor, has a side opening for the benefit of the inmates and to evade the Sunday law; four families occupy each floor, and a set of rooms consists of one or two dark closets, used as bedrooms, with a living room twelve feet by ten. The staircase is too often a dark well in the center of the house, and no direct through ventilation is possible, each family being separated from the other by partitions. Frequently the rear of the lot is occupied by another building of three stories high with two families on a floor." The picture is nearly as true today as ten years ago, and will be for a long time to come. The dim light admitted by the air shaft shines upon greater crowds than ever. Tenements are still "good property," and the poverty of the poor man his destruction. A barrack down-town where he *has to live* because he is poor brings in a third more rent than a decent flat house in Harlem. The statement once made a sensation that between seventy and eighty children had been found in one tenement. It no longer excites even passing attention, when the sanitary police report counting 101 adults and 91 children in a Crosby Street house, one of twins, built together. The children in the other, if I am not mistaken, numbered 89, a total of 180 for two tenements! Or when a midnight inspection in Mulberry Street unearths a hundred and fifty "lodgers" sleeping on filthy floors in two buildings. Spite of brown-stone trimmings, plate glass and mosaic vestibule floors, the water does not rise in summer to the second story, while the beer flows unchecked to the all-night picnics on the roof. The saloon with the side door and the landlord divide the prosperity of the place be-tween them, and the tenant, in sullen submission, foots the bills.

Where are the tenements of today? Say rather: where are they not? In fifty years they have crept up from the Fourth Ward slums and the Five Points the whole length of the island, and have polluted the An-nexed District to the Westchester line. Crowding all the lower wards, wherever business leaves a foot of ground unclaimed; strung along both rivers, like ball and chain tied to the foot of every street, and filling up Harlem with their restless, pent-up multitudes, they hold within their clutch the wealth and business of New York, hold them at their mercy in the day of mob rule and wrath. The bulletproof shut-ters, the stacks of hand grenades, and the Gatling guns of the Subtrea-sury are tacit admissions of the fact and of the quality of the mercy expected. The tenements today are New York, harboring three-fourths of its population. When another generation shall have doubled the census of our city, and to that vast army of workers, held captive by poverty, the very name of home shall be as a bitter mockery, what will the harvest be?

III

The Mixed Crowd

WHEN ONCE I ASKED the agent of a notorious Fourth Ward alley how many people might be living in it I was told: one hundred and forty families, one hundred Irish, thirty-eight Italian, and two that spoke the German tongue. Barring the agent herself, there was not a native-born individual in the court. The answer was characteristic of the cosmopolitan character of lower New York, very nearly so of the whole of it, wherever it runs to alleys and courts. One may find for the asking an Italian, a German, a French, African, Spanish, Bohemian, Russian, Scandinavian, Jewish, and Chinese colony. Even the Arab, who peddles "holy earth" from the Battery as a direct importation from Jerusalem, has his exclusive preserves at the lower end of Washington Street. The one thing you shall vainly ask for in the chief city of America is a distinctively American community. There is none; certainly not among the tenements. Where have they gone to, the old inhabitants? I put the question to one who might fairly be presumed to be of the number, since I had found him sighing for the "good old days" when the legend "no Irish need apply" was familiar in the advertising columns of the newspapers. He looked at me with a puzzled air. "I don't know," he said. "I wish I did. Some went to California in '49, some to the war and never came back. The rest, I expect, have gone to heaven, or somewhere. I don't see them 'round here."

Whatever the merit of the good man's conjectures, his eyes did not deceive him. They are not here. In their place has come this queer conglomerate mass of heterogeneous elements, ever striving and working like whiskey and water in one glass, and with the like result: final union and a prevailing taint of whiskey. The once unwelcome Irishman has been followed in his turn by the Italian, the Russian Jew, and the Chinaman, and has himself taken a hand at opposition, quite as bitter and quite as ineffectual, against these later hordes. Wherever these have gone they have crowded him out, possessing the block, the street, the ward with their denser swarms. But the Irishman's revenge is complete. Victorious in defeat over his recent as over his more ancient foe, the one who opposed his coming no less than the one who drove him out, he dictates to both their politics, and, secure in possession of the offices, returns the native his greeting with interest, while collecting the rents of the Italian whose house he has bought with the profits of his saloon. As a landlord he is picturesquely autocratic. An amusing instance of his methods came under my notice while writing these lines. An inspector of the Health Department found an Italian family paying a man with a Celtic name twenty-five dollars a month for three small rooms in a ramshackle rear tenement—more than twice what they were worth—and expressed his astonishment to the tenant, an ignorant Sicilian laborer. He replied that he had once asked the landlord to reduce the rent, but he would not do it.

"Well! What did he say?" asked the inspector.

"'Damma, man!' he said; 'if you speaka thata way to me, I fira you and your things in the streeta.'" And the frightened Italian paid the rent.

In justice to the Irish landlord it must be said that like an apt pupil he was merely showing forth the result of the schooling he had received, reenacting, in his own way, the scheme of the tenements. It is only his frankness that shocks. The Irishman does not naturally take kindly to tenement life, though with characteristic versatility he adapts himself to its conditions at once. It does violence, nevertheless, to the best that is in him, and for that very reason of all who come within its sphere soonest corrupts him. The result is a sediment, the product of more than a generation in the city's slums, that, as distinguished from the larger body of his class, justly ranks at the foot of tenement dwellers, the so-called "low Irish."

It is not to be assumed, of course, that the whole body of the population living in the tenements, of which New Yorkers are in the habit of speaking vaguely as "the poor," or even the larger part of it, is to be classed as vicious or as poor in the sense of verging on beggary.

New York's wage earners have no other place to live, more is the pity. They are truly poor for having no better homes; waxing poorer in purse as the exorbitant rents to which they are tied, as ever was serf to soil, keep rising. The wonder is that they are not all corrupted, and speedily, by their surroundings. If, on the contrary, there be a steady working up, if not out of the slough, the fact is a powerful argument for the optimist's belief that the world is, after all, growing better, not worse, and would go far toward disarming apprehension, were it not for the steadier growth of the sediment of the slums and its constant menace. Such an impulse toward better things there certainly is. The German ragpicker of thirty years ago, quite as low in the scale as his

Italian successor, is the thrifty tradesman or prosperous farmer of today.*

The Italian scavenger of our time is fast graduating into exclusive control of the corner fruit stands, while his black-eyed boy monopolizes the bootblacking industry in which a few years ago he was an intruder. The Irish hod carrier in the second generation has become a bricklayer, if not the Alderman of his ward, while the Chinese coolie is in almost exclusive possession of the laundry business. The reason is obvious. The poorest immigrant comes here with the purpose and ambition to better himself and, given half a chance, might be reasonably expected to make the most of it. To the false plea that he prefers the squalid homes in which his kind are housed there could be no better answer. The truth is, his half chance has too long been wanting, and for the bad result he has been unjustly blamed.

As emigration from east to west follows the latitude, so does the foreign influx in New York distribute itself along certain well-defined lines that waver and break only under the stronger pressure of a more gregarious race or the encroachments of inexorable business. A feeling of dependence upon mutual effort, natural to strangers in a strange land, unacquainted with its language and customs, sufficiently accounts for this.

The Irishman is the true cosmopolitan immigrant. All pervading, he shares his lodging with perfect impartiality with the Italian, the Greek, and the "Dutchman," yielding only to sheer force of numbers, and objects equally to them all. A map of the city, colored to designate nationalities, would show more stripes than on the skin of a zebra,

---

* The Sheriff Street Colony of ragpickers, long since gone, is an instance in point. The thrifty Germans saved up money during years of hard work in squalor and apparently wretched poverty to buy a township in a western state, and the whole colony moved out there in a body. There need be no doubt about their thriving there.

and more colors than any rainbow. The city on such a map would fall into two great halves, green for the Irish prevailing in the West Side tenement districts, and blue for the Germans on the East Side. But intermingled with these ground colors would be an odd variety of tints that would give the whole the appearance of an extraordinary crazy quilt. From down in the Sixth Ward, upon the site of the old Collect Pond[1] that in the days of the fathers drained the hills which are no more, the red of the Italian would be seen forcing its way northward along the line of Mulberry Street to the quarter of the French purple on Bleecker Street and South Fifth Avenue, to lose itself and reappear, after a lapse of miles, in the "Little Italy" of Harlem, east of Second Avenue. Dashes of red, sharply defined, would be seen strung through the Annexed District, northward to the city line. On the West Side the red would be seen overrunning the old Africa of Thompson Street, pushing the black of the Negro rapidly uptown, against querulous but unavailing protests, occupying his home, his church, his trade and all, with merciless impartiality. There is a church in Mulberry Street that has stood for two generations as a sort of milestone of these migrations. Built originally for the worship of staid New Yorkers of the "old stock," it was engulfed by the colored tide, when the draft-riots drove the Negroes out of reach of Cherry Street and the Five Points. Within the past decade the advance wave of the Italian onset reached it, and today the arms of United Italy adorn its front. The Negroes have made a stand at several points along Seventh and Eighth Avenues; but their main body, still pursued by the Italian foe, is on the march yet, and the black mark will be found overshadowing today many blocks on the East Side, with One Hundredth Street as the center, where colonies of them have settled recently.

Hardly less aggressive than the Italian, the Russian and Polish Jew, having overrun the district between Rivington and Division Streets, east of the Bowery, to the point of suffocation, is filling the tenements of the old Seventh Ward to the river front, and disputing with the Italian every foot of available space in the back alleys of Mulberry Street. The two races, differing hopelessly in much, have this in common: they carry their slums with them wherever they go, if allowed to do it. Little Italy already rivals its parent, the "Bend," in foulness. Other nationalities that begin at the bottom make a fresh start when crowded up the ladder. Happily both are manageable, the one by rabbinical, the other by the civil law. Between the dull gray of the Jew, his favorite color, and the Italian red, would be seen squeezed in on the map a sharp streak of yellow, marking the narrow boundaries of Chinatown. Dovetailed in with the German population, the poor but thrifty Bohemian might be picked out by the somber hue of his life as of his philosophy, struggling against heavy odds in the big human beehives of the East Side. Colonies of his people extend northward, with long lapses of space, from below the Cooper Institute more than three miles. The Bohemian is the only foreigner with any considerable representation in the city who counts no wealthy man of his race, none who has not to work hard for a living, or has got beyond the reach of the tenement.

Down near the Battery the West Side emerald would be soiled by a dirty stain, spreading rapidly like a splash of ink on a sheet of blotting paper, headquarters of the Arab tribe, that in a single year has swelled from the original dozen to twelve hundred, intent, every mother's son, on trade and barter. Dots and dashes of color here and there would show where the Finnish sailors worship their djumala (God), the Greek pedlars the ancient name of their race, and the Swiss the goddess of thrift. And so on to the end of the long register, all toiling together in the galling fetters of the tenement. Were the question raised who makes the most of life thus mortgaged, who resists most stubbornly its levelling tendency—knows how to drag even the barracks upward a part of the way at least toward the ideal plane of the home—the palm must be unhesitatingly awarded the Teuton. The Italian and the poor Jew rise only by compulsion. The Chinaman does not rise at all; here, as at home, he simply remains stationary. The Irishman's genius runs to public aifairs rather than domestic life; wherever he is mustered in force the saloon is the gorgeous center of political activity. The German struggles vainly to learn his trick; his Teutonic wit is too heavy, and the political ladder he raises from his saloon usually too short or too clumsy to reach the desired goal. The best part of his life is lived at home, and he makes himself a home independent of the surroundings, giving the lie to the saying, unhappily become a maxim of social truth, that pauperism and drunkenness naturally grow in the tenements. He makes the most of his tenement, and it should be added that whenever and as soon as he can save up money enough, he gets out and never crosses the threshold of one again.

son for dissenting from that observation. Glimpses caught of the parents watching the youngsters play from windows or open doorways will soon convince him that the native stock is in no way involved.

Leaving the Elevated Railroad where it dives under the Brooklyn Bridge at Franklin Square, scarce a dozen steps will take us where we wish to go. With its rush and roar echoing yet in our ears, we have turned the corner from prosperity to poverty. We stand upon the domain of the tenement. In the shadow of the great stone abutments the old Knickerbocker houses linger like ghosts of a departed day. Down the winding slope of Cherry Street—proud and fashionable Cherry Hill that was—their broad steps, sloping roofs, and dormer windows are easily made out; all the more easily for the contrast with the ugly barracks that elbow them right and left. These never had other design than to shelter, at as little outlay as possible, the greatest crowds out of which rent could be wrung. They were the bad afterthought of a heedless day. The years have brought to the old houses unhonored age, a querulous second childhood that is out of tune with the time, their tenants, the neighbors, and cries out against them and against you in fretful protest in every step on their rotten floors or squeaky stairs. Good cause have they for their fretting. This one, with its shabby front and poorly patched roof, what glowing firesides, what happy children may it once have owned? Heavy feet, too often with unsteady step, for the pot house is next door—where is it not next door in these slums?—have worn away the brownstone steps since; the broken columns at the door have rotted away at the base. Of the handsome cornice barely a trace is left. Dirt and desolation reign in the wide hallway, and danger lurks on the stairs. Rough pine boards fence off the roomy fireplaces—where coal is bought by the pail at the rate of twelve dollars a ton these have no place. The arched gateway leads no longer to a shady bower on the banks of the rushing stream, inviting to daydreams with its gentle repose, but to a dark

At the Cradle of the Tenement—Doorway of an Old-Fashioned Dwelling on Cherry Hill and nameless alley, shut in by high brick walls, cheerless as the lives of those they shelter. The wolf knocks loudly at the gate in the troubled dreams that come to this alley, echoes of the day's cares. A horde of dirty children play about the dripping hydrant, the only thing in the alley that thinks enough of its chance to make the most of it: it is the best it can do. These are the children of the tenements, the growing generation of the slums; this their home. From the great highway overhead, along which throbs the life tide of two great cities, one might drop a pebble into half a dozen such alleys.

One yawns just across the street; not very broadly, but it is not to blame. The builder of the old gateway had no thought of its ever becoming a public thoroughfare. Once inside it widens, but only to make room for a big box-like building with the worn and greasy look of the slum tenement that is stamped alike on the houses and their tenants down here, even on the homeless cur that romps with the children in yonder building lot, with an air of expectant interest plainly betraying the forlorn hope that at some stage of the game a meat-bone may show up in the role of "It." Vain hope, truly! Nothing more appetizing than a barelegged ragamuffin appears. Meat bones, not long since picked clean, are as scarce in Blind Man's Alley as elbowroom in any Fourth Ward backyard. The shouts of the children come hushed over the housetops, as if apologizing for the intrusion. Few glad noises make this old alley ring. Morning and evening it echoes with the gentle, groping tap of the blind man's staff as he feels his way to the street. Blind Man's Alley bears its name for a reason. Until little more than a year ago its dark burrows harbored a colony of blind beggars, tenants of a blind landlord, old Daniel Murphy, whom every child in the ward knows, if he never heard of the President of the United States. "Old Dan" made a big fortune—he told me once four hundred thousand dollars—out of his alley and the surrounding tenements, only to grow blind himself in extreme old age, sharing in the end the chief hardship of the wretched beings whose lot he had stubbornly refused to better that he might increase his wealth. Even when the Board of Health at last compelled him to repair and clean up the worst of the old buildings, under threat of driving out the tenants and locking the doors behind them, the work was accomplished against the old man's angry protests. He appeared in person before the Board to argue his case, and his argument was characteristic.

"I have made my will," he said. "My monument stands waiting for me in Calvary. I stand on the very brink of the grave, blind and helpless, and now (here the pathos of the appeal was swept under in a burst of angry indignation) do you want me to build and get skinned, skinned? These people are not fit to live in a nice house. Let them go where they can, and let my house stand."

In spite of the genuine anguish of the appeal, it was downright amusing to find that his anger was provoked less by the anticipated waste of luxury on his tenants than by distrust of his own kind, the builder. He knew intuitively what to expect. The result showed that Mr. Murphy had gauged his tenants correctly. The cleaning up process apparently destroyed the home-feeling of the alley; many of the blind people moved away and did not return. Some remained, however, and the name has clung to the place.

Some idea of what is meant by a sanitary "cleaning up" in these slums may be gained from the account of a mishap I met with once, in taking a flashlight picture of a group of blind beggars in one of the tenements down here. With unpractised hands I managed to set fire to the house. When the blinding effect of the flash had passed away and I could see once more, I discovered that a lot of paper and rags that hung on the wall were ablaze. There were six of us, five blind men and women who knew nothing of their danger, and myself, in an attic room with a dozen crooked, rickety stairs between us and the street, and as many households as helpless as the one whose guest I was all about us. The thought: how were they ever to be got out? made my blood run cold as I saw the flames creeping up the wall, and my first impulse was to bolt for the street and shout for help. The next was to smother the fire myself, and I did, with a vast deal of trouble. Afterward, when I came down to the street I told a friendly policeman of my trouble. For some reason he thought it rather a good joke, and laughed immoderately at my concern lest even then sparks should be burrowing in the rotten wall that might yet break out in flame and destroy the house with all that were in it. He told me why, when he found time to draw breath. "Why, don't you know," he said, "that house is the Dirty Spoon? It caught fire six times last winter, but it wouldn't burn. The dirt was so thick on the walls, it smothered the fire!" Which, if true, shows that water and dirt, not usually held to be harmonious elements, work together for the good of those who insure houses.

Sunless and joyless though it be, Blind Man's Alley has that which its compeers of the slums vainly yearn for. It has a payday. Once a year sunlight shines into the lives of its forlorn crew, past and present. In June, when the Superintendent of Outdoor Poor distributes the twenty thousand dollars annually allowed the poor blind by the city, in halfhearted recognition of its failure to otherwise provide for them, Blind Man's Alley takes a day off and goes to "see" Mr. Blake. That night it is noisy with unwonted merriment. There is scraping of squeaky fiddles in the dark rooms, and cracked old voices sing long-forgotten songs. Even the blind landlord rejoices, for much of the money goes into his coffers.

From their perch up among the rafters Mrs. Gallagher's blind boarders might hear, did they listen, the tramp of the policeman always on duty in Gotham Court, half a stone's throw away.[1] His beat, though it takes in but a small portion of a single block, is quite as

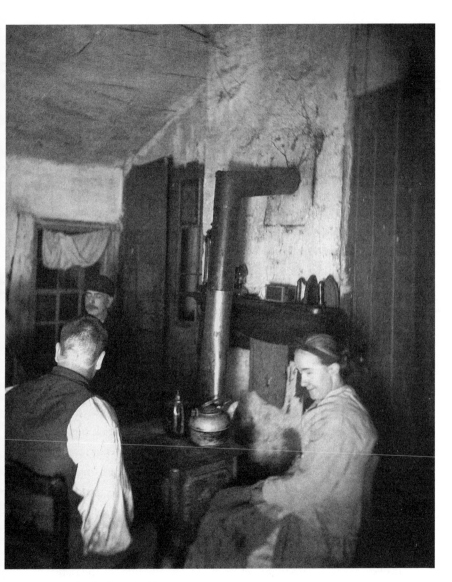

Upstairs in Blindman's Alley

lively as most larger patrol rounds. A double row of five-story tenements, back to back under a common roof, extending back from the
street two hundred and thirty-four feet, with barred openings in the
dividing wall, so that the tenants may see but cannot get at each other
from the stairs, makes the "court." Alleys—one wider by a couple of
feet than the other, whence the distinction Single and Double Alley—
skirt the barracks on either side. Such, briefly, is the tenement that
has challenged public attention more than any other in the whole city
and tested the power of sanitary law and rule for forty years. The
name of the pile is not down in the City Directory, but in the public
records it holds an unenviable place. It was here the mortality rose
during the last great cholera epidemic to the unprecedented rate of
195 in 1,000 inhabitants. In its worst days a full thousand could not be
packed into the court, though the number did probably not fall far
short of it. Even now, under the management of men of conscience,
and an agent, a King's Daughter,[2] whose practical energy, kindliness
and good sense have done much to redeem its foul reputation, the
swarms it shelters would make more than one fair-sized country village. The mixed character of the population, by this time about
equally divided between the Celtic and the Italian stock, accounts for
the iron bars and the policeman. It was an eminently Irish suggestion
that the latter was to be credited to the presence of two German families in the court, who "made trouble all the time." A Chinaman whom
I questioned as he hurried past the iron gate of the alley, put the matter in a different light. "Lem Ilish velly bad," he said. Gotham Court
has been the entering wedge for the Italian element, who until recently had not attained a foothold in the Fourth Ward, but are now
trailing across Chatham Street from their stronghold in "the Bend" in
ever increasing numbers, seeking, according to their wont, the lowest
level.

    It is curious to find that this notorious block, whose name was so long synonymous with all that was desperately bad, was originally built (in 1851) by a benevolent Quaker for the express purpose of rescuing the poor people from the dreadful rookeries they were then living in. How long it continued a model tenement is not on record. It could not have been very long, for already in 1862, ten years after it was finished, a sanitary official counted 146 cases of sickness in the court, including "all kinds of infectious disease," from smallpox down, and reported that of 138 children born in it in less than three years 61 had died, mostly before they were one year old. Seven years later the inspector of the district reported to the Board of Health that "nearly ten per cent. of the population is sent to the public hospitals each year." When the alley was finally taken in hand by the authorities, and, as a first step toward its reclamation, the entire population was driven out by the police, experience dictated, as one of the first improvements to be made, the putting in of a kind of sewer grating, so constructed, as the official report patiently puts it, "as to prevent the ingress of persons disposed to make a hiding-place" of the sewer and the cellars into which they opened. The fact was that the big vaulted sewers had long been a runway for thieves—the Swamp Angels—who through them easily escaped when chased by the police, as well as a storehouse for their plunder. The sewers are there today; in fact the two alleys are nothing but the roofs of these enormous tunnels in which a man may walk upright the full distance of the block and into the Cherry Street sewer—if he likes the fun and is not afraid of rats. Could their grimy walls speak, the big canals might tell many a startling tale. But they are silent enough, and so are most of those whose secrets they might betray. The floodgates connecting with the Cherry Street main are closed now, except when the water is drained off. Then there were no gates, and it is on record that the sewers were chosen as a short cut habitually by residents of the court whose business lay on the line of them, near a manhole, perhaps, in Cherry five hundred and thirty years of penal servitude, and he will tell you his opinion that the Fourth Ward, even the last twenty years, has turned out more criminals than all the rest of the city together.

But though the "Swamp Angels" have gone to their reward, their successors carry on business at the old stand as successfully, if not as boldly. There goes one who was once a shining light in thiefdom. He has reformed since, they say. The policeman on the corner, who is addicted to a professional unbelief in reform of any kind, will tell you that while on the Island once he sailed away on a shutter, paddling along until he was picked up in Hell Gate by a schooner's crew, whom he persuaded that he was a fanatic performing some sort of religious penance by his singular expedition. Over yonder, Tweed, the arch-thief, worked in a brush shop and earned an honest living before he took to politics. As we stroll from one narrow street to another the odd contrast between the low, old-looking houses in front and the towering tenements in the back yards grows even more striking, perhaps because we expect and are looking for it. Nobody who was not would suspect the presence of the rear houses, though they have been there long enough. Here is one seven stories high behind one with only three floors. Take a look into this Roosevelt Street alley; just about one step wide, with a five-story house on one side that gets its light and air—God help us for pitiful mockery!—from this slit between brick walls. There are no windows in the wall on the other side; it is perfectly blank. The fire escapes of the long tenement fairly touch it; but the rays of the sun, rising, setting, or at high noon, never do. It never shone into the alley from the day the devil planned and man built it. There was once an English doctor who experimented with the sunlight in the soldiers' barracks, and found that on the side that was shut off altogether from the sun the mortality was one hundred percent greater than on the light side, where its rays had free access. But then soldiers are of some account, have a fixed value, if not a very high one. The people who live here have not. The horse that pulls the dirt cart one of these laborers loads and unloads is of ever so much more account to the employer of his labor than he and all that belongs to him. Ask the owner; he will not attempt to deny it, if the horse is worth anything. The man too knows it. It is the one thought that occasionally troubles the owner of the horse in the enjoyment of his prosperity, built of and upon the successful assertion of the truth that all men are created equal.

With what a shock did the story of yonder Madison Street alley come home to New Yorkers one morning, eight or ten years ago, when a fire that broke out after the men had gone to their work swept up those narrow stairs and burned up women and children to the number of a full half score. There were fire escapes, yes! but so placed that they could not be reached. The firemen had to look twice before they could find the opening that passes for a thoroughfare; a stout man would never venture in. Some wonderfully heroic rescues were made at that fire by people living in the adjoining tenements. Danger and trouble—of the imminent kind, not the everyday sort that excites neither interest nor commiseration—run even this common clay into heroic moulds on occasion; occasions that help us to remember that the gap that separates the man with the patched coat from his wealthy neighbor is, after all, perhaps but a tenement. Yet, what a gap! and of whose making? Here, as we stroll along Madison Street, workmen are busy putting the finishing touches to the brownstone front of a tall new tenement. This one will probably be called an apartment house. They are carving satyrs' heads in the stone, with a crowd of gaping youngsters looking on in admiring wonder. Next door are two other tenements, likewise with brownstone fronts, fair to look at. The youngest of the children in the group is not too young to remember how their army of tenants was turned out by the health officers because the houses had been condemned as unfit for human beings to live in. The owner was a wealthy builder who "stood high in the community." Is it only in our fancy that the sardonic leer on the stone faces seems to list that way? Or is it an introspective grin? We will not ask if the new house belongs to the same builder. He too may have reformed.

We have crossed the boundary of the Seventh Ward. Penitentiary Row, suggestive name for a block of Cherry Street tenements, is behind us. Within recent days it has become peopled wholly with Hebrews, the overflow from Jewtown adjoining, pedlars and tailors, all of them. It is odd to read this legend from other days over the door: "No pedlars allowed in this house." These thrifty people are not only crowding into the tenements of this once exclusive district—they are buying them. The Jew runs to real estate as soon as he can save up enough for a deposit to clinch the bargain. As fast as the old houses are torn down, towering structures go up in their place, and Hebrews are found to be the builders. Here is a whole alley nicknamed after the intruder, Jews' Alley. But abuse and ridicule are not weapons to fight the Israelite with. He pockets them quietly with the rent and bides his time. He knows from experience, both sweet and bitter, that all things come to those who wait, including the houses and lands of their persecutors.

Here comes a pleasure party, as gay as any on the avenue, though the carryall is an ash cart. The father is the driver and he has taken his brown-legged boy for a ride. How proud and happy they both look up there on their perch! The queer old building they have halted in front of is "The Ship," famous for fifty years as a ramshackle tenement filled with the oddest crowd. No one knows why it is called "The Ship," though there is a tradition that once the river came clear up here to Hamilton Street, and boats were moored alongside it. More likely it is because it is as bewildering inside as a crazy old ship, with its ups and downs of ladders parading as stairs, and its unexpected pitfalls. But Hamilton Street, like Water Street, is not what it was. The missions drove from the latter the worst of its dives. A sailors' mission has lately made its appearance in Hamilton Street, but there are no dives there, nothing worse than the ubiquitous saloon and tough tenements.

Enough of them everywhere. Suppose we look into one? No. —Cherry Street. Be a little careful, please! The hall is dark and you might stumble over the children pitching pennies back there. Not that it would hurt them; kicks and cuffs are their daily diet. They have little else. Here where the hall turns and dives into utter darkness is a step, and another, another. A flight of stairs. You can feel your way, if you cannot see it. Close? Yes! What would you have? All the fresh air that ever enters these stairs comes from the hall door that is forever slamming, and from the windows of dark bedrooms that in turn receive from the stairs their sole supply of the elements God meant to be free, but man deals out with such niggardly hand. That was a woman filling her pail by the hydrant you just bumped against. The sinks are in the hallway, that all the tenants may have access—and all be poisoned alike by their summer stenches. Hear the pump squeak! It is the lullaby of tenement house babes. In summer, when a thousand thirsty throats pant for a cooling drink in this block, it is worked in vain. But the saloon, whose open door you passed in the hall, is always there. The smell of it has followed you up. Here is a door. Listen! That short hacking cough, that tiny, helpless wail—what do they mean? They mean that the soiled bow of white you saw on the door downstairs will have another story to tell—Oh! a sadly familiar story—before the day is at an end. The child is dying with measles. With half a chance it might have lived; but it had none. That dark bedroom killed it.

"It was took all of a suddint," says the mother, smoothing the throbbing little body with trembling hands. There is no unkindness in the rough voice of the man in the jumper, who sits by the window grimly smoking a clay pipe, with the little life ebbing out in his sight, bitter as his words sound: "Hush, Mary! If we cannot keep the baby, need we complain—such as we?"

Such as we! What if the words ring in your ears as we grope our way up the stairs and down from floor to floor, listening to the sounds behind the closed doors—some of quarrelling, some of coarse songs, more of profanity. They are true. When the summer heats come with their suffering they have meaning more terrible than words can tell. Come over here. Step carefully over this baby—it is a baby, spite of its rags and dirt—under these iron bridges called fire escapes, but loaded down, despite the incessant watchfulness of the firemen, with broken household goods, with washtubs and barrels, over which no man could climb from a fire. This gap between dingy brick walls is the yard. That strip of smoke-colored sky up there is the heaven of these people. Do you wonder the name does not attract them to the churches? That baby's parents live in the rear tenement here. She is at least as clean as the steps we are now climbing. There are plenty of houses with half a hundred such in. The tenement is much like the one in front we just left, only fouler, closer, darker—we will not say more cheerless. The word is a mockery. A hundred thousand people lived in rear tenements in New York last year. Here is a room neater than the rest. The woman, a stout matron with hard lines of care in her face, is at the washtub. "I try to keep the childer clean," she says, apologetically, but with a hopeless glance around. The spice of hot soapsuds is added to the air already tainted with the smell of boiling cabbage, of rags and uncleanliness all about. It makes an overpowering compound. It is Thursday, but patched linen is hung upon the pulley line from the window. There is no Monday cleaning in the tenements. It is washday all the week round, for a change of clothing is scarce among the poor. They are poverty's honest badge, these peren-

An Old Rear-Tenement in Roosevelt Street

nial lines of rags hung out to dry, those that are not the washerwoman's professional shingle. The true line to be drawn between pauperism and honest poverty is the clothesline. With it begins the effort to be clean that is the first and the best evidence of a desire to be honest.

What sort of an answer, think you, would come from these tenements to the question "Is life worth living?" were they heard at all in the discussion? It may be that this, cut from the last report but one of the Association for the Improvement of the Condition of the Poor, a long name for a weary task, has a suggestion of it: "In the depth of winter the attention of the Association was called to a Protestant family living in a garret in a miserable tenement in Cherry Street. The family's condition was most deplorable. The man, his wife, and three small children shivering in one room through the roof of which the pitiless winds of winter whistled. The room was almost barren of furniture; the parents slept on the floor, the elder children in boxes, and the baby was swung in an old shawl attached to the rafters by cords by way of a hammock. The father, a seaman, had been obliged to give up that calling because he was in consumption, and was unable to provide either bread or fire for his little ones."[5]

Perhaps this may be put down as an exceptional case, but one that came to my notice some months ago in a Seventh Ward tenement was typical enough to escape that reproach. There were nine in the family: husband, wife, an aged grandmother, and six children; honest, hardworking Germans, scrupulously neat, but poor. All nine lived in two rooms, one about ten feet square that served as parlor, bedroom, and eating room, the other, a small half room made into a kitchen. The rent was seven dollars and a half a month, more than a week's wages for the husband and father, who was the only breadwinner in the family. That day the mother had thrown herself out of the window, and was carried up from the street dead. She was "discouraged," said some of the other women from the tenement, who had come in to look after the children while a messenger carried the news to the father at the shop. They went stolidly about their task, although they were evidently not without feeling for the dead woman. No doubt she was wrong in not taking life philosophically, as did the four families a city missionary found housekeeping in the four corners of one room. They got along well enough together until one of the families took a boarder and made trouble. Philosophy, according to my optimistic friend, naturally inhabits the tenements. The people who live there come to look upon death in a different way from the rest of us—do not take it as hard. He has never found time to explain how the fact fits into his general theory that life is not unbearable in the tenements. Unhappily for the philosophy of the slums, it is too apt to be of the kind that readily recognizes the saloon, always handy, as the refuge from every trouble, and shapes its practice according to the discovery.

V

The Italian in New York

CERTAINLY A PICTURESQUE, if not very tidy, element has been added to the population in the "assisted" Italian immigrant who claims so large a share of public attention, partly because he keeps coming at such a tremendous rate, but chiefly because he elects to stay in New York, or near enough for it to serve as his base of operations, and here promptly reproduces conditions of destitution and disorder which, set in the framework of Mediterranean exuberance, are the delight of the artist, but in a matter-of-fact American community become its danger and reproach. The reproduction is made easier in New York because he finds the material ready to hand in the worst of the slum tenements; but even where it is not he soon reduces what he does find to his own level, if allowed to follow his natural bent.* The Italian comes in at the bottom, and in the genera-

---

*The process can be observed in the Italian tenements in Harlem (Little Italy), which, since their occupation by these people, have been gradually sinking to the slum level.

tion that came over the sea he stays there. In the slums he is welcomed as a tenant who "makes less trouble" than the contentious Irishman or the order-loving German, that is to say: is content to live in a pig-sty and submits to robbery at the hands of the rent collector without murmur. Yet this very tractability makes of him in good hands, when firmly and intelligently managed, a really desirable tenant. But it is not his good fortune often to fall in with other hospitality upon his coming than that which brought him here for its own profit, and has no idea of letting go its grip upon him as long as there is a cent to be made out of him.

Recent Congressional inquiries have shown the nature of the "as-sistance" he receives from greedy steamship agents and "bankers," who persuade him by false promises to mortgage his home, his few belongings, and his wages for months to come for a ticket to the land where plenty of work is to be had at princely wages.[1] The padrone—the "banker," is nothing else—having made his ten percent out of him en route, receives him at the landing and turns him to double account as a wage earner and a rent payer. In each of these roles he is made to yield a profit to his unscrupulous countryman, whom he trusts im-plicitly with the instinct of utter helplessness. The man is so ignorant that, as one of the sharpers who prey upon him put it once, it "would be downright sinful not to take him in." His ignorance and uncon-querable suspicion of strangers dig the pit into which he falls. He not only knows no word of English, but he does not know enough to learn. Rarely only can he write his own language. Unlike the German, who begins learning English the day he lands as a matter of duty, or the Polish Jew, who takes it up as soon as he is able as an investment, the Italian learns slowly, if at all. Even his boy, born here, often speaks his native tongue indifferently. He is forced, therefore, to have con-stant recourse to the middleman, who makes him pay handsomely at every turn. He hires him out to the railroad contractor, receiving a commission from the employer as well as from the laborer, and repeats the performance monthly, or as often as he can have him dismissed. In the city he contracts for his lodgings, subletting to him space in the vilest tenements at extortionate rents, and sets an example that does not lack imitators. The "princely wages" have vanished with his coming, and in their place hardships and a dollar a day, beheft with the padrone's merciless mortgage, confront him. Bred to even worse fare, he takes both as a matter of course, and, applying the maxim that it is not what one makes but what he saves that makes him rich, manages to turn the very dirt of the streets into a hoard of gold, with which he either returns to his Southern home, or brings over his family to join in his work and in his fortunes the next season.

The discovery was made by earlier explorers that there is money in New York's ash barrel, but it was left to the genius of the padrone to develop the full resources of the mine that has become the exclusive preserve of the Italian immigrant. Only a few years ago, when rag-picking was carried on in a desultory and irresponsible sort of way, the city hired gangs of men to trim the ash scows before they were sent out to sea. The trimming consisted in levelling out the dirt as it was dumped from the carts, so that the scow might be evenly loaded. The men were paid a dollar and a half a day, kept what they found that was worth having, and allowed the swarms of Italians who hung about the dumps to do the heavy work for them, letting them have their pick of the loads for their trouble. Today Italians contract for the work, paying large sums to be permitted to do it. The city received not less than $80,000 last year for the sale of this privilege to the contractors, who in addition have to pay gangs of their countrymen for sorting out the bones, rags, tin cans and other waste that are found in the ashes and form the staples of their trade and their sources of revenue. The effect has been to vastly increase the power of the padrone, or his ally, the contractor, by giving him exclusive control of the one

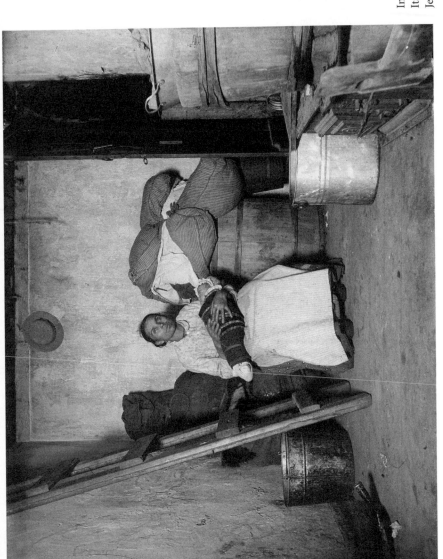

In the Home of an
Italian Rag-Picker,
Jersey Street

industry in which the Italian was formerly an independent "dealer," and reducing him literally to the plane of the dump. Whenever the back of the sanitary police is turned, he will make his home in the filthy burrows where he works by day, sleeping and eating his meals under the dump, on the edge of slimy depths and amid surroundings full of unutterable horror. The city did not bargain to house, though it is content to board, him so long as he can make the ash barrels yield the food to keep him alive, and a vigorous campaign is carried on at intervals against these unlicensed dump settlements; but the temptation of having to pay no rent is too strong, and they are driven from one dump only to find lodgement under another a few blocks farther up or down the river. The fiercest warfare is waged over the patronage of the dumps by rival factions represented by opposing contractors, and it has happened that the defeated party has endeavored to capture by strategy what he failed to carry by assault. It augurs unsuspected adaptability in the Italian to our system of self-government that these rivalries have more than once been suspected of being behind the sharpening of city ordinances, that were apparently made in good faith to prevent meddling with the refuse in the ash barrels or in transit.

Did the Italian always adapt himself as readily to the operation of the civil law as to the manipulation of political "pull" on occasion, he would save himself a good deal of unnecessary trouble. Ordinarily he is easily enough governed by authority—always excepting Sunday, when he settles down to a game of cards and lets loose all his bad passions. Like the Chinese, the Italian is a born gambler. His soul is in the game from the moment the cards are on the table, and very frequently his knife is in it too before the game is ended. No Sunday has passed in New York since "the Bend" became a suburb of Naples without one or more of these murderous affrays coming to the notice of the police. As a rule that happens only when the man the game went against is either dead or so badly wounded as to require instant surgical help. As to the other, unless he be caught red-handed, the chances that the police will ever get him are slim indeed. The wounded man can seldom be persuaded to betray him. He wards off all inquiries with a wicked "I fix him myself," and there the matter rests until he either dies or recovers. If the latter, the community hears after a while of another Italian affray, a man stabbed in a quarrel, dead or dying, and the police know that "he" has been fixed, and the account squared.

With all his conspicuous faults, the swarthy Italian immigrant has his redeeming traits. He is as honest as he is hotheaded. There are no Italian burglars in the Rogues' Gallery; the ex-brigand toils peacefully with pickaxe and shovel on American ground. His boy occasionally shows, as a pickpocket, the results of his training with the toughs of the Sixth Ward slums. The only criminal business to which the father occasionally lends his hand, outside of murder, is a bunco game, of

VI

The Bend

WHERE MULBERRY STREET CROOKS like an elbow within hail of the old depravity of the Five Points, is "the Bend," foul core of New York's slums.[1] Long years ago the cows coming home from the pasture trod a path over this hill. Echoes of tinkling bells linger there still, but they do not call up memories of green meadows and summer fields; they proclaim the homecoming of the ragpicker's cart. In the memory of man the old cow path has never been other than a vast human pigsty. There is but one "Bend" in the world, and it is enough. The city authorities, moved by the angry protests of ten years of sanitary reform effort, have decided that it is too much and must come down. Another Paradise Park[2] will take its place and let in sunlight and air to work such transformation as at the Five Points, around the corner of the next block. Never was change more urgently needed. Around "the Bend" cluster the bulk of the tenements that are stamped as altogether bad, even by the optimists of the Health Department. Incessant raids cannot keep down the crowds that make them their home. In the scores of back alleys, of stable lanes and hidden byways, of which the rent-collector alone can keep track, they share such shelter as the ramshackle structures afford with every kind of abomination rifled from the dumps and ash barrels of the city. Here, too, shunning the light, skulks the unclean beast of dishonest idleness. "The Bend" is the home of the tramp as well as the ragpicker.

It is not much more than twenty years since a census of "the Bend" district returned only twenty-four of the six hundred and nine tenements as in decent condition.[3] Three-fourths of the population of the "Bloody Sixth" Ward were then Irish. The army of tramps that grew up after the disbandment of the armies in the field, and has kept up its muster roll, together with the inrush of the Italian tide, have ever since opposed a stubborn barrier to all efforts at permanent improvement. The more that has been done, the less it has seemed to accomplish in the way of real relief, until it has at last become clear that nothing short of entire demolition will ever prove of radical benefit. Corruption could not have chosen ground for its stand with better promise of success. The whole district is a maze of narrow, often unsuspected passageways—necessarily, for there is scarce a lot that has not two, three, or four tenements upon it, swarming with unwholesome crowds. What a bird's-eye view of "the Bend" would be like is a matter of bewildering conjecture. Its everyday appearance, as seen from the corner of Bayard Street on a sunny day, is one of the sights of New York.

Bayard Street is the high road to Jewtown across the Bowery, picketed from end to end with the outposts of Israel. Hebrew faces, Hebrew signs, and incessant chatter in the queer lingo that passes for Hebrew on the East Side attend the curious wanderer to the very corner of Mulberry Street. But the moment he turns the corner the scene changes abruptly. Before him lies spread out what might better be the marketplace in some town in southern Italy than a street in New York —all but the houses; they are still the same old tenements of the un-romantic type. But for once they do not make the foreground in a slum picture from the American metropolis. The interest centers not in them, but in the crowd they shelter only when the street is not pref-erable, and that with the Italian is only when it rains or he is sick. When the sun shines the entire population seeks the street, carrying on its household work, its bargaining, its lovemaking on street or sidewalk, or idling there when it has nothing better to do, with the reverse of the impulse that makes the Polish Jew coop himself up in his den with the thermometer at stewing heat. Along the curb women sit in rows, young and old alike with the odd head covering, pad or turban, that is their badge of servitude—hers to bear the burden as long as she lives—haggling over baskets of frowsy weeds, some sort of salad probably, stale tomatoes, and oranges not above suspicion. Ash barrels serve them as counters, and not infrequently does the ar-rival of the official cart en route for the dump cause a temporary sus-pension of trade until the barrels have been emptied and restored. Hucksters' and pedlars' carts make two rows of booths in the street itself, and along the houses is still another—a perpetual market doing a very lively trade in its own queer staples, found nowhere on Ameri-can ground save in "the Bend." Two old hags, camping on the pave-ment, are dispensing stale bread, baked not in loaves, but in the shape of big wreaths like exaggerated crullers, out of bags of dirty bedtick. There is no use disguising the fact: they look like and they probably are old mattresses mustered into service under the pressure of a rush of trade. Stale bread was the one article the health officers, after a raid on the market, once reported as "not unwholesome." It was only dis-gusting. Here is a brawny butcher, sleeves rolled up above the elbows and clay pipe in mouth, skinning a kid that hangs from his hook.

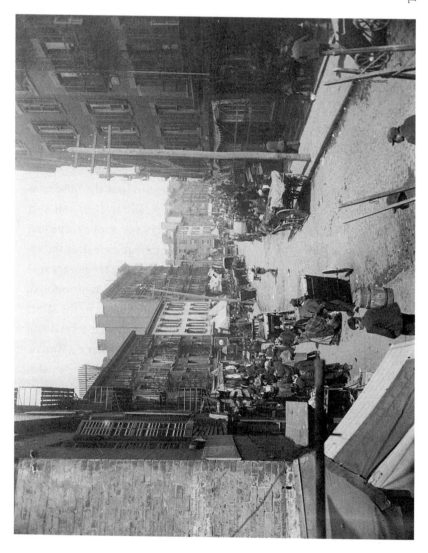

They will tell you with a laugh at the Elizabeth Street police station that only a few days ago when a dead goat had been reported lying in Pell Street it was mysteriously missing by the time the offal cart came to take it away. It turned out that an Italian had carried it off in his sack to a wake or feast of some sort in one of the back alleys.

On either side of the narrow entrance to Bandit's Roost, one of the most notorious of these, is a shop that is a fair sample of the sort of invention necessity is the mother of in "the Bend." It is not enough that trucks and ash barrels have provided four distinct lines of shops that are not down on the insurance maps, to accommodate the crowds. Here have the very hallways been made into shops. Three feet wide by four deep, they have just room for one, the shopkeeper, who, himself within, does his business outside, his wares displayed on a board hung across what was once the hall door. Back of the rear wall of this unique shop a hole has been punched from the hall into the alley and the tenants go that way. One of the shops is a "tobacco bureau," presided over by an unknown saint, done in yellow and red—there is not a shop, a stand, or an ash barrel doing duty for a counter, that has not its patron saint—the other is a fish stand full of slimy, odd-looking creatures, fish that never swam in American waters, or if they did, were never seen on an American fish stand, and snails. Big, awkward sausages, anything but appetizing, hang in the grocer's doorway, knocking against the customer's head as if to remind him that they are there waiting to be bought. What they are I never had the courage to ask. Down the street comes a file of women carrying enormous bundles of firewood on their heads, loads of decaying vegetables from the market wagons in their aprons, and each a baby at the breast supported by a sort of sling that prevents it from tumbling down. The women do all the carrying, all the work one sees going on in "the Bend." The men sit or stand in the streets, on trucks, or in the open doors of the saloons smoking black clay pipes, talking and gesticulating as if forever on the point of coming to blows. Near a particularly boisterous group, a really pretty girl with a string of amber beads twisted artlessly in the knot of her raven hair has been bargaining long and earnestly with an old granny, who presides over a wheelbarrow load of secondhand stockings and faded cotton yarn, industriously darning the biggest holes while she extols the virtues of her stock. One of the rude swains, with patched overalls tucked into his boots, to whom the girl's eyes have strayed more than once, steps up and gallantly offers to pick her out the handsomest pair, whereat she laughs and pushes him away with a gesture which he interprets as an invitation to stay; and he does, evidently to the satisfaction of the beldame, who forthwith raises her prices fifty percent without being detected by the girl.

Red bandannas and yellow kerchiefs are everywhere; so is the Italian tongue, infinitely sweeter than the harsh gutturals of the Russian Jew around the corner. So are the "ristorantes" of innumerable Pasquales; half of the people in "the Bend" are christened Pasquale, or get the name in some other way. When the police do not know the name of an escaped murderer, they guess at Pasquale and send the name out on alarm; in nine cases out of ten it fits. So are the "banks" that hang out their shingle as tempting bait on every hand.[4] There are half a dozen in the single block, steamship agencies, employment offices, and savings banks, all in one. So are the toddling youngsters, bowlegged half of them, and so are no end of mothers, present and prospective, some of them scarce yet in their teens. Those who are not in the street are hanging halfway out of the windows, shouting at someone below. All "the Bend" must be, if not altogether, at least half out-of-doors when the sun shines.

In the street, where the city wields the broom, there is at least an effort at cleaning up. There has to be, or it would be swamped in filth overrunning from the courts and alleys where the ragpickers live. It requires more than ordinary courage to explore these on a hot day. The undertaker has to do it then, the police always. Right here, in the tenement on the east side of the street, they found little Antonia Candia, victim of fiendish cruelty, "covered," says the account found in the records of the Society for the Prevention of Cruelty to Children, "with sores, and her hair matted with dried blood." Abuse is the normal condition of "the Bend," murder its everyday crop, with the tenants not always the criminals. In this block between Bayard, Park, Mulberry, and Baxter Streets, "the Bend" proper, the late Tenement House Commission counted 155 deaths of children* in a specimen year (1882).[5] Their percentage of the total mortality in the block was 68.28, while for the whole city the proportion was only 46.20. The infant mortality in any city or place as compared with the whole number of deaths is justly considered a good barometer of its general sanitary condition. Here, in this tenement, No. 59½, next to Bandit's Roost, fourteen persons died that year, and eleven of them were children; in No. 61 eleven, and eight of them not yet five years old. According to the records in the Bureau of Vital Statistics only thirty-nine people lived in No. 59½ in the year 1888, nine of them little children. There were five baby funerals in that house the same year. Out of the alley itself, No. 59, nine dead were carried in 1888, five in baby coffins. Here is the record of the year for the whole block, as furnished by the Registrar of Vital Statistics, Dr. Roger S. Tracy:

The general death rate for the whole city that year was 26.27.

These figures speak for themselves, when it is shown that in the model tenement across the way at Nos. 48 and 50, where the same class of people live in greater swarms (161, according to the record), but under good management, and in decent quarters, the hearse

---

* The term *child* means in the mortality tables a person under five years of age. Children five years old and over figure in the tables as adults.

Deaths and Death Rates in 1888 in Baxter and Mulberry Streets, between Park and Bayard Streets

	POPULATION			DEATHS				DEATH RATE		
	5 years old and over	Under 5 years	Total	5 years old and over	Under 5 years	Total	5 years old and over	Under 5 years	General
Baxter Street	1,918	315	2,233	26	46	72	13.56	146.02 [146.03]	32.24
Mulberry Street	2,788	629	3,417	44	86	130	15.78	136.70 [136.72]	38.05
Total	4,706	944	5,650	70	132	202	14.87	139.83	35.75

EDITOR'S NOTE: The death rate given in this table and the text is expressed in the customary form of deaths per thousand live persons. Printer's or arithmetical errors were made in the categories of Baxter Street, under five years, and Mulberry Street, under five years; these should read 146.03 and 136.72 respectively.

called that year only twice, once for a baby. The agent of the Christian people who built that tenement will tell you that Italians are good tenants, while the owner of the alley will oppose every order to put his property in repair with the claim that they are the worst of a bad lot. Both are right, from their different standpoints. It is the standpoint that makes the difference—and the tenant.

What if I were to tell you that this alley, and more tenement property in "the Bend," all of it notorious for years as the vilest and worst to be found anywhere, stood associated on the tax books all through the long struggle to make its owners responsible, which has at last resulted in a qualified victory for the law, with the name of an honored family, one of the "oldest and best," rich in possessions and in influence, and high in the councils of the city's government? It would be but the plain truth. Nor would it be the only instance by very many that stand recorded on the Health Department's books of a kind that has come near to making the name of landlord as odious in New York as it has become in Ireland.

Bottle Alley is around the corner in Baxter Street; but it is a fair specimen of its kind, wherever found. Look into any of these houses, everywhere the same piles of rags, of malodorous bones and musty paper, all of which the sanitary police flatter themselves they have banished to the dumps and the warehouses. Here is a "flat" of "parlor" and two pitch-dark coops called bedrooms. Truly, the bed is all there is room for. The family teakettle is on the stove, doing duty for the time being as a washboiler. By night it will have returned to its proper use again, a practical illustration of how poverty in "the Bend" makes both ends meet. One, two, three beds are there, if the old boxes and heaps of foul straw can be called by that name; a broken stove with crazy pipe from which the smoke leaks at every joint, a table of rough boards propped up on boxes, piles of rubbish in the corner. The closeness and smell are appalling. How many people sleep here?

Bandit's Roost

The woman with the red bandanna shakes her head sullenly, but the barelegged girl with the bright face counts on her fingers—five, six!

"Six, sir!" Six grown people and five children.

"Only five," she says with a smile, swathing the little one on her lap in its cruel bandage. There is another in the cradle—actually a cradle. And how much the rent?

Nine and a half, and "please, sir! he won't put the paper on."

"He" is the landlord. The "paper" hangs in musty shreds on the wall.

Well do I recollect the visit of a health inspector to one of these tenements on a July day when the thermometer outside was climbing high in the nineties; but inside, in that awful room, with half a dozen persons washing, cooking, and sorting rags, lay the dying baby alongside the stove, where the doctor's thermometer ran up to 115°! Perishing for the want of a breath of fresh air in this city of untold charities! Did not the manager of the Fresh Air Fund write to the pastor of an Italian church only last year* that "no one asked for Italian children," and hence he could not send any to the country?

Half a dozen blocks up Mulberry Street there is a ragpickers' settlement, a sort of overflow from "the Bend," that exists today in all its pristine nastiness. Something like forty families are packed into five old two-story and attic houses that were built to hold five, and out in the yards additional crowds are, or were until very recently, accommodated in sheds built of all sorts of old boards and used as drying racks for the Italian tenants' "stock." I found them empty when I visited the settlement while writing this. The last two tenants had just left. Their fate was characteristic. The "old man," who lived in the corner coop, with barely room to crouch beside the stove—there would not have been room for him to sleep had not age crooked his frame to

---

* See City Mission Report, February, 1890, page 77.

Bottle Alley

showed that in "the Bend" district, between Broadway and the Bowery and Canal and Chatham Streets, in a total of four thousand three hundred and sixty-seven "apartments" only nine were for the moment vacant, while in the old "Africa," west of Broadway, that receives the overflow from Mulberry Street and is rapidly changing its character, the notice "standing room only" is up. Not a single vacant room was found there. Nearly a hundred and fifty "lodgers" were driven out of two adjoining Mulberry Street tenements, one of them aptly named "the House of Blazes," during that census. What squalor and degradation inhabit these dens the health officers know. Through the long summer days their carts patrol "the Bend," scattering disinfectants in streets and lanes, in sinks and cellars, and hidden hovels where the tramp burrows. From midnight till far into the small hours of the morning the policeman's thundering rap on closed doors is heard, with his stern command, "Apri port'!" on his rounds gathering evidence of illegal overcrowding. The doors are opened unwillingly enough—but the order means business, and the tenant knows it even if he understands no word of English—upon such scenes as the one presented in the picture. It was photographed by flashlight on just such a visit. In a room not thirteen feet either way slept twelve men and women, two or three in bunks set in a sort of alcove, the rest on the floor. A kerosene lamp burned dimly in the fearful atmosphere, probably to guide other and later arrivals to their "beds," for it was only just past midnight. A baby's fretful wail came from an adjoining hall room, where, in the semidarkness, three recumbent figures could be made out. The "apartment" was one of three in two adjoining buildings we had found, within half an hour, similarly crowded. Most of the men were lodgers, who slept there for five cents a spot.

Another room on the top floor, that had been examined a few nights before, was comparatively empty. There were only four per-

Lodgers in a Crowded Bayard Street Tenement—"Five Cents a Spot"

sons in it, two men, an old woman, and a young girl. The landlord opened the door with alacrity, and exhibited with a proud sweep of his hand the sacrifice he had made of his personal interests to satisfy the law. Our visit had been anticipated. The policeman's back was probably no sooner turned than the room was reopened for business.

kind of war correspondent—groped its way in single file through the narrow rift between slimy walls to the tenements in the rear. Twice during our trip we stumbled over tramps, both women, asleep in the passage. They were quietly passed to the rear, receiving sundry prods and punches on the trip, and headed for the station in the grip of a policeman as a sort of advance guard of the coming army. After what seemed half a mile of groping in the dark we emerged finally into the alley proper, where light escaping through the cracks of closed shutters on both sides enabled us to make out the contour of three rickety frame tenements. Snatches of ribald songs and peals of coarse laughter reached us from now this, now that of the unseen burrows.

"School is in," said the sergeant drily as we stumbled down the worn steps of the next cellarway. A kick of his boot heel sent the door flying into the room.

A room perhaps a dozen feet square, with walls and ceiling that might once have been clean—assuredly the floor had not in the memory of man, if indeed there was other floor than hard-trodden mud—but were now covered with a brown crust that, touched with the end of a club, came off in shuddering showers of crawling bugs, revealing the blacker filth beneath. Grouped about a beer keg that was propped on the wreck of a broken chair, a foul and ragged host of men and women, on boxes, benches, and stools. Tomato cans filled at the keg were passed from hand to hand. In the center of the group a sallow, wrinkled hag, evidently the ruler of the feast, dealt out the hideous stuff. A pile of copper coins rattled in her apron, the very pennies received with such showers of blessings upon the giver that afternoon; the faces of some of the women were familiar enough from the streets as those of beggars forever whining for a penny, "to keep a family from starving." Their whine and boisterous hilarity were alike hushed now. In sullen, cowed submission they sat, evidently knowing what to expect. At the first glimpse of the uniform in the open door some in the group, customers with a record probably, had turned their heads away to avoid the searching glance of the officer; while a few, less used to such scenes, stared defiantly.

A single stride took the sergeant into the middle of the room, and with a swinging blow of his club he knocked the faucet out of the keg and the half-filled can from the boss hag's hand. As the contents of both splashed upon the floor, half a dozen of the group made a sudden dash, and with shoulders humped above their heads to shield their skulls against the dreaded locust broke for the door. They had not counted upon the policemen outside. There was a brief struggle, two or three heavy thumps, and the runaways were brought back to where their comrades crouched in dogged silence.

"Thirteen!" called the sergeant, completing his survey. "Take them out. 'Revolvers'[1] all but one. Good for six months on the island, the whole lot." The exception was a young man not much if any over twenty, with a hard look of dissipation on his face. He seemed less unconcerned than the rest, but tried hard to make up for it by putting on the boldest air he could. "Come down early," commented the officer, shoving him along with his stick. "There is need of it. They don't last long at this. That stuff is brewed to kill at long range."

At the head of the cellar steps we encountered a similar procession from farther back in the alley, where still another was forming to take up its march to the station. Out in the street was heard the tramp of the hosts already pursuing that well-trodden path, as with a fresh complement of men we entered the next stale-beer alley. There were four dives in one cellar here. The filth and the stench were utterly unbearable; even the sergeant turned his back and fled after scattering the crowd with his club and starting them toward the door. The very dog in the alley preferred the cold flags for a berth to the stifling cellar. We found it lying outside. Seventy-five tramps, male and female, were arrested in the four small rooms. In one of them, where the air seemed thick enough to cut with a knife, we found a woman, a mother with a newborn babe on a heap of dirty straw. She was asleep and was left until an ambulance could be called to take her to the hospital.

Returning to the station with this batch, we found every window in the building thrown open to the cold October wind, and the men from the sergeant down smoking the strongest cigars that could be obtained by way of disinfecting the place. Two hundred and seventy-five tramps had been jammed into the cells to be arraigned next morning in the police court on the charge of vagrancy, with the certain prospect of six months "on the Island." Of the sentence at least they were sure. As to the length of the men's stay the experienced official at the desk was sceptical, it being then within a month of an important election. If tramps have nothing else to call their own they have votes, and votes that are for sale cheap for cash. About election time this gives them a "pull," at least by proxy. The sergeant observed, as if it were the most natural thing in the world, that he had more than once seen the same tramp sent to Blackwell's Island twice in twenty-four hours for six months at a time.

As a thief never owns to his calling, however devoid of moral scruples, preferring to style himself a speculator, so this real home product of the slums, the stale-beer dive, is known about "the Bend" by the more dignified name of the two-cent restaurant. Usually, as in this instance, it is in some cellar giving on a back alley. Doctored, unlicensed beer is its chief ware. Sometimes a cup of "coffee" and a stale roll may be had for two cents. The men pay the score. To the women —unutterable horror of the suggestion—the place is free. The beer is collected from the kegs put on the sidewalk by the saloonkeeper to await the brewer's cart, and is touched up with drugs to put a froth on it. The privilege to sit all night on a chair, or sleep on a table, or in a barrel, goes with each round of drinks. Generally an Italian, some-

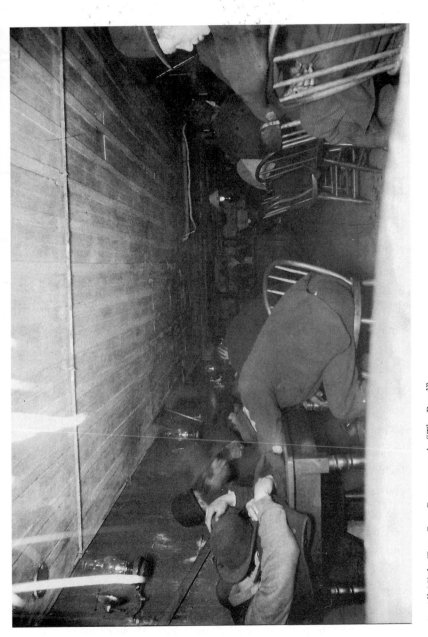

An All-Night Two-Cent Restaurant, in "The Bend"

times a Negro, occasionally a woman, "runs" the dive. Their customers, alike homeless and hopeless in their utter wretchedness, are the professional tramps, and these only. The meanest thief is infinitely above the stale-beer level. Once upon that plane there is no escape. To sink below it is impossible; no one ever rose from it. One night spent in a stale-beer dive is like the traditional putting on of the uniform of the caste, the discarded rags of an old tramp. That stile once crossed, the lane has no longer a turn; and contrary to the proverb, it is usually not long either.

With the gravitation of the Italian tramp landlord toward the old stronghold of the African on the West Side, a share of the stale-beer traffic has left "the Bend"; but its headquarters will always remain there, the real home of trampdom, just as Fourteenth Street is its limit. No real tramp crosses that frontier after nightfall and in the daytime only to beg. Repulsive as the business is, its profits to the Italian dive-keeper are considerable; in fact, barring a slight outlay in the ingredients that serve to give "life" to the beer dregs, it is all profit. The "banker" who curses the Italian colony does not despise taking a hand in it, and such a thing as a stale-beer trust on a Mulberry Street scale may yet be among the possibilities. One of these bankers, who was once known to the police as the keeper of one notorious stale-beer dive and the active backer of others, is today an extensive manufacturer of macaroni, the owner of several big tenements and other real estate; and the capital, it is said, has all come out of his old business. Very likely it is true.

On hot summer nights it is no rare experience when exploring the worst of the tenements in "the Bend" to find the hallways occupied by rows of "sitters," tramps whom laziness or hard luck has prevented from earning enough by their day's "labor" to pay the admission fee to a stale-beer dive, and who have their reasons for declining the hospitality of the police station lodging rooms. Huddled together in loathsome files, they squat there over night, or until an inquisitive policeman breaks up the congregation with his club, which in Mulberry Street has always free swing. At that season the woman tramp predominates. The men, some of them at least, take to the railroad track and to camping out when the nights grow warm, returning in the fall to prey on the city and to recruit their ranks from the lazy, the shiftless, and the unfortunate. Like a foul loadstone, "the Bend" attracts and brings them back, no matter how far they have wandered. For next to idleness the tramp loves rum; next to rum stale beer, its equivalent of the gutter. And the first and last go best together.

As "sitters" they occasionally find a job in the saloons about Chatham and Pearl Streets on cold winter nights, when the hallway is not practicable, that enables them to pick up a charity drink now and then and a bite of an infrequent sandwich. The barkeeper permits them to sit about the stove and by shivering invite the sympathy of transient customers. The dodge works well, especially about Christmas and election time, and the sitters are able to keep comfortably filled up to the advantage of their host. But to look thoroughly miserable they must keep awake. A tramp placidly dozing at the fire would not be an object of sympathy. To make sure that they do keep awake, the wily bartender makes them sit constantly swinging one foot like the pendulum of a clock. When it stops the slothful "sitter" is roused with a kick and "fired out." It is said by those who profess to know that habit has come to the rescue of over-sleepy tramps and that the old rounders can swing hand or foot in their sleep without betraying themselves. In some saloons "sitters" are let in at these seasons in fresh batches every hour.

On one of my visits to "the Bend" I came across a particularly ragged and disreputable tramp, who sat smoking his pipe on the rung of a ladder with such evident philosophic contentment in the busy labor of a score of ragpickers all about him, that I bade him sit for a picture, offering him ten cents for the job. He accepted the offer with hardly a nod, and sat patiently watching me from his perch until I got ready for work. Then he took the pipe out of his mouth and put it in his pocket, calmly declaring that it was not included in the contract, and that it was worth a quarter to have it go in the picture. The pipe, by the way, was of clay, and of the two-for-a-cent kind. But I had to give in. The man, scarce ten seconds employed at honest labor, even at sitting down, at which he was an undoubted expert, had gone on strike. He knew his rights and the value of "work," and was not to be cheated out of either.

Whence these tramps, and why the tramping? are questions oftener asked than answered. Ill-applied charity and idleness answer the first query. They are the whence, and to a large extent the why also. Once started on the career of a tramp, the man keeps to it because it is the laziest. Tramps and toughs profess the same doctrine, that the world owes them a living, but from standpoints that tend in different directions. The tough does not become a tramp, save in rare instances, when old and broken down. Even then usually he is otherwise disposed of. The devil has various ways of taking care of his own. Nor is the tramps' army recruited from any certain class. All occupations and most grades of society yield to it their contingent of idleness. Occasionally, from one cause or another, a recruit of a better stamp is forced into the ranks; but the first acceptance of alms puts a brand on the able-bodied man which his moral nature rarely hold out to efface. He seldom recovers his lost caste. The evolution is gradual, keeping step with the increasing shabbiness of his clothes and corresponding loss of self-respect, until he reaches the bottom in "the Bend."

Of the tough the tramp doctrine that the world owes him a living makes a thief; of the tramp a coward. Numbers only make him bold unless he has to do with defenceless women. In the city the policemen

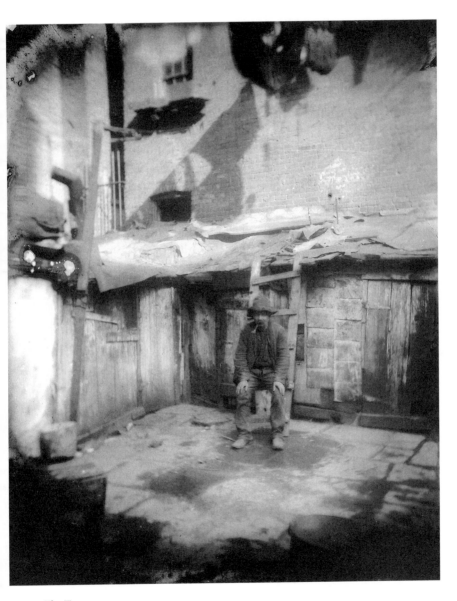

The Tramp

keep him straight enough. The women rob an occasional clothesline when no one is looking, or steal the pail and scrubbing brush with which they are set to clean up in the station house lodging rooms after their night's sleep. At the police station the roads of the tramp and the tough again converge. In midwinter, on the coldest nights, the sanitary police corral the tramps here and in their lodging houses and vaccinate them, despite their struggles and many oaths that they have recently been "scraped." The station house is the sieve that sifts out the chaff from the wheat, if there be any wheat there. A man goes from his first night's sleep on the hard slab of a police station lodging room to a deckhand's berth on an out-going steamer, to the recruiting office, to any work that is honest, or he goes "to the devil or the dives, same thing," says my friend, the sergeant, who knows.

magistrate: "The ten-cent lodging houses more than counterbalance the good done by the free reading room, lectures, and all other agencies of reform. Such lodging houses have caused more destitution, more beggary and crime than any other agency I know of." A very slight acquaintance with the subject is sufficient to convince the observer that neither authority overstates the fact. The two officials had reference, however, to two different grades of lodging houses. The cost of a night's lodging makes the difference. There is a wider gap between the "hotel"—they are all hotels—that charges a quarter and the one that furnishes a bed for a dime than between the bridal suite and the everyday hall bedroom of the ordinary hostelry.

The metropolis is to lots of people like a lighted candle to the moth. It attracts them in swarms that come year after year with the vague idea that they can get along here if anywhere; that something is bound to turn up among so many. Nearly all are young men, unsettled in life, many—most of them, perhaps—fresh from good homes, beyond a doubt with honest hopes of getting a start in the city and making a way for themselves. Few of them have much money to waste while looking around, and the cheapness of the lodging offered is an object. Fewer still know anything about the city and its pitfalls. They have come in search of crowds, of "life," and they gravitate naturally to the Bowery, the great democratic highway of the city, where the twenty-five-cent lodging houses take them in. In the alleged reading rooms of these great barracks, that often have accommodations, such as they are, for two, three, and even four hundred guests, they encounter three distinct classes of associates: the great mass adventurers like themselves, waiting there for something to turn up; a much smaller class of respectable clerks or mechanics, who, too poor or too lonely to have a home of their own, live this way from year to year; and lastly the thief in search of recruits for his trade. The sights the young stranger sees, and the company he keeps, in the Bowery are not of a kind to strengthen any moral principle he may have brought away from home, and by the time his money is gone, with no work yet in sight, and he goes down a step, a long step, to the fifteen-cent lodging house, he is ready for the tempter whom he finds waiting for him there, reinforced by the contingent of ex-convicts returning from the prisons after having served out their sentences for robbery or theft. Then it is that the something he has been waiting for turns up. The police returns have the record of it. "In nine cases out of ten," says Inspector Byrnes, "he turns out a thief, or a burglar, if, indeed, he does not sooner or later become a murderer." As a matter of fact, some of the most atrocious of recent murders have been the result of schemes of robbery hatched in these houses, and so frequent and bold have become the depredations of the lodging house thieves, that the authorities have been compelled to make a public demand for more effective laws that shall make them subject at all times to police regulation.

Inspector Byrnes observes that in the last two or three years at least four hundred young men have been arrested for petty crimes that originated in the lodging houses, and that in many cases it was their first step in crime. He adds his testimony to the notorious fact that three-fourths of the young men called on to plead to generally petty offences in the courts are under twenty years of age, poorly clad, and without means. The bearing of the remark is obvious. One of the, to the police, well-known thieves who lived, when out of jail, at the Windsor, a well-known lodging house in the Bowery, went to Johnstown after the flood and was shot and killed there while robbing the dead.

An idea of just how this particular scheme of corruption works, with an extra touch of infamy thrown in, may be gathered from the story of David Smith, the "New York Fagin," who was convicted and sent to prison last year through the instrumentality of the Society for the Prevention of Cruelty to Children. Here is the account from the Society's last report:

"The boy, Edward Mulhearn, fourteen years old, had run away from his home in Jersey City, thinking he might find work and friends in New York. He may have been a trifle wild. He met Smith on the Bowery and recognized him as an acquaintance. When Smith offered him a supper and bed he was only too glad to accept. Smith led the boy to a vile lodging house on the Bowery, where he introduced him to his 'pals' and swore he would make a man of him before he was a week older. Next day he took the unsuspecting Edward all over the Bowery and Grand Street, showed him the sights and drew his attention to the careless way the ladies carried their bags and purses and the easy thing it was to get them. He induced Edward to try his hand. Edward tried and won. He was richer by three dollars! It did seem easy. 'Of course it is,' said his companion. From that time Smith took the boy on a number of thieving raids, but he never seemed to become adept enough to be trusted out of range of the 'Fagin's' watchful eye. When he went out alone he generally returned empty-handed. This did not suit Smith. It was then he conceived the idea of turning this little inferior thief into a superior beggar. He took the boy into his room and burned his arms with a hot iron. The boy screamed and entreated in vain. The merciless wretch pressed the iron deep into the tender flesh, and afterward applied acid to the raw wound.

"Thus prepared, with his arm inflamed, swollen, and painful, Edward was sent out every day by this fiend, who never let him out of his sight, and threatened to burn his arm off if he did not beg money enough. He was instructed to tell people the wound had been caused by acid falling upon his arm at the works. Edward was now too much under the man's influence to resist or disobey him. He begged hard and handed Smith the pennies faithfully. He received in return bad food and worse treatment."[2]

The reckoning came when the wretch encountered the boy's father, in search of his child, in the Bowery, and fell under suspicion of knowing more than he pretended of the lad's whereabouts. He was found in his den with a half dozen of his chums revelling on the proceeds of the boy's begging for the day.

The twenty-five cent lodging house keeps up the pretence of a bedroom, though the head-high partition enclosing a space just large enough to hold a cot and a chair and allow the man room to pull off his clothes is the shallowest of all pretences. The fifteen-cent bed stands boldly forth without screen in a room full of bunks with sheets as yellow and blankets as foul. At the ten-cent level the locker for the sleeper's clothes disappears. There is no longer need of it. The tramp limit is reached, and there is nothing to lock up save, on general principles, the lodger. Usually the ten- and seven-cent lodgings are different grades of the same abomination. Some sort of an apology for a bed, with mattress and blanket, represents the aristocratic purchase of the tramp who, by a lucky stroke of beggary, has exchanged the chance of an empty box or ash barrel for shelter on the quality floor of one of these "hotels." A strip of canvas, strung between rough timbers, without covering of any kind, does for the couch of the seven-cent lodger who prefers the questionable comfort of a red-hot stove close to his elbow to the revelry of the stale-beer dive. It is not the most secure perch in the world. Uneasy sleepers roll off at intervals, but they have not far to fall to the next tier of bunks, and the commotion that ensues is speedily quieted by the boss and his club. On cold winter nights, when every bunk had its tenant, I have stood in such a lodging room more than once, and listening to the snoring of the sleepers like the regular strokes of an engine, and the slow creaking of the beams under their restless weight, imagined myself on shipboard and experienced the very real nausea of seasickness. The one thing that did not favor the deception was the air; its character could not be mistaken.

The proprietor of one of these seven-cent houses was known to

Bunks in a Seven-Cent Lodging House, Pell Street

me as a man of reputed wealth and respectability. He "ran" three such establishments and made, it was said, $8,000 a year clear profit on his investment. He lived in a handsome house quite near to the stylish precincts of Murray Hill, where the nature of his occupation was not suspected. A notice that was posted on the wall of the lodgers' room suggested at least an effort to maintain his uptown standing in the slums. It read: "No swearing or loud talking after nine o'clock." Before nine no exceptions were taken to the natural vulgarity of the place; but that was the limit.

There are no licensed lodging houses known to me which charge less than seven cents for even such a bed as this canvas strip, though there are unlicensed ones enough where one may sleep on the floor for five cents a spot, or squat in a sheltered hallway for three. The police station lodging house, where the soft side of a plank is the regulation couch, is next in order. The manner in which this police bed is "made up" is interesting in its simplicity. The loose planks that make the platform are simply turned over, and the job is done, with an occasional coat of whitewash thrown in to sweeten things. I know of only one easier way, but, so far as I am informed, it has never been introduced in this country. It used to be practised, if report spoke truly, in certain old-country towns. The "bed" was represented by clotheslines stretched across the room upon which the sleepers hung by the armpits for a penny a night. In the morning the boss woke them up by simply untying the line at one end and letting it go with its load; a laborsaving device certainly, and highly successful in attaining the desired end.

According to the police figures, 4,974,025 separate lodgings were furnished last year by these dormitories, between two and three hundred in number, and, adding the 147,634 lodgings furnished by the station houses, the total of the homeless army was 5,121,659, an average of over fourteen thousand homeless men* for every night in the year! The health officers, professional optimists always in matters that trench upon their official jurisdiction, insist that the number is not quite so large as here given. But, apart from any slight discrepancy in the figures the more important fact remains that last year's record of lodgers is an all round increase over the previous year's of over three hundred thousand, and that this has been the ratio of growth of the business during the last three years, the period of which Inspector Byrnes complains as turning out so many young criminals with

---

* Deduct 69,111 women lodgers in the police stations.

the lodging house stamp upon them. More than half of the lodging houses are in the Bowery district, that is to say, the Fourth, Sixth, and Tenth Wards, and they harbor nearly three-fourths of their crowds. The calculation that more than nine thousand homeless young men lodge nightly along Chatham Street and the Bowery, between the City Hall and the Cooper Union, is probably not far out of the way. The City Missionary finds them there far less frequently than the thief in need of helpers. Appropriately enough, nearly one-fifth of all the pawnshops in the city and one-sixth of all the saloons are located here, while twenty-seven percent of all the arrests on the police books have been credited to the district for the last two years.

About election time, especially in Presidential elections, the lodging houses come out strong on the side of the political boss who has the biggest "barrel." The victory in political contests, in the three wards I have mentioned of all others, is distinctly to the general with the strongest battalions, and the lodging houses are his favorite recruiting ground. The colonization of voters is an evil of the first magnitude, none the less because both parties smirch their hands with it, and for that reason next to hopeless. Honors are easy, where the two "machines," intrenched in their strongholds, outbid each other across the Bowery in open rivalry as to who shall commit the most flagrant frauds at the polls. Semi-occasionally a champion offender is caught and punished, as was, not long ago, the proprietor of one of the biggest Bowery lodging houses. But such scenes are largely spectacular, if not prompted by some hidden motive of revenge that survives from the contest. Beyond a doubt Inspector Byrnes speaks by the card when he observes that "usually this work is done in the interest of some local political boss, who stands by the owner of the house, in case the latter gets into trouble." For standing by, read twisting the machinery of outraged justice so that its hand shall fall not too heavily upon the culprit, or miss him altogether. One of the houses that achieved profitable notoriety in this way in many successive elections, a notorious tramps' resort in Houston Street, was lately given up, and has most appropriately been turned into a bar factory, thus still contributing, though in a changed from, to the success of "the cause." It must be admitted that the black tramp who herds in the West Side "hotels" is more discriminating in this matter of electioneering than his white brother. He at least exhibits some real loyalty in invariably selling his vote to the Republican bidder for a dollar, while he charges the Democratic boss a dollar and a half. In view of the well-known facts, there is a good deal of force in the remark made by a friend of ballot reform during the recent struggle over that hotly contested issue, that real ballot reform will do more to knock out cheap lodging houses than all the regulations of police and health officers together.

The experiment made by a well-known stove manufacturer a winter or two ago in the way of charity, might have thrown much desired light on the question of the number of tramps in the city, could it have been carried to a successful end. He opened a sort of breakfast shop for the idle and unemployed in the region of Washington Square, offering to all who had no money a cup of coffee and a roll for nothing. The first morning he had a dozen customers, the next about two hundred. The number kept growing until one morning, at the end of two weeks, found by actual count 2,014 shivering creatures in line waiting their turn for a seat at his table. The shop was closed that day. It was one of the rare instances of too great a rush of custom wrecking a promising business, and the great problem remained unsolved.

Chinatown

ETWEEN THE TABERNACLES of Jewry and the shrines of the
Bend, Joss[1] has cheekily planted his pagan worship of idols, chief
among which are the celestial worshipper's own gain and lusts. Whatever may be said about the Chinaman being a thousand years behind
the age on his own shores, here he is distinctly abreast of it in his successful scheming to "make it pay." It is doubtful if there is anything he
does not turn to a paying account, from his religion down, or up, as
one prefers. At the risk of distressing some well-meaning, but, I fear,
too trustful people, I state it in advance as my opinion, based on the
steady observation of years, that all attempts to make an effective
Christian of John Chinaman will remain abortive in this generation;
of the next I have, if anything, less hope. Ages of senseless idolatry, a
mere grub-worship, have left him without the essential qualities for
appreciating the gentle teachings of a faith whose motive and unselfish spirit are alike beyond his grasp. He lacks the handle of a strong

faith in something, anything, however wrong, to catch him by. There is nothing strong about him, except his passions when aroused. I am convinced that he adopts Christianity, when he adopts it at all, as he puts on American clothes, with what the politicians would call an ulterior motive, some sort of gain in the near prospect—washing, a Christian wife, perhaps, anything he happens to rate for the moment above his cherished pigtail. It may be that I judge him too harshly. Exceptions may be found. Indeed, for the credit of the race, I hope there are such. But I am bound to say my hope is not backed by lively faith.

Chinatown as a spectacle is disappointing. Next door neighbor to the Bend, it has little of its outdoor stir and life, none of its gaily colored rags or picturesque filth and poverty. Mott Street is clean to distraction: the laundry stamp is on it, though the houses are chiefly of the conventional tenement house type, with nothing to rescue them from the everyday dismal dreariness of their kind save here and there a splash of dull red or yellow, a sign, hung endways and with streamers of red flannel tacked on, that announces in Chinese characters that Dr. Chay Yen Chong sells Chinese herb medicines, or that Won Lung & Co.—queer contradiction—take in washing, or deal out tea and groceries. There are some gimcracks in the second story fire escape of one of the houses, signifying that Joss or a club has a habitation there. An American patent medicine concern has seized the opportunity to decorate the background with its cabalistic trademark, that in this company looks as foreign as the rest. Doubtless the privilege was bought for cash. It will buy anything in Chinatown, Joss himself included, as indeed, why should it not? He was bought for cash across the sea and came here under the law that shuts out the live Chinaman, but lets in his dead god on payment of the statutory duty on bric-a-brac. Red and yellow are the holiday colors of Chinatown as of the Bend, but they do not lend brightness in Mott Street as around the corner in Mulberry. Rather, they seem to descend to the level of the general dullness, and glower at you from doors and windows, from the telegraph pole that is the official organ of Chinatown and from the store signs, with blank, unmeaning stare, suggesting nothing, asking no questions, and answering none. Fifth Avenue is not duller on a rainy day than Mott Street to one in search of excitement. Whatever is on foot goes on behind closed doors. Stealth and secretiveness are as much part of the Chinaman in New York as the cat-like tread of his felt shoes. His business, as his domestic life, shuns the light, less because there is anything to conceal than because that is the way of the man. Perhaps the attitude of American civilization toward the stranger, whom it invited in, has taught him that way. At any rate, the very doorways of his offices and shops are fenced off by queer, forbidding partitions suggestive of a continual state of siege. The stranger who enters through the crooked approach is received with sudden silence, a sullen stare, and an angry "Vat you vant?" that breathes annoyance and distrust.

Trust not him who trusts no one, is as safe a rule in Chinatown as out of it. Were not Mott Street overawed in its isolation, it would not be safe to descend this open cellarway, through which come the pungent odor of burning opium and the clink of copper coins on the table. As it is, though safe, it is not profitable to intrude. At the first footfall of leather soles on the steps the hum of talk ceases, and the group of celestials, crouching over their game of fan-tan, stop playing and watch the comer with ugly looks. Fan-tan is their ruling passion. The average Chinaman, the police will tell you, would rather gamble than eat any day, and they have ample experience to back them. Only the fellow in the bunk smokes away, indifferent to all else but his pipe and his own enjoyment. It is a mistake to assume that Chinatown is honeycombed with opium "joints." There are a good many more outside of it than in it. The celestials do not monopolize the pipe. In

Mott Street there is no need of them. Not a Chinese home or bur-
row there, but has its bunk and its layout, where they can be enjoyed
safe from police interference. The Chinaman smokes opium as Cau-
casians smoke tobacco, and apparently with little worse effect upon
himself. But woe unto the white victim upon which his pitiless drug
gets it grip!

The bloused pedlars who, with arms buried half to the elbow in
their trousers' pockets, lounge behind their stock of watermelon seed
and sugarcane, cut in lengths to suit the purse of the buyer, disdain to
offer the barbarian their wares. Chinatown, that does most things by
contraries, rules it holiday style to carry its hands in its pockets, and
its denizens follow the fashion, whether in blue blouse, in gray, or in
brown, with shining and braided pigtail dangling below the knees, or
with hair cropped short above a coat collar of "Melican" cut. All kinds
of men are met, but no women—none at least with almond eyes. The
reason is simple: there are none. A few, a very few, Chinese merchants
have wives of their own color, but they are seldom or never seen in
the street. The "wives" of Chinatown are of a different stock that
comes closer home.

From the teeming tenements to the right and left of it come the
white slaves of its dens of vice and their infernal drug, that have in-
fused into the "Bloody Sixth" Ward a subtler poison than ever the
stale-beer dives know, or the "sudden death" of the Old Brewery.
There are houses, dozens of them, in Mott and Pell Streets, that are
literally jammed, from the "joint" in the cellar to the attic, with these
hapless victims of a passion which, once acquired, demands the sacrifice of every instinct of decency to its insatiate desire. There is a
church in Mott Street, at the entrance to Chinatown, that stands as
a barrier between it and the tenements beyond. Its young men have
waged unceasing war upon the monstrous wickedness for years,
but with very little real result. I have in mind a house in Pell Street

that has been raided no end of times by the police, and its population emptied upon Blackwell's Island, or into the reformatories, yet is today honeycombed with scores of the conventional households of the Chinese quarter: the men worshippers of Joss; the women, all white, girls hardly yet grown to womanhood, worshipping nothing save the pipe that has enslaved them body and soul. Easily tempted from homes that have no claim upon the name, they rarely or never return. Mott Street gives up its victims only to the Charity Hospital or the Potter's Field. Of the depth of their fall no one is more thoroughly aware than these girls themselves; no one less concerned about it. The calmness with which they discuss it, while insisting illogically upon the fiction of a marriage that deceives no one, is disheartening. Their misery is peculiarly fond of company, and an amount of visiting goes on in these households that makes it extremely difficult for the stranger to untangle them. I came across a company of them "hitting the pipe" together, on a tour through their dens one night with the police captain of the precinct. The girls knew him, called him by name, offered him a pipe, and chatted with him about the incidents of their acquaintance, how many times he had "sent them up," and their chances of "lasting" much longer. There was no shade of regret in their voices, nothing but utter indifference and surrender.

One thing about them was conspicuous: their scrupulous neatness. It is the distinguishing mark of Chinatown, outwardly and physically. It is not altogether by chance the Chinaman has chosen the laundry as his distinctive field. He is by nature as clean as the cat, which he resembles in his traits of cruel cunning, and savage fury when aroused. On this point of cleanliness he insists in his domestic circle, yielding in others with crafty submissiveness to the caprice of the girls, who "boss" him in a very independent manner, fretting vengefully under the yoke they loathe, but which they know right well they can never shake off, once they have put the pipe to their lips and given Mott

In a Chinese Joint

Street a mortgage upon their souls for all time. To the priest, whom they call in when the poison racks the body, they pretend that they are yet their own masters; but he knows that it is an idle boast, least of all believed by themselves. As he walks with them the few short steps to the Potter's Field, he hears the sad story he has heard told over and over again, of father, mother, home, and friends given up for the accursed pipe, and stands hopeless and helpless before the colossal evil for which he knows no remedy.

The frequent assertions of the authorities that at least no girls under age are wrecked on this Chinese shoal, are disproved by the observation of those who go frequently among these dens, though the smallest girl will invariably, and usually without being asked, insist that she is sixteen, and so of age to choose the company she keeps. Such assertions are not to be taken seriously. Even while I am writing, the morning returns from one of the precincts that pass through my hands report the arrest of a Chinaman for "inveigling little girls into his laundry," one of the hundred outposts of Chinatown that are scattered all over the city, as the outer threads of the spider's web that holds its prey fast. Reference to case no. 39,499 in this year's report of the Society for the Prevention of Cruelty to Children, will discover one of the much travelled roads to Chinatown. The girl whose story it tells was thirteen, and one of six children abandoned by a dissipated father. She had been discharged from an Eighth Avenue store, where she was employed as cash girl, and, being afraid to tell her mother, floated about until she landed in a Chinese laundry. The judge heeded her tearful prayer, and sent her home with her mother, but she was back again in a little while despite all promises of reform.

Her tyrant knows well that she will come, and patiently bides his time. When her struggles in the web have ceased at last, he rules no longer with gloved hand. A specimen of celestial logic from the home circle at this period came home to me with a personal application, one evening when I attempted, with a policeman, to stop a Chinaman whom we found beating his white "wife" with a broom handle in a Mott Street cellar. He was angry at our interference, and declared vehemently that she was "bad."

"S'ppose your wifee bad, you no lickee her?" he asked, as if there could be no appeal from such a commonsense proposition as that. My assurance that I did not, that such a thing could not occur to me, struck him dumb with amazement. He eyed me a while in stupid silence, poked the linen in his tub, stole another look, and made up his mind. A gleam of intelligence shone in his eye, and pity and contempt struggled in his voice. "Then, I guess, she lickee you," he said.

No small commotion was caused in Chinatown once upon the occasion of an expedition I undertook, accompanied by a couple of police detectives, to photograph Joss. Some conscienceless wag spread the report, after we were gone, that his picture was wanted for the Rogues' Gallery at Headquarters. The insult was too gross to be passed over without atonement of some sort. Two roast pigs made matters all right with his offended majesty of Mott Street, and with his attendant priests, who bear a very practical hand in the worship by serving as the divine stomach, as it were. They eat the good things set before their rice-paper master, unless, as once happened, some sacrilegious tramp sneaks in and gets ahead of them. The practical way in which this people combine worship with business is certainly admirable. I was told that the scrawl covering the wall on both sides of the shrine stood for the names of the pillars of the church or club—the Joss House is both—that they might have their reward in this world, no matter what happened to them in the next. There was another inscription overhead that needed no interpreter. In familiar English letters, copied bodily from the trade dollar, was the sentiment: "In God we trust." The priest pointed to it with undisguised pride and attempted an explanation, from which I gathered that the inscription was intended as a diplomatic courtesy, a delicate international compliment to the "Melican Joss," the almighty dollar.

Chinatown has enlisted the telegraph for the dissemination of public intelligence, but it has got hold of the contrivance by the wrong end. As the wires serve us in newspaper making, so the Chinaman makes use of the pole for the same purpose. The telegraph pole, of which I spoke as the real official organ of Chinatown, stands not far from the Joss House in Mott Street, in full view from Chatham Square. In it centers the real life of the colony, its gambling news. Every day yellow and red notices are posted upon it by unseen hands, announcing that in such and such a cellar a fan-tan game will be running that night, or warning the faithful that a raid is intended on this

"The Official Organ of Chinatown"

or that game through the machination of a rival interest. A constant
stream of plotting and counterplotting makes up the round of Chinese social and political existence. I do not pretend to understand the
exact political structure of the colony, or its internal government.
Even discarding as idle the stories of a secret cabal with power over
life and death, and authority to enforce its decrees, there is evidence
enough that the Chinese consider themselves subject to the laws of
the land only when submission is unavoidable, and that they are governed by a code of their own, the very essence of which is rejection of
all other authority except under compulsion. If now and then some

horrible crime in the Chinese colony, a murder of such hideous ferocity as one I have a very vivid recollection of, where the murderer
stabbed his victim (both Chinamen, of course) in the back with a
meat knife, plunging it in to the hilt no less than seventeen times,
arouses the popular prejudice to a suspicion that it was "ordered,"
only the suspected themselves are to blame, for they appear to rise up
as one man to shield the criminal. The difficulty of tracing the motive
of the crime and the murderer is extreme, and it is the rarest of all
results that the police get on the track of either. The obstacles in the
way of hunting down an Italian murderer are as nothing to the opposition encountered in Chinatown. Nor is the failure of the pursuit
wholly to be ascribed to the familiar fact that to Caucasian eyes "all
Chinamen look alike," but rather to their acting "alike," in a body, to
defeat discovery at any cost.

Withal the police give the Chinese the name of being the "quiet-
est people down there," meaning in the notoriously turbulent Sixth
Ward; and they are. The one thing they desire above all is to be let
alone, a very natural wish perhaps, considering all the circumstances.
If it were a laudable or even an allowable ambition that prompts it,
they might be humored with advantage, probably, to both sides. But
the facts show too plainly that it is not, and that in their very exclu-
siveness and reserve they are a constant and terrible menace to society, wholly regardless of their influence upon the industrial problems which their presence confuses. The severest official scrutiny, the
harshest repressive measures are justifiable in Chinatown, orderly as
it appears on the surface, even more than in the Bend, and the case is
infinitely more urgent. To the peril that threatens there all the senses
are alert, whereas the poison that proceeds from Mott Street puts
mind and body to sleep, to work out its deadly purpose in the corruption of the soul.

This again may be set down as a harsh judgment. I may be accused of inciting persecution of an unoffending people. Far from it.

Granted, that the Chinese are in no sense a desirable element of the population, that they serve no useful purpose here, whatever they may have done elsewhere in other days, yet to this it is a sufficient answer that they are here, and that, having let them in, we must make the best of it. This is a time for very plain speaking on this subject. Rather than banish the Chinaman, I would have the door opened wider—for his wife; make it a condition of his coming or staying that he bring his wife with him. Then, at least, he might not be what he now is and remains, a homeless stranger among us. Upon this hinges the real Chinese question, in our city at all events, as I see it. To assert that the victims of his drug and his base passions would go to the bad anyhow, is begging the question. They might and they might not. The chance is the span between life and death. From any other form of dissipation than that for which Chinatown stands there is recovery; for the victims of any other vice, hope. For these there is neither hope nor recovery; nothing but death—moral, mental, and physical death.

oughly has the chosen people crowded out the Gentiles in the Tenth Ward that, when the great Jewish holidays come around every year, the public schools in the district have practically to close up. Of their thousands of pupils scarce a handful come to school. Nor is there any suspicion that the rest are playing hookey. They stay honestly home to celebrate. There is no mistaking it: we are in Jewtown.

It is said that nowhere in the world are so many people crowded together on a square mile as here. The average five-story tenement adds a story or two to its stature in Ludlow Street and an extra build-ing on the rear lot, and yet the sign "To Let" is the rarest of all there. Here is one seven stories high. The sanitary policeman whose beat this is will tell you that it contains thirty-six families, but the term has a widely different meaning here and on the avenues. In this house, where a case of smallpox was reported, there were fifty-eight babies and thirty-eight children that were over five years of age. In Essex Street two small rooms in a six-story tenement were made to hold a "family" of father and mother, twelve children, and six boarders. The boarder plays as important a part in the domestic economy of Jew-town as the lodger in the Mulberry Street Bend. These are samples of the packing of the population that has run up the record here to the rate of three hundred and thirty thousand per square mile. The dens-est crowding of Old London, I pointed out before, never got beyond a hundred and seventy-five thousand. Even the alley is crowded out. Through dark hallways and filthy cellars, crowded, as is every foot of the street, with dirty children, the settlements in the rear are reached. Thieves know how to find them when pursued by the police, and the tramps that sneak in on chilly nights to fight for the warm spot in the yard over some baker's oven. They are out of place in this hive of busy industry, and they know it. It has nothing in common with them or with their philosophy of life, that the world owes the idler a living. Life here means the hardest kind of work almost from the

A Tramp's Nest in Ludlow Street

cradle. The world as a debtor has no credit in Jewtown. Its promise to pay wouldn't buy one of the old hats that are hawked about Hester Street, unless backed by security representing labor done at lowest market rates. But this army of workers must have bread. It is cheap and filling, and bakeries abound. Wherever they are in the tenements the tramp will skulk in, if he can. There is such a tramps' roost in the rear of a tenement near the lower end of Ludlow Street, that is never without its tenants in winter. By a judicious practice of flopping over on the stone pavement at intervals, and thus warming one side at a time, and with an empty box to put the feet in, it is possible to keep reasonably comfortable there even on a rainy night. In summer the yard is the only one in the neighborhood that does not do duty as a public dormitory.

Thrift is the watchword of Jewtown, as of its people the world over. It is at once its strength and its fatal weakness, its cardinal virtue and its foul disgrace. Become an overmastering passion with these people who come here in droves from Eastern Europe to escape persecution, from which freedom could be bought only with gold, it has enslaved them in bondage worse than that from which they fled. Money is their God. Life itself is of little value compared with even the leanest bank account. In no other spot does life wear so intensely bald and materialistic an aspect as in Ludlow Street. Over and over again I have met with instances of these Polish or Russian Jews deliberately starving themselves to the point of physical exhaustion, while working night and day at a tremendous pressure to save a little money. An avenging nemesis pursues this headlong hunt for wealth; there is no worse paid class anywhere. I once put the question to one of their own people, who, being a pawnbroker, and an unusually intelligent and charitable one, certainly enjoyed the advantage of a practical view of the situation: "Whence the many wretchedly poor people in such a colony of workers, where poverty, from a misfortune, has become a reproach, dreaded as the plague?"

"Immigration," he said, "brings us a lot. In five years it has averaged twenty-five thousand a year, of which more that seventy percent have stayed in New York. Half of them require and receive aid from the Hebrew Charities from the very start, lest they starve. That is one explanation. There is another class than the one that cannot get work: those who have had too much of it; who have worked and hoarded and lived, crowded together like pigs, on the scantiest fare and the worst to be got, bound to save whatever their earnings, until, worn out, they could work no longer. Then their hoards were soon exhausted. That is their story." And I knew that what he said was true.

Penury and poverty are wedded everywhere to dirt and disease, and Jewtown is no exception. It could not well be otherwise in such crowds, considering especially their low intellectual status. The managers of the Eastern Dispensary, which is in the very heart of their district, told the whole story when they said: "The diseases these people suffer from are not due to intemperance or immorality, but to ignorance, want of suitable food, and the foul air in which they live and work."* The homes of the Hebrew quarter are its workshops also. Reference will be made to the economic conditions under which they work in a succeeding chapter. Here we are concerned simply with the fact. You are made fully aware of it before you have travelled the length of a single block in any of these East Side streets, by the whir of a thousand sewing machines, worked at high pressure from earliest dawn till mind and muscle give out together. Every member of the family, from the youngest to the oldest, bears a hand, shut in the qualmy rooms, where meals are cooked and clothing washed and dried besides, the livelong day. It is not unusual to find a dozen persons—men, women, and children—at work in a single small room. The fact accounts for the contrast that strikes with wonder the observer who comes across from the Bend. Over there the entire population seems possessed of an uncontrollable impulse to get out into the street; here all its energies appear to be bent upon keeping in and away from it. Not that the streets are deserted. The overflow from these tenements is enough to make a crowd anywhere. The children alone would do it. Not old enough to work and no room for play, that is their story. In the home the child's place is usurped by the lodger, who performs the service of the Irishman's pig—pays the rent. In the street the army of hucksters crowd him out. Typhus fever and smallpox are bred here, and help solve the question what to do with him. Filth diseases both, they sprout naturally among the hordes that bring the germs with them from across the sea, and whose first instinct is to hide their sick lest the authorities carry them off to the hospital to be slaughtered, as they firmly believe. The health officers are on constant

* Report of Eastern Dispensary for 1889.

and sharp lookout for hidden fever nests. Considering that half of the ready-made clothes that are sold in the big stores, if not a good deal more than half, are made in these tenement rooms, this is not excessive caution. It has happened more than once that a child recovering from smallpox, and in the most contagious stage of the disease, has been found crawling among heaps of half-finished clothing that the next day would be offered for sale on the counter of a Broadway store; or that a typhus fever patient has been discovered in a room whence perhaps a hundred coats had been sent home that week, each one with the wearer's death warrant, unseen and unsuspected, basted in the lining.

The health officers call the Tenth the typhus ward; in the office where deaths are registered it passes as the "suicide ward," for reasons not hard to understand; and among the police as the "crooked ward," on account of the number of "crooks," petty thieves and their allies, the "fences," receivers of stolen goods, who find the dense crowds congenial. The nearness of the Bowery, the great "thieves' highway," helps to keep up the supply of these, but Jewtown does not support its dives. Its troubles with the police are the characteristic crop of its intense business rivalries. Oppression, persecution, have not shorn the Jew of his native combativeness one whit. He is as ready to fight for his rights, or what he considers his rights, in a business transaction—synonymous generally with his advantage—as if he had not been robbed of them for eighteen hundred years. One strong impression survives with him from his days of bondage: the power of the law. On the slightest provocation he rushes off to invoke it for his protection. Doubtless the sensation is novel to him, and therefore pleasing. The police at the Eldridge Street station are in a constant turmoil over these everlasting fights. Somebody is always denouncing somebody else, and getting his enemy or himself locked up; frequently both, for the prisoner, when brought in, has generally as plausible a story to tell as his accuser, and as hot a charge to make. The day closes on a wild conflict of rival interests. Another dawns with the prisoner in court, but no complainant. Over night the case has been settled on a business basis, and the police dismiss their prisoner in deep disgust.

These quarrels have sometimes a comic aspect. Thus, with the numerous dancing schools that are scattered among the synagogues, often keeping them company in the same tenement. They are generally kept by some man who works in the daytime at tailoring, cigarmaking, or something else. The young people in Jewtown are inordinately fond of dancing, and after their day's hard work will flock to these "schools" for a night's recreation. But even to their fun they carry their business preferences, and it happens that a school adjourns in a body to make a general raid on the rival establishment across the street, without the ceremony of paying the admission fee. Then the dance breaks up in a general fight, in which, likely enough, someone is badly hurt. The police come in, as usual, and ring down the curtain.

Bitter as are his private feuds, it is not until his religious life is invaded that a real inside view is obtained of this Jew, whom the history of Christian civilization has taught nothing but fear and hatred. There are two or three missions in the district conducting a hopeless propagandism for the Messiah whom the Tenth Ward rejects, and they attract occasional crowds, who come to hear the Christian preacher as the Jews of old gathered to hear the apostles expound the new doctrine. The result is often strikingly similar. "For once," said a certain well-known minister of an uptown church to me, after such an experience, "I felt justified in comparing myself to Paul preaching salvation to the Jews. They kept still until I spoke of Jesus Christ as

the Son of God. Then they got up and fell to arguing among themselves and to threatening me, until it looked as if they meant to take me out in Hester Street and stone me." As at Jerusalem, the Chief Captain was happily at hand with his centurions, in the person of a sergeant and three policemen, and the preacher was rescued. So, in all matters pertaining to their religious life that tinges all their customs, they stand, these East Side Jews, where the new day that dawned on Calvary left them standing, stubbornly refusing to see the light. A visit to a Jewish house of mourning is like bridging the gap of two thousand years. The inexpressibly sad and sorrowful wail for the dead, as it swells and rises in the hush of all sounds of life, comes back from the ages like a mournful echo of the voice of Rachel "weeping for her children and refusing to be comforted, because they are not."

Attached to many of the synagogues, which among the poorest Jews frequently consist of a scantily furnished room in a rear tenement, with a few wooden stools or benches for the congregation, are Talmudic schools that absorb a share of the growing youth. The schoolmaster is not rarely a man of some attainments who has been stranded there, his native instinct for moneymaking having been smothered in the process that has made of him a learned man. It was of such a school in Eldridge Street that the wicked Isaac Iacob, who killed his enemy, his wife, and himself in one day, was janitor. But the majority of the children seek the public schools, where they are received sometimes with some misgivings on the part of the teachers, who find it necessary to inculcate lessons of cleanliness in the worst cases by practical demonstrations with washbowl and soap. "He took hold of the soap as if it were some animal," said one of these teachers to me after such an experiment upon a new pupil, "and wiped three fingers across his face. He called that washing." In the Allen Street public school the experienced principal has embodied among the elementary lessons, to keep constantly before the children the duty that clearly lies next to their hands, a characteristic exercise. The question is asked daily from the teacher's desk: "What must I do to be healthy?" and the whole school responds:

I must keep my skin clean,
Wear clean clothes,
Breathe pure air,
And live in the sunlight.

It seems little less than biting sarcasm to hear them say it, for to not a few of them all these things are known only by name. In their everyday life there is nothing even to suggest any of them. Only the demand of religious custom has power to make their parents clean up at stated intervals, and the young naturally are no better. As scholars, the children of the most ignorant Polish Jew keep fairly abreast of their more favored playmates, until it comes to mental arithmetic, when they leave them behind with a bound. It is surprising to see how strong the instinct of dollars and cents is in them. They can count, and correctly, almost before they can talk.

Within a few years the police captured on the East Side a band of firebugs who made a business of setting fire to tenements for the insurance on their furniture. There has, unfortunately, been some evidence in the past year that another such conspiracy is on foot. The danger to which these fiends expose their fellow tenants is appalling. A fire panic at night in a tenement, by no means among the rare experiences in New York, with the surging, half-smothered crowds on stairs and fire escapes, the frantic mothers and crying children, the wild struggle to save the little that is their all, is a horror that has few parallels in human experience.

I cannot think without a shudder of one such scene in a First Avenue tenement. It was in the middle of the night. The fire had swept up with sudden fury from a restaurant on the street floor, cutting off esford a whole. It took more than ten years of persistent effort on the part of the sanitary authorities to drive the trade in live fowl from the streets to the fowl market on Gouverneur Slip, where the killing is now done according to Jewish rite by priests detailed for the purpose by the chief rabbi. Since then they have had a characteristic rumpus, that involved the entire Jewish community, over the fees for killing and the mode of collecting them. Here is a woman churning horseradish on a machine she has chained and padlocked to a tree on the sidewalk, lest someone steal it. Beside her a butcher's stand with cuts at prices the avenues never dreamed of. Old coats are hawked for fifty cents, "as good as new," and "pants"—there are no trousers in Jewtown, only pants—at anything that can be got. There is a knot of half a dozen "pants" pedlars in the middle of the street, twice as many men of their own race fingering their wares and plucking at the seams with the anxious scrutiny of would-be buyers, though none of them has the least idea of investing in a pair. Yes, stop! This baker, fresh from his trough, bareheaded and with bare arms, has made an offer: for this pair thirty cents; a dollar and forty was the price asked. The pedlar shrugs his shoulders, and turns up his hands with a half pitying, wholly indignant air. What does the baker take him for? Such pants—. The baker has turned to go. With a jump like a panther's, the man with the pants has him by the sleeve. Will he give eighty cents? Sixty? Fifty? So help him, they are dirt cheap at that. Lose, will he, on the trade, lose all the profit of his day's pedling. The baker goes on unmoved. Forty then? What, not forty? Take them then for thirty, and wreck the life of a poor man. And the baker takes them and goes, well knowing that at least twenty cents of the thirty, two hundred percent, were clear profit, if indeed the "pants" cost the pedlar anything.

The suspender pedlar is the mystery of the pig market, omnipresent and unfathomable. He is met at every step with his wares dangling over his shoulder, down his back, and in front. Millions of suspend-

The Old Clo'e's Man—in the Jewish Quarters

ers thus perambulate Jewtown all day on a sort of dress parade. Why
suspenders, is the puzzle, and where do they all go to? The "pants"
of Jewtown hang down with a common accord, as if they had never
known the support of suspenders. It appears to be as characteristic a
trait of the race as the long beard and the Sabbath silk hat of ancient
pedigree. I have asked again and again. No one has ever been able to
tell me what becomes of the suspenders of Jewtown. Perhaps they are
hung up as bric-a-brac in its homes, or laid away and saved up as the
equivalent of cash. I cannot tell. I only know that more suspenders
are hawked about the pig market every day than would supply the
whole of New York for a year, were they all bought and turned to use.

The crowds that jostle each other at the wagons and about the
sidewalk shops, where a gutter plank on two ash barrels does duty
for a counter! Pushing, struggling, babbling, and shouting in foreign
tongues, a veritable Babel of confusion. An English word falls upon
the ear almost with a sense of shock, as something unexpected and
strange. In the midst of it all there is a sudden wild scattering, a hus-
tling of things from the street into dark cellars, into backyards and
byways, a slamming and locking of doors hidden under the impro-
vised shelves and counters. The health officers' cart is coming down
the street, preceded and followed by stalwart policemen, who shovel
up with scant ceremony the eatables—musty bread, decayed fish and
stale vegetables—indifferent to the curses that are showered on them
from stoops and windows, and carry them off to the dump. In the
wake of the wagon, as it makes its way to the East River after the raid,
follow a line of despoiled hucksters shouting defiance from a safe
distance. Their clamor dies away with the noise of the market. The
endless panorama of the tenements, rows upon rows, between stony
streets, stretches to the north, to the south, and to the west as far as
the eye reaches.

XI

The Sweaters of Jewtown

A NYTHING LIKE AN exhaustive discussion of the economical problem presented by the Tenth Ward* is beset by difficulties that increase in precise proportion to the efforts put forth to remove them.[1] I have too vivid a recollection of weary days and nights spent in those stewing tenements, trying to get to the bottom of the vexatious question only to find myself in the end as far from the truth as at the beginning, asking with rising wrath Pilate's question, "What is truth?" to attempt to weary the reader by dragging him with me over that sterile and unprofitable ground. Nor are these pages the place for such a discussion. In it, let me confess it at once and have done with it, I should be like the blind leading the blind; between the real and apparent poverty, the hidden hoards and the unhesitating mendacity

---

* I refer to the Tenth Ward always as typical. The district embraced in the discussion really includes the Thirteenth Ward, and in a growing sense large portions of the Seventh and contiguous wards as well.

of these people, where they conceive their interests to be concerned in one way or another, the reader and I would fall together into the ditch of doubt and conjecture in which I have found company before.

The facts that lie on the surface indicate the causes as clearly as the nature of the trouble. In effect both have been already stated. A friend of mine who manufactures cloth once boasted to me that nowadays, on cheap clothing, New York "beats the world." "To what," I asked, "do you attribute it?" "To the cutter's long knife* and the Polish Jew," he said. Which of the two has cut deepest into the workman's wages is not a doubtful question. Practically the Jew has monopolized the business since the battle between East Broadway and Broadway ended in a complete victory for the East Side and cheap labor, and transferred to it the control of the trade in cheap clothing.[2] Yet, not satisfied with having won the field, he strives as hotly with his own for the profit of half a cent as he fought with his Christian competitor for the dollar. If the victory is a barren one, the blame is his own. His price is not what he can get, but the lowest he can live for and underbid his neighbor. Just what that means we shall see. The manufacturer knows it, and is not slow to take advantage of his knowledge. He makes him hungry for work by keeping it from him as long as possible; then drives the closest bargain he can with the sweater.

Many harsh things have been said of the "sweater," that really apply to the system in which he is a necessary, logical link. It can at least be said of him that he is no worse than the conditions that created him. The sweater is simply the middleman, the subcontractor, a workman like his fellows, perhaps with the single distinction from the rest that he knows a little English; perhaps not even that, but with the accidental possession of two or three sewing machines, or of credit enough

---

* An invention that cuts many garments at once, where the scissors could cut only a few.

to hire them, as his capital, who drums up work among the clothing houses. Of workmen he can always get enough. Every shipload
from German ports brings them to his door in droves, clamoring for
work. The sun sets upon the day of the arrival of many a Polish Jew,
finding him at work in an East Side tenement, treading the machine
and "learning the trade." Often there are two, sometimes three, sets
of sweaters on one job. They work with the rest when they are not
drumming up trade, driving their "hands" as they drive their machine, for all they are worth, and making a profit on their work, of
course, though in most cases not nearly as extravagant a percentage,
probably, as is often supposed. If it resolves itself into a margin of
five or six cents, or even less, on a dozen pairs of boys' trousers, for
instance, it is nevertheless enough to make the contractor with his
thrifty instincts independent. The workman growls, not at the hard
labor, or poor pay, but over the pennies another is coining out of his
sweat, and on the first opportunity turns sweater himself, and takes
his revenge by driving an even closer bargain than his rival tyrant,
thus reducing his profits.

The sweater knows well that the isolation of the workman in his
helpless ignorance is his sure foundation, and he has done what he
could—with merciless severity where he could—to smother every
symptom of awakening intelligence in his slaves. In this effort to perpetuate his despotism he has had the effectual assistance of his own
system and the sharp competition that keep the men on starvation
wages; of their constitutional greed, that will not permit the sacrifice
of temporary advantage, however slight, for permanent good, and
above all, of the hungry hordes of immigrants to whom no argument
appeals save the cry for bread. Within very recent times he has, however, been forced to partial surrender by the organization of the men
to a considerable extent into trades unions, and by experiments in
cooperation, under intelligent leadership, that presage the sweater's

doom. But as long as the ignorant crowds continue to come and to herd in these tenements, his grip can never be shaken off. And the supply across the seas is apparently inexhaustible. Every fresh persecution of the Russian or Polish Jew on his native soil starts greater hordes hitherward to confound economical problems, and recruit the sweater's phalanx. The curse of bigotry and ignorance reaches halfway across the world, to sow its bitter seed in fertile soil in the East Side tenements. If the Jew himself was to blame for the resentment he aroused over there, he is amply punished. He gathers the first fruits of the harvest here.

The bulk of the sweater's work is done in the tenements, which the law that regulates factory labor does not reach. To the factories themselves that are taking the place of the rear tenements in rapidly growing numbers, letting in bigger day-crowds than those the health officers banished, the tenement shops serve as a supplement through which the law is successfully evaded. Ten hours is the legal workday in the factories, and nine o'clock the closing hour at the latest. Forty-five minutes at least must be allowed for dinner, and children under sixteen must not be employed unless they can read and write English; none at all under fourteen. The very fact that such a law should stand on the statute book, shows how desperate the plight of these people. But the tenement has defeated its benevolent purpose. In it the child works unchallenged from the day he is old enough to pull a thread. There is no such thing as a dinner hour; men and women eat while they work, and the "day" is lengthened at both ends far into the night. Factory hands take their work with them at the close of the lawful day to eke out their scanty earnings by working overtime at home. Little chance on this ground for the campaign of education that alone can bring the needed relief; small wonder that there are whole settlements on this East Side where English is practically an unknown tongue, though the people be both willing and anxious to learn. "When shall we find time to learn?" asked one of them of me once. I owe him the answer yet.

Take the Second Avenue Elevated Railroad at Chatham Square and ride up half a mile through the sweaters' district. Every open window of the big tenements, that stand like a continuous brick wall on both sides of the way, gives you a glimpse of one of these shops as the train speeds by. Men and women bending over their machines, or ironing clothes at the window, half-naked. Proprieties do not count on the East Side; nothing counts that cannot be converted into hard cash. The road is like a big gangway through an endless workroom where vast multitudes are forever laboring. Morning, noon, or night, it makes no difference; the scene is always the same. At Rivington Street let us get off and continue our trip on foot. It is Sunday evening west of the Bowery. Here, under the rule of Mosaic law, the week of work is under full headway, its first day far spent. The hucksters' wagons are absent or stand idle at the curb; the saloons admit the thirsty crowds through the side door labelled "Family Entrance"; a tin sign in a store window announces that a "Sunday School" gathers in stray children of the new dispensation; but beyond these things there is little to suggest the Christian Sabbath. Men stagger along the sidewalk groaning under heavy burdens of unsewn garments, or enormous black bags stuffed full of finished coats and trousers. Let us follow one to his home and see how Sunday passes in a Ludlow Street tenement.

Up two flights of dark stairs, three, four, with new smells of cabbage, of onions, of frying fish, on every landing, whirring sewing machines behind closed doors betraying what goes on within, to the door that opens to admit the bundle and the man. A sweater, this, in a small way. Five men and a woman, two young girls, not fifteen, and a boy who says unasked that he is fifteen, and lies in saying it, are at the machines sewing knickerbockers, "knee-pants" in the Ludlow Street dialect. The floor is littered ankle-deep with half-sewn garments. In the alcove, on a couch of many dozens of "pants" ready for the finisher, a barelegged baby with pinched face is asleep. A fence of piled-up clothing keeps him from rolling off on the floor. The faces, hands, and arms to the elbows of everyone in the room are black with the color of the cloth on which they are working. The boy and the woman alone look up at our entrance. The girls shoot sidelong glances, but at a warning look from the man with the bundle they tread their machines more energetically than ever. The men do not appear to be aware even of the presence of a stranger.

They are "learners," all of them, says the woman, who proves to be the wife of the boss, and have "come over" only a few weeks ago. She is disinclined to talk at first, but a few words in her own tongue from our guide* set her fears, whatever they are, at rest, and she grows almost talkative. The learners work for week's wages, she says. How much do they earn? She shrugs her shoulders with an expressive gesture. The workers themselves, asked in their own tongue, say indifferently, as though the question were of no interest: from two to five dollars. The children—there are four of them—are not old enough to work. The oldest is only six. They turn out one hundred and twenty dozen "knee-pants" a week, for which the manufacturer pays seventy cents a dozen. Five cents a dozen is the clear profit, but her own and her husband's work brings the family earnings up to twenty-five dollars a week, when they have work all the time. But often half the time is put in looking for it. They work no longer than to nine o'clock at night, from daybreak. There are ten machines in the room; six are hired at two dollars a month. For the two shabby, smoke-begrimed rooms, one somewhat larger than ordinary, they pay twenty dollars a month. She does not complain, though "times are not what they

---

*I was always accompanied on these tours of inquiry by one of their own people who knew of and sympathized with my mission. Without that precaution my errand would have been fruitless; even with him it was often nearly so.

were, and it costs a good deal to live." Eight dollars a week for the family of six and two boarders. How do they do it? She laughs, as she goes over the bill of fare, at the silly question: Bread, fifteen cents a day, of milk two quarts a day at four cents a quart, one pound of meat for dinner at twelve cents, butter one pound a week at "eight cents a quarter of a pound." Coffee, potatoes, and pickles complete the list. At the least calculation, probably, this sweater's family hoards up thirty dollars a month, and in a few years will own a tenement somewhere and profit by the example set by their landlord in rent collecting. It is the way the savings of Jewtown are universally invested, and with the natural talent of its people for commercial speculation the investment is enormously profitable.

On the next floor, in a dimly lighted room with a big red-hot stove to keep the pressing irons ready for use, is a family of man, wife, three children, and a boarder. "Knee-pants" are made there too, of a still lower grade. Three cents and a half is all he clears, says the man, and lies probably out of at least two cents. The wife makes a dollar and a half finishing, the man about nine dollars at the machine. The boarder pays sixty-five cents a week. He is really only a lodger, getting his meals outside. The rent is two dollars and twenty-five cents a week, cost of living five dollars. Every floor has at least two, sometimes four, such shops. Here is one with a young family for which life is bright with promise. Husband and wife work together; just now the latter, a comely young woman, is eating her dinner of dry bread and green pickles. Pickles are favorite food in Jewtown. They are filling, and keep the children from crying with hunger. Those who have stomachs like ostriches thrive in spite of them and grow strong— plain proof that they are good to eat. The rest? "Well, they die," says our guide, dryly. No thought of untimely death comes to disturb this family with life all before it. In a few years the man will be a prosperous sweater. Already he employs an old man as ironer at three dollars

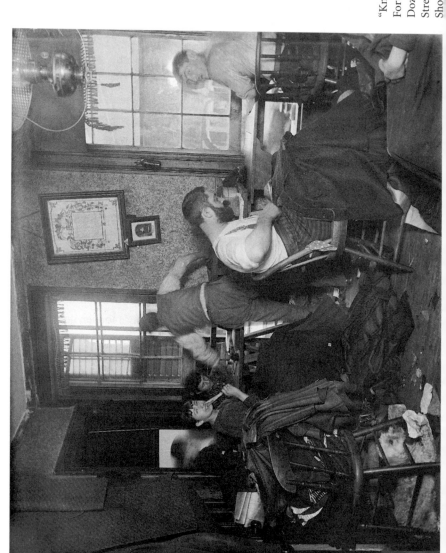

"Knee-Pants" at Forty-five Cents a Dozen—A Ludlow Street Sweater's Shop a week, and a sweet-faced little Italian girl as finisher at a dollar and a half. She is twelve, she says, and can neither read nor write; will probably never learn. How should she? The family clears from ten to eleven dollars a week in brisk times, more than half of which goes into the bank.

A companion picture from across the hall. The man works on the machine for his sweater twelve hours a day, turning out three dozen "knee-pants," for which he receives forty-two cents a dozen. The finisher who works with him gets ten, and the ironer eight cents a dozen; buttonholes are extra, at eight to ten cents a hundred. This operator has four children at his home in Stanton Street, none old enough to work, and a sick wife. His rent is twelve dollars a month; his wages for a hard week's work less than eight dollars. Such as he, with their consuming desire for money thus smothered, recruit the ranks of the anarchists, won over by the promise of a general "divide"; and an enlightened public sentiment turns up its nose at the vicious foreigner for whose perverted notions there is no room in this land of plenty.

Turning the corner into Hester Street, we stumble upon a nest of cloak makers in their busy season. Six months of the year the cloak maker is idle, or nearly so. Now is his harvest. Seventy-five cents a cloak, all complete, is the price in this shop. The cloak is of cheap plush, and might sell for eight or nine dollars over the store counter. Seven dollars is the weekly wage of this man with wife and two children, and nine dollars and a half rent to pay per month. A boarder pays about a third of it. There was a time when he made ten dollars a week and thought himself rich. But wages have come down fearfully in the last two years. Think of it: "come down" to this. The other cloak makers aver that they can make as much as twelve dollars a week, when they are employed, by taking their work home and sewing till midnight. One exhibits his account book with a Ludlow Street sweater. It shows that he and his partner, working on first-class garments for a Broadway house in the four busiest weeks of the season, made together from \$15.15 to \$19.20 a week by striving from 6 A.M. to 11 P.M., that is to say, from \$7.58 to \$9.60 each.* The sweaters on this work probably made as much as fifty percent at least on their labor. Not far away is a factory in a rear yard where the factory inspector reports teams of tailors making men's coats at an average of twenty-seven cents a coat, all complete except buttons and buttonholes.

Turning back, we pass a towering double tenement in Ludlow Street, owned by a well-known Jewish liquor dealer and politician, a triple combination that bodes ill for his tenants. As a matter of fact, the cheapest "apartment," three rear rooms on the sixth floor, only one of which deserves the name, is rented for \$13 a month. Here is a reminder of the Bend, a hallway turned into a shoemaker's shop. Two hallways side by side in adjoining tenements, would be sinful waste in Jewtown, when one would do as well by knocking a hole in the wall. But this shoemaker knows a trick the Italian's ingenuity did not suggest. He has his "flat" as well as his shop there. A curtain hung back of his stool in the narrow passage half conceals his bed that fills it entirely from wall to wall. To get into it he has to crawl over the footboard, and he must come out the same way. Expedients more odd than this are born of the East Side crowding. In one of the houses we left, the coalbin of a family on the fourth floor was on the roof of the adjoining tenement. A quarter of a ton of coal was being dumped there while we talked with the people.

We have reached Broome Street. The hum of industry in this six-story tenement on the corner leaves no doubt of the aspect Sunday wears within it. One flight up, we knock at the nearest door. The grocer, who keeps the store, lives on the "stoop," the first floor in East

---

* The strike of the cloak makers last summer, that ended in victory, raised their wages considerably, at least for the time being.

to send for them. Their breakfast, eaten at the workbench, consists of a couple of rolls at a cent a piece, and a draught of water, milk when business has been very good, a square meal at noon in a restaurant, and the morning meal over again at night. This square meal, that is the evidence of a very liberal disposition on the part of the consumer, is an affair of more than ordinary note; it may be justly called an institution. I know of a couple of restaurants at the lower end of Orchard Street that are favorite resorts for the Polish Jews, who remember the injunction that the ox that treadeth out the corn shall not be muzzled. Being neighbors, they are rivals of course, and cutting under. When I was last there one gave a dinner of soup, meat stew, bread, pie, pickles, and a "schooner" of beer for thirteen cents; the other charged fifteen cents for a similar dinner, but with two schooners of beer and a cigar, or a cigarette, as the extra inducement. The two cents had won the day, however, and the thirteen-cent restaurant did such a thriving business that it was about to spread out into the adjoining store to accommodate the crowds of customers. At this rate the lodger of Jewtown can "live like a lord," as he says himself, for twenty-five cents a day, including the price of his bed, that ranges all the way from thirty to forty and fifty cents a week, and save money, no matter what his earnings. He does it, too, so long as work is to be had at any price, and by the standard he sets up Jewtown must abide.

It has thousands upon thousands of lodgers who help to pay its extortionate rents. At night there is scarce a room in all the district that has not one or more of them, some above half a score, sleeping on cots, or on the floor. It is idle to speak of privacy in these "homes." The term carries no more meaning with it than would a lecture on social ethics to an audience of Hottentots. The picture is not overdrawn. In fact, in presenting the home life of these people I have been at some pains to avoid the extreme of privation, taking the cases just as they came to hand on the safer middle ground of average earnings.

Yet even the direct apparent poverty in Jewtown, unless dependent on absolute lack of work, would, were the truth known, in nine cases out of ten have a silver lining in the shape of a margin in bank.

These are the economical conditions that enable my manufacturing friend to boast that New York can "beat the world" on cheap clothing. In support of his claim he told me that a single Bowery firm last year sold fifteen thousand suits at $1.95 that averaged in cost $1.12½. With the material at fifteen cents a yard, he said, children's suits of assorted sizes can be sold at wholesale for seventy-five cents, and boys' cape overcoats at the same price. They are the same conditions that have perplexed the committee of benevolent Hebrews in charge of Baron de Hirsch's munificent gift of ten thousand dollars a month for the relief of the Jewish poor in New York.[3] To find proper channels through which to pour this money so that it shall effect its purpose without pauperizing, and without perpetuating the problem it is sought to solve, by attracting still greater swarms, is indeed no easy task. Colonization has not in the past been a success with these people. The great mass of them are too gregarious to take kindly to farming, and their strong commercial instinct hampers the experiment. To herd them in model tenements, though it relieve the physical suffering in a measure, would be to treat a symptom of the disease rather than strike at its root, even if land could be got cheap enough where they gather to build on a sufficiently large scale to make the plan a success. Trade schools for manual training could hardly be made to reach the adults, who in addition would have to be supported for months while learning. For the young this device has proved most excellent under the wise management of the United Hebrew Charities, an organization that gathers to its work the best thought and effort of many of our most public-spirited citizens. One, or all, of these plans may be tried, probably will. I state but the misgivings as to the result of some of the practical minds that have busied themselves with the problem. Its keynote evidently is the ignorance of the immigrants. They must be taught the language of the country they have chosen as their home, as the first and most necessary step. Whatever may follow, that is essential, absolutely vital. That done, it may well be that the case in its new aspect will not be nearly so hard to deal with.

Evening has worn into night as we take up our homeward journey through the streets, now no longer silent. The thousands of lighted windows in the tenements glow like dull red eyes in a huge stone wall. From every door multitudes of tired men and women pour forth for a half-hour's rest in the open air before sleep closes the eyes weary with incessant working. Crowds of half-naked children tumble in the street and on the sidewalk, or doze fretfully on the stone steps. As we stop in front of a tenement to watch one of these groups, a dirty baby in a single brief garment—yet a sweet, human little baby despite its dirt and tatters—tumbles off the lowest step, rolls over once, clutches my leg with unconscious grip, and goes to sleep on the flagstones, its curly head pillowed on my boot.

XII

The Bohemians—Tenement House Cigarmaking

E VIL AS THE PART IS which the tenement plays in Jewtown as the pretext for circumventing the law that was made to benefit and relieve the tenant, we have not far to go to find it in even a worse role. If the tenement is here continually dragged into the eye of public condemnation and scorn, it is because in one way or another it is found directly responsible for, or intimately associated with, three-fourths of the miseries of the poor. In the Bohemian quarter it is made the vehicle for enforcing upon a proud race a slavery as real as any that ever disgraced the South. Not content with simply robbing the tenant, the owner, in the dual capacity of landlord and employer, reduces him to virtual serfdom by making his becoming *his* tenant, on such terms as he sees fit to make, the condition of employment at wages likewise of his own making. It does not help the case that this landlord employer, almost always a Jew, is frequently of the thrifty Polish race just described.

Perhaps the Bohemian quarter is hardly the proper name to give to the colony, for though it has distinct boundaries it is scattered over a wide area on the East Side, in wedge-like streaks that relieve the monotony of the solid German population by their strong contrasts. The two races mingle no more on this side of the Atlantic than on the rugged slopes of the Bohemian mountains; the echoes of the Thirty Years' War ring in New York, after two centuries and a half, with as fierce a hatred as the gigantic combat bred among the vanquished Czechs. A chief reason for this is doubtless the complete isolation of the Bohemian immigrant. Several causes operate to bring this about: his singularly harsh and unattractive language, which he can neither easily himself unlearn nor impart to others, his stubborn pride of race, and a popular prejudice which has forced upon him the unjust stigma of a disturber of the public peace and an enemy of organized labor. I greatly mistrust that the Bohemian on our shores is a much-abused man. To his traducer, who casts up anarchism against him, he replies that the last census (1880) shows his people to have the fewest criminals of all in proportion to numbers. In New York a Bohemian criminal is such a rarity that the case of two firebugs of several years ago is remembered with damaging distinctness. The accusation that he lives like the "rat" he is, cutting down wages by his underpaid labor, he throws back in the teeth of the trades unions with the counter charge that they are the first cause of his attitude to the labor question.

A little way above Houston Street the first of his colonies is encountered, in Fifth Street and thereabouts. Then for a mile and a half scarce a Bohemian is to be found, until Thirty-eighth Street is reached. Fifty-fourth and Seventy-third Streets in their turn are the centers of populous Bohemian settlements. The location of the cigar factories, upon which he depends for a living, determines his choice of home, though there is less choice about it than with any other class in the community, save perhaps the colored people. Probably more than half of all the Bohemians in this city are cigarmakers, and it is the herding of these in great numbers in the so-called tenement factories, where the cheapest grade of work is done at the lowest wages, that constitutes at once their greatest hardship and the chief grudge of other workmen against them. The manufacturer who owns, say, from three or four, to a dozen or more tenements contiguous to his shop, fills them up with these people, charging them outrageous rents, and demanding often even a preliminary deposit of five dollars "key money"; deals them out tobacco by the week, and devotes the rest of his energies to the paring down of wages to within a peg or two of the point where the tenant rebels in desperation. When he does rebel, he is given the alternative of submission, or eviction with entire loss of employment. His needs determine the issue. Usually he is not in a position to hesitate long. Unlike the Polish Jew, whose example of untiring industry he emulates, he has seldom much laid up against a rainy day. He is fond of a glass of beer, and likes to live as well as his means will permit. The shop triumphs, and fetters more galling than ever are forged for the tenant. In the opposite case, the newspapers have to record the throwing upon the street of a small army of people, with pitiful cases of destitution and family misery.

Men, women and children work together seven days in the week in these cheerless tenements to make a living for the family, from the break of day till far into the night. Often the wife is the original cigarmaker from the old home, the husband having adopted her trade here as a matter of necessity, because, knowing no word of English, he could get no other work. As they state the cause of the bitter hostility of the trades unions, she was the primary bone of contention in the day of the early Bohemian immigration. The unions refused to admit the women, and, as the support of the family depended upon her to a large extent, such terms as were offered had to be accepted. The

manufacturer has ever since industriously fanned the antagonism between the unions and his hands, for his own advantage. The victory
rests with him, since the Court of Appeals decided that the law, passed
a few years ago, to prohibit cigarmaking in tenements was unconsti-
tutional, and thus put an end to the struggle. While it lasted, all sorts
of frightful stories were told of the shocking conditions under which
people lived and worked in these tenements, from a sanitary point of
view especially, and a general impression survives to this day that
they are particularly desperate. The Board of Health, after a careful
canvass, did not find them so then. I am satisfied from personal inspection, at a much later day, guided in a number of instances by the
union cigarmakers themselves to the tenements which they considered the worst, that the accounts were greatly exaggerated. Doubtless
the people are poor, in many cases very poor; but they are not un-
cleanly, rather the reverse; they live much better than the clothing
makers in the Tenth Ward, and in spite of their sallow look, that may
be due to the all-pervading smell of tobacco, they do not appear to be
less healthy than other indoor workers. I found on my tours of investigation several cases of consumption, of which one at least was said
by the doctor to be due to the constant inhalation of tobacco fumes.
But an examination of the death records in the Health Department
does not support the claim that the Bohemian cigarmakers are peculiarly prone to that disease. On the contrary, the Bohemian percentage of deaths from consumption appears quite low. This, however, is
a line of scientific inquiry which I leave others to pursue, along with
the more involved problem whether the falling off in the number of
children, sometimes quite noticeable in the Bohemian settlements, is,
as has been suggested, dependent upon the character of the parents'
work. The sore grievances I found were the miserable wages and the
enormous rents exacted for the minimum of accommodation. And
surely these stand for enough of suffering.

Take a row of houses in East Tenth Street as an instance. They contained thirty-five families of cigarmakers, with probably not half a dozen persons in the whole lot of them, outside of the children, who could speak a word of English, though many had been in the country half a lifetime. This room with two windows giving on the street, and a rear attachment without windows, called a bedroom by courtesy, is rented at $12.25 a month. In the front room man and wife work at the bench from six in the morning till nine at night. They make a team, stripping the tobacco leaves together; then he makes the filler, and she rolls the wrapper on and finishes the cigar. For a thousand they receive $3.75, and can turn out together three thousand cigars a week. The point has been reached where the rebellion comes in, and the workers in these tenements are just now on a strike, demanding $5.00 and $5.50 for their work. The manufacturer having refused, they are expecting hourly to be served with notice to quit their homes, and the going of a stranger among them excites their resentment, until his errand is explained. While we are in the house, the ultimatum of the "boss" is received. He will give $3.75 a thousand, not another cent. Our host is a man of seeming intelligence, yet he has been nine years in New York and knows neither English nor German. Three bright little children play about the floor.

His neighbor on the same floor has been here fifteen years, but shakes his head when asked if he can speak English. He answers in a few broken syllables when addressed in German. With $11.75 rent to pay for like accommodation, he has the advantage of his oldest boy's work besides his wife's at the bench. Three properly make a team, and these three can turn out four thousand cigars a week, at $3.75. This Bohemian has a large family; there are four children, too small to work, to be cared for. A comparison of the domestic bill of fare between Tenth and Ludlow Streets result, in the discovery that this Bohemian's butcher's bill for the week, with meat at twelve cents a pound as in Ludlow Street, is from two dollars and a half to three dollars. The Polish Jew fed as big a family on one pound of meat a day. The difference proves to be typical. Here is a suite of three rooms, two dark, three flights up. The ceiling is partly down in one of the rooms. "It is three months since we asked the landlord to fix it," says the oldest son, a very intelligent lad who has learned English in the evening school. His father has not had that advantage, and has sat at his bench, deaf and dumb to the world about him except his own, for six years. He has improved his time and become an expert at his trade. Father, mother, and son together, a full team, make from fifteen to sixteen dollars a week.

A man with venerable beard and keen eyes answers our questions through an interpreter, in the next house. Very few brighter faces would be met in a day's walk among American mechanics, yet he has in nine years learned no syllable of English. German he probably does not want to learn. His story supplies the explanation, as did the stories of the others. In all that time he has been at work grubbing to earn bread. Wife and he by constant labor make three thousand cigars a week, earning $11.25 when there is no lack of material; when in winter they receive from the manufacturer tobacco for only two thousand, the rent of $10 for two rooms, practically one with a dark alcove, has nevertheless to be paid in full, and six mouths to be fed. He was a blacksmith in the old country, but cannot work at his trade here because he does not understand "Engliska." If he could, he says, with a bright look, he could do better work than he sees done here. It would seem happiness to him to knock off at 6 o'clock instead of working, as he now often has to do, till midnight. But how? He knows of no Bohemian blacksmith who can understand him; he should starve. Here, with his wife, he can make a living at least. "Aye," says she, turning, from listening, to her household duties, "it would be nice for sure to have father work at his trade." Then what a home she could make for

Bohemian
Cigarmakers at
Work in Their
Tenement

them, and how happy they would be. Here is an unattainable ideal, indeed, of a workman in the most prosperous city in the world! There is genuine, if unspoken, pathos in the soft tap she gives her husband's hand as she goes about her work with a half-suppressed little sigh.

The very ash barrels that stand in front of the big rows of tenements in Seventy-first and Seventy-third Streets advertise the business that is carried on within. They are filled to the brim with the stems of stripped tobacco leaves. The rank smell that waited for us on the corner of the block follows us into the hallways, penetrates every nook and cranny of the houses. As in the settlement farther down town, every room here has its workbench with its stumpy knife and queer pouch of bedtick, worn brown and greasy, fastened in front the whole length of the bench to receive the scraps of waste. This landlord-employer at all events gives three rooms for $12.50, if two be dark, one wholly and the other getting some light from the front room. The mother of the three barefooted little children we met on the stairs was taken to the hospital the other day when she could no longer work. She will never come out alive. There is no waste in these tenements. Lives, like clothes, are worn through and out before put aside. Her place at the bench is taken already by another who divides with the head of the household his earnings of $15.50 a week. He has just come out successful of a strike that brought the pay of these tenements up to $4.50 per thousand cigars. Notice to quit had already been served on them, when the employer decided to give in, frightened by the prospective loss of rent. Asked how long he works, the man says: "from they can see till bedtime." Bedtime proves to be eleven o'clock. Seventeen hours a day, seven days in the week, at thirteen cents an hour for the two, six cents and a half for each! Good average earnings for a tenement house cigarmaker in summer. In winter it is at least one-fourth less. In spite of it all, the rooms are cleanly kept. From the bedroom farthest back the woman brings out a pile of moist tobacco leaves to be stripped. They are kept there, under cover lest they dry and crack, from Friday to Friday, when an accounting is made and fresh supplies given out. The people sleep there too, but the smell, offensive to the unfamiliar nose, does not bother them. They are used to it.

In a house around the corner that is not a factory-tenement, lives now the cigarmaker I spoke of as suffering from consumption which the doctor said was due to the tobacco fumes. Perhaps the lack of healthy exercise had as much to do with it. His case is interesting from its own standpoint. He too is one with a—for a Bohemian—large family. Six children sit at his table. By trade a shoemaker, for thirteen years he helped his wife make cigars in the manufacturer's tenement. She was a very good hand, and until his health gave out two years ago they were able to make from $17 to $25 a week, by lengthening the day at both ends. Now that he can work no more, and the family under the doctor's orders has moved away from the smell of tobacco, the burden of its support has fallen upon her alone, for none of the children are old enough to help. She has work in the shop at eight dollars a week, and this must go round; it is all there is. Happily, this being a tenement for revenue only, unmixed with cigars, the rent is cheaper: seven dollars for two bright rooms on the top floor. No housekeeping is attempted. A woman in Seventy-second Street supplies their cooking, which the wife and mother fetches in a basket, her husband being too weak. Breakfast of coffee and hardtack, or black bread, at twenty cents for the whole eight; a good many, the little woman says with a brave, patient smile, and there is seldom anything to spare, but——. The invalid is listening, and the sentence remains unfinished. What of dinner? One of the children brings it from the cook. Oh! it is a good dinner, meat, soup, greens and bread, all for thirty cents. It is the principal family meal. Does she come home for dinner? No; she cannot leave the shop, but gets a bite at her bench. The question: A bite of what? seems as merciless as the surgeon's knife, and she winces under it as one shrinks from physical pain. Bread, then. But at night they all have supper together—sausage and bread. For ten cents they can eat all they want. Can they not? she says, stroking the hair of the little boy at her knee; his eyes glisten hungrily at the thought, as he nods stoutly in support of his mother. Only, she adds, the week the rent is due, they have to shorten rations to pay the landlord.

But what of his being an Anarchist, this Bohemian—an infidel—I hear somebody say. Almost one might be persuaded by such facts as these—and they are everyday facts, not fancy—to retort: what more natural? With every hand raised against him in the old land and the new, in the land of his hoped-for freedom, what more logical than that his should be turned against society that seems to exist only for his oppression? But the charge is not half true. Naturally the Bohemian loves peace, as he loves music and song. As someone has said: He does not seek war, but when attacked knows better how to die than how to surrender. The Czech is the Irishman of Central Europe, with all his genius and his strong passions, with the same bitter traditions of landlord robbery, perpetuated here where he thought to forget them; like him ever and on principle in the opposition, "agin the government" wherever he goes. Among such a people, ground by poverty until their songs have died in curses upon their oppressors, hopelessly isolated and ignorant of our language and our laws, it would not be hard for bad men at any time to lead a few astray. And this is what has been done. Yet, even with the occasional noise made by the few, the criminal statistics already alluded to quite dispose of the charge that they incline to turbulence and riot. So it is with the infidel propaganda, the legacy perhaps of the fierce contention through hundreds of years between Catholics and Protestants on Bohemia's soil, of bad faith and savage persecutions in the name of the Christians' God that disgrace its history. The Bohemian clergyman, who spoke for his people at the Christian Conference held in Chickering Hall two years ago, took even stronger ground. "They are Roman Catholics by birth, infidels by necessity, and Protestants by history and inclination," he said. Yet he added his testimony in the same breath to the fact that, though the Freethinkers had started two schools in the immediate neighborhood of his church to counteract its influence, his flock had grown in a few years from a mere handful at the start to proportions far beyond his hopes, gathering in both Anarchists and Freethinkers, and making good church members of them.

Thus the whole matter resolves itself once more into a question of education, all the more urgent because these people are poor, miserably poor almost to a man. "There is not," said one of them, who knew thoroughly what he was speaking of, "there is not one of them all, who, if he were to sell all he was worth tomorrow, would have money enough to buy a house and lot in the country."

XIII

The Color Line in New York

THE COLOR LINE MUST be drawn through the tenements to give the picture its proper shading. The landlord does the drawing, does it with an absence of pretence, a frankness of despotism, that is nothing if not brutal. The Czar of all the Russias is not more absolute upon his own soil than the New York landlord in his dealings with colored tenants. Where he permits them to live, they go; where he shuts the door, stay out. By his grace they exist at all in certain localities; his ukase banishes them from others. He accepts the responsibility, when laid at his door, with unruffled complacency. It is business, he will tell you. And it is. He makes the prejudice in which he traffics pay him well, and that, as he thinks it quite superfluous to tell you, is what he is there for.

That his pencil does not make quite as black a mark as it did, that the hand that wields it does not bear down as hard as only a short half dozen years ago, is the hopeful sign of an awakening public conscience under the stress of which the line shows signs of wavering. But for this the landlord deserves no credit. It has come, is coming about despite him. The line may not be wholly effaced while the name of the Negro, alone among the world's races, is spelled with a small *n*.[1] Natural selection will have more or less to do beyond a doubt in every age with dividing the races; only so, it may be, can they work out together their highest destiny. But with the despotism that deliberately assigns to the defenceless Black the lowest level for the purpose of robbing him there that has nothing to do. Of such slavery, different only in degree from the other kind that held him as a chattel, to be sold or bartered at the will of his master, this century, if signs fail not, will see the end in New York.

Ever since the war New York has been receiving the overflow of colored population from the southern cities. In the last decade this migration has grown to such proportions that it is estimated that our Blacks have quite doubled in number since the Tenth Census. Whether the exchange has been of advantage to the Negro may well be questioned. Trades of which he had practical control in his southern home are not open to him here. I know that it may be answered that there is no industrial proscription of color; that it is a matter of choice. Perhaps so. At all events he does not choose then. How many colored carpenters or masons has anyone seen at work in New York? In the South there are enough of them and, if the testimony of the most intelligent of their people is worth anything, plenty of them have come here. As a matter of fact the colored man takes in New York, without a struggle, the lower level of menial service for which his past traditions and natural love of ease perhaps as yet fit him best. Even the colored barber is rapidly getting to be a thing of the past. Along shore, at any unskilled labor, he works unmolested; but he does not appear to prefer the job. His sphere thus defined, he naturally takes his stand among the poor, and in the homes of the poor. Until very recent times—the years since a change was wrought can be counted on the fingers of one hand—he was practically restricted in the choice of a home to a narrow section on the West Side, that nevertheless had a social top and bottom to it—the top in the tenements on the line of Seventh Avenue as far north as Thirty-second Street, where he was allowed to occupy the houses of unsavory reputation which the police had cleared and for which decent white tenants could not be found; the bottom in the vile rookeries of Thompson Street and South Fifth Avenue, the old "Africa" that is now fast becoming a modern Italy. Today there are black colonies in Yorkville and Morrisania. The encroachment of business and the Italian below, and the swelling of the population above, have been the chief agents in working out his second emancipation, a very real one, for with his cutting loose from the old tenements there has come a distinct and gratifying improvement in the tenant, that argues louder than theories or speeches the influence of vile surroundings in debasing the man. The colored citizen whom this year's census man found in his Ninety-ninth Street "flat" is a very different individual from the "nigger" his predecessor counted in the black-and-tan slums of Thompson and Sullivan Streets. There is no more clean and orderly community in New York than the new settlement of colored people that is growing up on the East Side from Yorkville to Harlem.[2]

Cleanliness is the characteristic of the Negro in his new surroundings, as it was his virtue in the old. In this respect he is immensely the superior of the lowest of the whites, the Italians and the Polish Jews, below whom he has been classed in the past in the tenant scale. Nevertheless, he has always had to pay higher rents than even these for the poorest and most stinted rooms. The exceptions I have come across, in which the rents, though high, have seemed more nearly on a level with what was asked for the same number and size of rooms in the average tenement, were in the case of tumbledown rookeries in which no one else would live, and were always coupled with the condition that the landlord should "make no repairs." It can readily be seen, that his profits were scarcely curtailed by his "humanity." The reason advanced for this systematic robbery is that white people will not live in the same house with colored tenants, or even in a house recently occupied by Negroes, and that consequently its selling value is injured. The prejudice undoubtedly exists, but it is not lessened by the house agents, who have set up the maxim "once a colored house, always a colored house."

There is method in the maxim, as shown by an inquiry made last year by the *Real Estate Record*.[3] It proved agents to be practically unanimous in the endorsement of the Negro as a clean, orderly, and "profitable" tenant. Here is the testimony of one of the largest real estate firms in the city: "We would rather have Negro tenants in our poorest class of tenements than the lower grades of foreign white people. We find the former cleaner than the latter, and they do not destroy the property so much. We also get higher prices. We have a tenement on Nineteenth Street, where we get $10 for two rooms which we could not get more than $7.50 for from white tenants previously. We have a four-story tenement on our books on Thirty-third Street, between Sixth and Seventh Avenues, with four rooms per floor —a parlor, two bedrooms, and a kitchen. We get $20 for the first floor, $24 for the second, $23 for the third and $20 for the fourth, in all $87 or $1,044 per annum. The size of the building is only 21 × 55." Another firm declared that in a specified instance they had saved fifteen to twenty percent on the gross rentals since they changed their white tenants for colored ones. Still another gave the following case of a front and rear tenement that had formerly been occupied by tenants of a "low European type," who had been turned out on account of filthy habits and poor pay. The Negroes proved cleaner, better, and steadier tenants. Instead, however, of having their rents reduced in consequence, the comparison stood as follows:

Rents under White Tenants		Rents under Colored Tenants	
Floor	Per Month	Floor	Per Month
Front		Front	
1st (store, etc.)	$21	1st (store, etc.)	$21
2nd	13	2nd	14
3rd	13	3rd	14
4th (and rear)	21	4th	14
Rear		Rear	
2nd	12	2nd	12
3rd	12	3rd	13
4th	(see front)	4th	13
Rear House		Rear House	
1st	8	1st	10
2nd	10	2nd	12
3rd	9	3rd	11
4th	8	4th	10
Total	$127	Total	$144

An increased rental of $17 per month, or $204 a year, and an advance of nearly thirteen and one-half percent on the gross rental "in favor" of the colored tenant. Profitable, surely!

I have quoted these cases at length in order to let in light on the quality of this landlord despotism that has purposely confused the public mind, and for its own selfish ends is propping up a waning prejudice. It will be cause for congratulation if indeed its time has come at last. Within a year, I am told by one of the most intelligent and best informed of our colored citizens, there has been evidence, simultaneous with the colored hegira from the low downtown tenements, of a movement toward less exorbitant rents. I cannot pass from this subject without adding a leaf from my own experience that to look for when the sun shines unclouded in a clear sky. His home surroundings, except when he is utterly depraved, reflect his blithesome temper. The poorest Negro housekeeper's room in New York is bright with gaily colored prints of his beloved "Abe Linkum," General Grant, President Garfield, Mrs. Cleveland, and other national celebrities, and cheery with flowers and singing birds. In the art of putting the best foot foremost, of disguising his poverty by making a little go a long way, our Negro has no equal. When a fair share of prosperity is his, he knows how to make life and home very pleasant to those about him. Pianos and parlor furniture abound in the uptown homes of colored tenants and give them a very prosperous air. But even where the wolf howls at the door, he makes a bold and gorgeous front. The amount of "style" displayed on fine Sundays on Sixth and Seventh Avenues by colored holidaymakers would turn a pessimist black with wrath. The Negro's great ambition is to rise in the social scale to which his color has made him a stranger and an outsider, and he is quite willing to accept the shadow for the substance where that is the best he can get. The claw-hammer coat and white tie of a waiter in a first-class summer hotel, with the chance of taking his ease in six months of winter, are to him the next best thing to mingling with the white quality he serves, on equal terms. His festive gatherings, preeminently his cakewalks, at which a sugared and frosted cake is the proud prize of the couple with the most aristocratic step and carriage, are comic mixtures of elaborate ceremonial and the joyous abandon of the natural man. With all his ludicrous incongruities, his sensuality and his lack of moral accountability, his superstition and other faults that are the effect of temperament and of centuries of slavery, he has his eminently good points. He is loyal to the backbone, proud of being an American and of his newfound citizenship. He is at least as easily moulded for good as for evil. His churches are crowded to the doors on Sunday nights when the colored colony turns out to worship. His people own church property in this city upon which they have paid half a million dollars out of the depth of their poverty, with comparatively little assistance from their white brethren. He is both willing and anxious to learn, and his intellectual status is distinctly improving. If his emotions are not very deeply rooted, they are at least sincere while they last, and until the tempter gets the upper hand again.

Of all the temptations that beset him, the one that troubles him and the police most is his passion for gambling. The game of policy is a kind of unlawful penny lottery specially adapted to his means, but patronized extensively by poor white players as well. It is the meanest of swindles, but reaps for its backers rich fortunes wherever colored people congregate. Between the fortune teller and the policy shop, closely allied frauds always, the wages of many a hard day's work are wasted by the Negro; but the loss causes him few regrets. Penniless, but with undaunted faith in his ultimate "luck," he looks forward to the time when he shall once more be able to take a hand at "beating policy." When periodically the Negro's lucky numbers, 4–11–44, come out on the slips of alleged daily drawings, that are supposed to be held in some far-off western town, intense excitement reigns in Thompson Street and along the Avenue, where someone is always the winner. An immense impetus is given then to the bogus business that has no existence outside of the cigar stores and candy shops where it hides from the law, save in some cunning Bowery "broker's" back office, where the slips are printed and the "winnings" apportioned daily with due regard to the backer's interests.

It is a question whether "Africa" has been improved by the advent of the Italian, with the tramp from the Mulberry Street Bend in his train. The moral turpitude of Thompson Street has been notorious for years, and the mingling of the three elements does not seem to have wrought any change for the better. The borderland where the

A Black-and-Tan
Dive in "Africa"

white and black races meet in common debauch, the aptly-named black-and-tan saloon, has never been debatable ground from a moral standpoint. It has always been the worst of the desperately bad. Than this commingling of the utterly depraved of both sexes, white and black, on such ground, there can be no greater abomination. Usually it is some foul cellar dive, perhaps run by the political "leader" of the district, who is "in with" the police. In any event it gathers to itself all the lawbreakers and all the human wrecks within reach. When a fight breaks out during the dance a dozen razors are handy in as many bootlegs, and there is always a job for the surgeon and the ambulance. The black "tough" is as handy with the razor in a fight as his peaceably inclined brother is with it in pursuit of his honest trade. As the Chinaman hides his knife in his sleeve and the Italian his stiletto in the bosom, so the Negro goes to the ball with a razor in his bootleg, and on occasion does as much execution with it as both of the others together. More than three-fourths of the business the police have with the colored people in New York arises in the black-and-tan district, now no longer fairly representative of their color.

I have touched briefly upon such facts in the Negro's life as may serve to throw light on the social condition of his people in New York. If, when the account is made up between the races, it shall be claimed that he falls short of the result to be expected from twenty-five years of freedom, it may be well to turn to the other side of the ledger and see how much of the blame is borne by the prejudice and greed that have kept him from rising under a burden of responsibility to which he could hardly be equal. And in this view he may be seen to have advanced much farther and faster than before suspected, and to promise, after all, with fair treatment, quite as well as the rest of us, his white-skinned fellow citizens, had any right to expect.

XIV

The Common Herd

THERE IS ANOTHER LINE NOT always so readily drawn in the tenements, yet the real boundary line of the Other Half: the one that defines the "flat." The law does not draw it at all, accounting all flats tenements without distinction. The health officer draws it from observation, lumping all those which in his judgment have nothing, or not enough, to give them claim upon the name, with the common herd, and his way is, perhaps, on the whole, the surest and best. The outside of the building gives no valuable clue. Brass and brownstone go well sometimes with dense crowds and dark and dingy rooms; but the first attempt to enter helps draw the line with tolerable distinctness. A locked door is a strong point in favor of the flat. It argues that the first step has been taken to secure privacy, the absence of which is the chief curse of the tenement. Behind a locked door the hoodlum is not at home, unless there be a jailor in place of a janitor to guard it. Not that the janitor and the doorbell are infallible. There may be a

The Open Door

tenement behind a closed door; but never a "flat" without it. The hall
that is a highway for all the world by night and by day is the tenement's proper badge. The Other Half ever receives with open doors.

   With this introduction we shall not seek it long anywhere in the
city. Below Houston Street the doorbell in our age is as extinct as the
dodo. East of Second Avenue, and west of Ninth Avenue as far up as
the Park, it is practically an unknown institution. The nearer the river
and the great workshops the more numerous the tenements. The kind
of work carried on in any locality to a large extent determines their
character. Skilled and well-paid labor puts its stamp on a tenement

even in spite of the open door, and usually soon supplies the missing bell. Gashouses, slaughterhouses and the docks, that attract the roughest crowds and support the vilest saloons, invariably form slum centers. The city is full of such above the line of Fourteenth Street, that is erroneously supposed by some to fence off the good from the bad, separate the chaff from the wheat. There is nothing below that line that can outdo in wickedness Hell's Kitchen,[1] in the region of three-cent whiskey, or its counterpoise at the other end of Thirty-ninth Street, on the East River, the home of the infamous Rag Gang. Cherry Street is not "tougher" than Battle Row in East Sixty-third Street, or "the village" at Twenty-ninth Street and First Avenue, where stores of broken bricks, ammunition for the nightly conflicts with the police, are part of the regulation outfit of every tenement. The Mulberry Street Bend is scarce dirtier than Little Italy in Harlem. Even across the Harlem River, Frog Hollow challenges the admiration of the earlier slums for the boldness and pernicious activity of its home gang. There are enough of these sore spots. We shall yet have occasion to look into the social conditions of some of them; were I to draw a picture of them here as they are, the subject, I fear, would outgrow alike the limits of this book and the reader's patience.

It is true that they tell only one side of the story; that there is another to tell. A story of thousands of devoted lives, laboring earnestly to make the most of their scant opportunities for good; of heroic men and women striving patiently against fearful odds and by their very courage coming off victors in the battle with the tenement; of womanhood pure and undefiled. That it should blossom in such an atmosphere is one of the unfathomable mysteries of life. And yet it is not an uncommon thing to find sweet and innocent girls, singularly untouched by the evil around them, true wives and faithful mothers, literally "like jewels in a swine's snout," in the worst of the infamous barracks. It is the experience of all who have intelligently observed this side of life in a great city, not to be explained—unless on the theory of my friend, the priest in the Mulberry Street Bend, that inherent purity revolts instinctively from the naked brutality of vice as seen in the slums—but to be thankfully accepted as the one gleam of hope in an otherwise hopeless desert.

But the relief is not great. In the dull content of life bred on the tenement house dead level there is little to redeem it, or to calm apprehension for a society that has nothing better to offer its toilers; while the patient efforts of the lives finally attuned to it to render the situation tolerable, and the very success of these efforts, serve only to bring out in stronger contrast the general gloom of the picture by showing how much farther they might have gone with half a chance. Go into any of the "respectable" tenement neighborhoods—the fact

Bird's-Eye View of an East Side Tenement Block (From a Drawing by Charles F. Wingate, Esq.)

EDITOR'S NOTE: Charles Frederick Wingate (1848–1909) was a civil engineer and editor of the trade journal *The Plumber and Sanitary Engineer* in 1879 when that magazine ran its disastrous architectural contest which resulted in the "dumbell tenement" design. In 1884 he served with Felix Adler on the New York Senate Tenement House Commission which Riis covered for the *New York Tribune*.

that there are not more than two saloons on the corner, nor over three or four in the block will serve as a fair guide—where live the great body of hardworking Irish and German immigrants and their descendants, who accept naturally the conditions of tenement life, because for them there is nothing else in New York; be with and among its people until you understand their ways, their aims, and the quality of their ambitions, and unless you can content yourself with the scriptural promise that the poor we shall have always with us, or with the menagerie view that, if fed, they have no cause of complaint, you shall come away agreeing with me that, humanly speaking, life there does not seem worth the living. Take at random one of these uptown tenement blocks, not of the worst nor yet of the most prosperous kind, within hail of what the newspapers would call a "fine residential section." These houses were built since the last cholera scare made people willing to listen to reason. The block is not like the one over on the East Side in which I actually lost my way once. There were thirty or forty rear houses in the heart of it, three or four on every lot, set at all sorts of angles, with odd, winding passages, or no passage at all, only "runways" for the thieves and toughs of the neighborhood. These yards are clear. There is air there, and it is about all there is. The view between brick walls outside is that of a stony street; inside, of rows of unpainted board fences, a bewildering maze of clothes posts and lines; underfoot, a desert of brown, hard-baked soil from which every blade of grass, every stray weed, every speck of green, has been trodden out, as must inevitably be every gentle thought and aspiration above the mere wants of the body in those whose moral natures such home surroundings are to nourish. In self-defense, you know, all life eventually accommodates itself to its environment, and human life is no exception. Within the house there is nothing to supply the want thus left unsatisfied. Tenement houses have no aesthetic resources. If any are to be brought to bear on them, they must come from the outside. There is the common hall with doors opening softly on every landing as the strange step is heard on the stairs, the air shaft that seems always so busy letting out foul stenches from below that it has no time to earn its name by bringing down fresh air, the squeaking pumps that hold no water, and the rent that is never less than one week's wages out of the four, quite as often half of the family earnings.

Why complete the sketch? It is drearily familiar already. Such as it is, it is the frame in which are set days, weeks, months, and years of unceasing toil, just able to fill the mouth and clothe the back. Such as it is, it is the world, and all of it, to which these weary workers return nightly to feed heart and brain after wearing out the body at the bench, or in the shop. To it come the young with their restless yearnings, perhaps to pass on the threshold one of the daughters of sin, driven to the tenement by the police when they raided her den, sallying forth in silks and fine attire after her day of idleness. These in their coarse garments—girls with the love of youth for beautiful things, with this hard life before them—who shall save them from the tempter? Down in the street the saloon, always bright and gay, gathering to itself all the cheer of the block, beckons the boys. In many such blocks the census taker found two thousand men, women, and children, and over, who called them home.

The picture is faithful enough to stand for its class wherever along both rivers the Irish brogue is heard. As already said, the Celt falls most readily victim to tenement influences since shantytown and its original free-soilers have become things of the past. If he be thrifty and shrewd his progress thenceforward is along the plane of the tenement, on which he soon assumes to manage without improving things. The German has an advantage over his Celtic neighbor in his strong love for flowers, which not all the tenements on the East Side have power to smother. His garden goes with him wherever he goes.

Not that it represents any high moral principle in the man; rather
perhaps the capacity for it. He turns his saloon into a shrubbery as
soon as his backyard. But wherever he puts it in a tenement block it
does the work of a dozen police clubs. In proportion as it spreads the
neighborhood takes on a more orderly character. As the green dies
out of the landscape and increases in political importance, the police
find more to do. Where it disappears altogether from sight, lapsing
into a mere sentiment, police beats are shortened and the force pa-
trols double at night. Neither the man nor the sentiment is wholly
responsible for this. It is the tenement unadorned that is. The changing of Tompkins Square from a sand lot into a beautiful park put an
end for good and all to the Bread and Blood riots of which it used
to be the scene, and transformed a nest of dangerous agitators into a
harmless, beer-craving band of anarchists. They have scarcely been
heard of since. Opponents of the small parks system as a means of
relieving the congested population of tenement districts, please take
note.

With the first hot nights in June police dispatches, that record the
killing of men and women by rolling off roofs and windowsills while
asleep, announce that the time of greatest suffering among the poor is
at hand. It is in hot weather, when life indoors is well-nigh unbearable with cooking, sleeping, and working, all crowded into the small
rooms together, that the tenement expands, reckless of all restraint.
Then a strange and picturesque life moves upon the flat roofs. In the
day and early evening mothers air their babies there, the boys fly their
kites from the housetops, undismayed by police regulations, and the
young men and girls court and pass the growler. In the stifling July
nights, when the big barracks are like fiery furnaces, their very walls
giving out absorbed heat, men and women lie in restless, sweltering
rows, panting for air and sleep. Then every truck in the street, every
crowded fire escape, becomes a bedroom, infinitely preferable to any

The White Badge of Mourning

the house affords. A cooling shower on such a night is hailed as a heaven-sent blessing in a hundred thousand homes.

Life in the tenements in July and August spells death to an army of little ones whom the doctor's skill is powerless to save. When the white badge of mourning flutters from every second door, sleepless mothers walk the streets in the gray of the early dawn, trying to stir a cooling breeze to fan the brow of the sick baby. There is no sadder sight than this patient devotion striving against fearfully hopeless odds. Fifty "summer doctors," especially trained to this work, are then sent into the tenements by the Board of Health, with free advice and medicine for the poor. Devoted women follow in their track with care and nursing for the sick. Fresh-air excursions run daily out of New York on land and water; but despite all efforts the gravediggers in Calvary work overtime, and little coffins are stacked mountains high on the deck of the Charity Commissioners' boat when it makes its semi-weekly trips to the city cemetery.

Under the most favorable circumstances, an epidemic, which the well-to-do can afford to make light of as a thing to be got over or avoided by reasonable care, is excessively fatal among the children of the poor, by reason of the practical impossibility of isolating the patient in a tenement. The measles, ordinarily a harmless disease, furnishes a familiar example. Tread it ever so lightly on the avenues, in the tenements it kills right and left. Such an epidemic ravaged three crowded blocks in Elizabeth Street on the heels of the grippe last winter, and, when it had spent its fury, the death maps in the Bureau of Vital Statistics looked as if a black hand had been laid across those blocks, overshadowing in part the contiguous tenements in Mott Street, and with the thumb covering a particularly packed settlement of half a dozen houses in Mulberry Street. The track of the epidemic through these teeming barracks was as clearly defined as the track of a tornado through a forest district. There were houses in which as many as eight little children had died in five months. The records showed that respiratory diseases, the common heritage of the grippe and the measles, had caused death in most cases, discovering the trouble to be, next to the inability to check the contagion in those crowds, in the poverty of the parents and the wretched home conditions that made proper care of the sick impossible. The fact was emphasized by the occurrence here and there of a few isolated deaths from diphtheria and scarlet fever. In the case of these diseases, considered more dangerous to the public health, the health officers exercised summary powers of removal to the hospital where proper treatment could be had, and the result was a low death rate.

These were tenements of the tall, modern type. A little more than a year ago, when a census was made of the tenements and compared with the mortality tables, no little surprise and congratulation was caused by the discovery that as the buildings grew taller the death rate fell. The reason is plain, though the reverse had been expected by most people. The biggest tenements have been built in the last ten years of sanitary reform rule, and have been brought, in all but the crowding, under its laws. The old houses that from private dwellings were made into tenements, or were run up to house the biggest crowds in defiance of every moral and physical law, can be improved by no device short of demolition. They will ever remain the worst.

That ignorance plays its part, as well as poverty and bad hygienic surroundings, in the sacrifice of life is of course inevitable. They go usually hand in hand. A message came one day last spring summoning me to a Mott Street tenement in which lay a child dying from some unknown disease. With the "charity doctor" I found the patient on the top floor, stretched upon two chairs in a dreadfully stifling room. She was gasping in the agony of peritonitis that had already written its death sentence on her wan and pinched face. The whole family, father, mother, and four ragged children, sat around looking on with the stony resignation of helpless despair that had long since given up the fight against fate as useless. A glance around the wretched room left no doubt as to the cause of the child's condition. "Improper nourishment," said the doctor, which, translated to suit the place, meant starvation. The father's hands were crippled from lead poisoning. He had not been able to work for a year. A contagious disease of the eyes, too long neglected, had made the mother and one of the boys nearly blind. The children cried with hunger. They had

In Poverty Gap, West Twenty-eighth Street. An English Coal-Heaver's Home

Suspicions of murder, in the case of a woman who was found dead, covered with bruises, aft a day's running fight with her husband, in which the beer jug had been the bone of contention, brought me to this house, a ramshackle tenement on the tail end of a lot over near the North River docks. The family in the picture lived above the rooms where the dead woman lay on a bee of straw, overrun by rats, and had been uninterested witnesses of the affray that was an everyday occurrence in the house. A patched and shaky stairway led up to their one bare and miserable room, in comparison with which a whitewashed prison cell seemed a real palace. A heap of old rags, in which the baby slept serenely, served as the common sleeping bunk of father, mother, an children—two bright and pretty girls, singularly out of keeping in their clean, if coarse, dresses, with their surroundings. The father, a slow-going, honest English coal-heaver, earned on the average five dollars a week, "when work was fairly brisk," at the docks. But there were long seaso: when it was very "slack," he said, doubtfully. Yet the prospect did not seem to discourage them. The mother, a pleasant-faced woman, was cheerful, even lighthearted. Her smile seemed the mo: sadly hopeless of all in the utter wretchedness of the place, cheery though it was meant to be and really was. It seemed doomed to certain disappointment—the one thing there that was yet to know a greater depth of misery.

not broken their fast that day, and it was then near noon. For months the family had subsisted on two dollars a week from the priest, and a few loaves and a piece of corned beef which the sisters sent them on Saturday. The doctor gave direction for the treatment of the child, knowing that it was possible only to alleviate its sufferings until death should end them, and left some money for food for the rest. An hour later, when I returned, I found them feeding the dying child with ginger ale, bought for two cents a bottle at the pedlar's cart down the street. A pitying neighbor had proposed it as the one thing she could think of as likely to make the child forget its misery. There was enough in the bottle to go round to the rest of the family. In fact, the wake had already begun; before night it was under way in dead earnest.

Every once in a while a case of downright starvation gets into the newspapers and makes a sensation. But this is the exception. Were the whole truth known, it would come home to the community with a shock that would rouse it to a more serious effort than the spasmodic undoing of its purse strings. I am satisfied from my own observation that hundreds of men, women, and children are every day slowly starving to death in the tenements with my medical friend's complaint of "improper nourishment." Within a single week I have had this year three cases of insanity, provoked directly by poverty and want. One was that of a mother who in the middle of the night got up to murder her child, who was crying for food; another was the case of an Elizabeth Street truck driver whom the newspapers never heard of. With a family to provide for, he had been unable to work for many months. There was neither food, nor a scrap of anything upon which money could be raised, left in the house; his mind gave way under the combined physical and mental suffering. In the third case I was just in time with the police to prevent the madman from murdering his whole family. He had the sharpened hatchet in his pocket when we seized him. He was an Irish laborer, and had been working in the sewers until the poisonous gases destroyed his health. Then he was laid off, and scarcely anything had been coming in all winter but the oldest child's earnings as cashgirl in a store, $2.50 a week. There were seven children to provide for, and the rent of the Mulberry Street attic in which the family lived was $10 a month. They had borrowed as long as anybody had a cent to lend. When at last the man got an odd job that would just buy the children bread, the week's wages only served to measure the depth of their misery. "It came in so on the tail end of everything," said his wife in telling the story, with unconscious eloquence. The outlook worried him through sleepless nights until it destroyed his reason. In his madness he had only one conscious thought: that the town should not take the children. "Better that I take care of them myself," he repeated to himself as he ground the axe to an edge. Help came in abundance from many almost as poor as they when the desperate straits of the family became known through his arrest. The readiness of the poor to share what little they have with those who have even less is one of the few moral virtues of the tenements. Their enormous crowds touch elbow in a closeness of sympathy that is scarcely to be understood out of them, and has no parallel except among the unfortunate women whom the world scorns as outcasts. There is very little professed sentiment about it to draw a sentimental tear from the eye of romantic philanthropy. The hard fact is that the instinct of self-preservation impels them to make common cause against the common misery.

No doubt intemperance bears a large share of the blame for it; judging from the standpoint of the policeman perhaps the greater share. Two such entries as I read in the police returns on successive days last March, of mothers in West Side tenements, who, in their drunken sleep, lay upon and killed their infants, go far to support such a position. And they are far from uncommon. But my experi-

ence has shown me another view of it, a view which the last report
of the Society for Improving the Condition of the Poor seems more
than half inclined to adopt in allotting to "intemperance the cause of
distress, or distress the cause of intemperance," forty percent of the
cases it is called upon to deal with.[2] Even if it were all true, I should
still load over upon the tenement the heaviest responsibility. A single
factor, the scandalous scarcity of water in the hot summer when the
thirst of the million tenants must be quenched, if not in that in something else, has in the past years more than all other causes encouraged
drunkenness among the poor. But to my mind there is a closer connection between the wages of the tenements and the vices and improvidence of those who dwell in them than, with the guilt of the
tenement upon our heads, we are willing to admit even to ourselves.
Weak tea with a dry crust is not a diet to nurse moral strength. Yet
how much better might the fare be expected to be in the family of this
"widow with seven children, very energetic and prudent"—I quote
again from the report of the Society for the Improvement of the Condition of the Poor—whose "eldest girl was employed as a learner in
a tailor's shop at small wages, and one boy had a place as 'cash' in a
store. There were two other little boys who sold papers and sometimes earned one dollar. The mother finishes pantaloons and can do
three pairs in a day, thus earning thirty-nine cents. Here is a family of
eight persons with rent to pay and an income of less than six dollars a
week."

And yet she was better off in point of pay than this Sixth Street
mother, who "had just brought home four pairs of pants to finish,
at seven cents a pair. She was required to put the canvas in the bottom, basting and sewing three times around; to put the linings in the
waistbands; to tack three pockets, three corners to each; to put on two
stays and eight buttons, and make six buttonholes; to put the buckle
on the back strap and sew on the ticket, all for seven cents." Better off

than the "churchgoing mother of six children," and with a husband
sick to death, who to support the family made shirts, averaging an
income of one dollar and twenty cents a week, while her oldest girl,
aged thirteen, was "employed downtown cutting out Hamburg edg-
ings at one dollar and a half a week—two and a half cents per hour for
ten hours of steady labor—making the total income of the family two
dollars and seventy cents per week." Than the Harlem woman, who
was "making a brave effort to support a sick husband and two children by taking in washing at thirty-five cents for the lot of fourteen
large pieces, finding coal, soap, starch, and bluing herself, rather than
depend on charity in any form." Specimen wages of the tenements
these, seemingly inconsistent with the charge of improvidence.

But the connection on second thought is not obscure. There is
nothing in the prospect of a sharp, unceasing battle for the bare nec-
essaries of life, to encourage looking ahead, everything to discourage
the effort. Improvidence and wastefulness are natural results. The instalment plan secures to the tenant who lives from hand to mouth his
few comforts; the evil day of reckoning is put off till a tomorrow that
may never come. When it does come, with failure to pay and the loss
of hard-earned dollars, it simply adds another hardship to a life measured from the cradle by such incidents. The children soon catch the
spirit of this sort of thing. I remember once calling at the home of a
poor washerwoman, living in an East Side tenement, and finding the
door locked. Some children in the hallway stopped their play and
eyed me attentively while I knocked. The biggest girl volunteered the
information that Mrs. Smith was out; but while I was thinking of how
I was to get a message to her, the child put a question of her own: "Are
you the spring man or the clock man?" When I assured her that I was
neither one nor the other, but had brought work for her mother, Mrs.
Smith, who had been hiding from the instalment collector, speedily
appeared.

Perhaps of all the disheartening experiences of those who have devoted lives of unselfish thought and effort, and their number is not
so small as often supposed, to the lifting of this great load, the indifference of those they would help is the most puzzling. They will not
be helped. Dragged by main force out of their misery, they slip back
again on the first opportunity, seemingly content only in the old rut.
The explanation was supplied by two women of my acquaintance in
an Elizabeth Street tenement, whom the missionaries had taken from
their wretched hovel and provided with work and a decent home
somewhere in New Jersey. In three weeks they were back, saying that
they preferred their dark rear room to the stumps out in the country. But to me the oldest, the mother, who had struggled along with
her daughter making cloaks at half a dollar apiece, twelve long years
since the daughter's husband was killed in a street accident and the
city took the children, made the bitter confession: "We do get so kind
o' downhearted living this way, that we have to be where something is
going on, or we just can't stand it." And there was sadder pathos to me
in her words than in the whole long story of their struggle with poverty; for unconsciously she voiced the sufferings of thousands, mis-
judged by a happier world, deemed vicious because they are human
and unfortunate.

It is a popular delusion, encouraged by all sorts of exaggerated stories when nothing more exciting demands public attention, that there
are more evictions in the tenements of New York every year "than in
all Ireland." I am not sure that it is doing much for the tenant to upset
this fallacy. To my mind, to be put out of a tenement would be the
height of good luck. The fact is, however, that evictions are not nearly
as common in New York as supposed. The reason is that in the civil
courts, the judges of which are elected in their districts, the tenant
voter has solid ground to stand upon at last. The law that takes his
side to start with is usually twisted to the utmost to give him time and

Dispossessed

save him expense. In the busiest East Side court, that has been very appropriately dubbed the "Poor Man's Court," fully five thousand dispossess warrants are issued in a year, but probably not fifty evictions take place in the district. The landlord has only one vote, while there may be forty voters hiring his rooms in the house, all of which the judge takes into careful account as elements that have a direct bearing on the case. And so they have—on his case. There are sad cases, just as there are "rounders" who prefer to be moved at the landlord's expense and save the rent, but the former at least are unusual enough to attract more than their share of attention.

If his very poverty compels the tenant to live at a rate if not in a style that would beggar a Vanderbilt, paying four prices for everything he needs, from his rent and coal down to the smallest item in his housekeeping account, fashion, no less inexorable in the tenements than on the avenue, exacts of him that he must die in a style that is finally and utterly ruinous. The habit of expensive funerals—I know of no better classification for it than along with the opium habit and similar grievous plagues of mankind—is a distinctively Irish inheritance, but it has taken root among all classes of tenement dwellers, curiously enough most firmly among the Italians, who have taken amazingly to the funeral coach, perhaps because it furnishes the one opportunity of their lives for a really grand turnout with a free ride thrown in. It is not at all uncommon to find the hoards of a whole lifetime of hard work and self-denial squandered on the empty show of a ludicrous funeral parade and a display of flowers that ill comports with the humble life it is supposed to exalt. It is easier to understand the wake as a sort of consolation cup for the survivors for whom there is—as one of them, doubtless a heathenish pessimist, put it to me once—"no such luck." The press and the pulpit have denounced the wasteful practice that often entails bitter want upon the relatives of the one buried with such pomp, but with little or no apparent result. Rather, the undertaker's business prospers more than ever in the tenements since the genius of politics has seen its way clear to make capital out of the dead voter as well as of the living, by making him the means of a useful "show of strength" and count of noses.[3]

The Trench in the Potter's Field

One free excursion awaits young and old whom bitter poverty has denied the poor privilege of the choice of the home in death they were denied in life, the ride up the Sound to the Potter's Field, charitably styled the City Cemetery. But even there they do not escape their fate. In the common trench of the Poor Burying Ground they lie packed three stories deep, shoulder to shoulder, crowded in death as they were in life, to "save space"; for even on that desert island the ground is not for the exclusive possession of those who cannot afford to pay for it. There is an odd coincidence in this, that year by year the lives that are begun in the gutter, the little nameless waifs whom the police pick up and the city adopts as its wards, are balanced by the even more forlorn lives that are ended in the river. I do not know how or why it happens, or that it is more than a mere coincidence. But there it is. Year by year the balance is struck—a few more, a few less—substantially the same when the record is closed.

XV

The Problem of the Children

THE PROBLEM OF THE CHILDREN BECOMES, in these swarms, to the last degree perplexing. Their very number make one stand aghast. I have already given instances of the packing of the child population in East Side tenements. They might be continued indefinitely until the array would be enough to startle any community. For, be it remembered, these children with the training they receive—or do not receive—with the instincts they inherit and absorb in their growing up, are to be our future rulers, if our theory of government is worth anything. More than a working majority of our voters now register from the tenements. I counted the other day the little ones, up to ten years or so, in a Bayard Street tenement that for a yard has a triangular space in the center with sides fourteen or fifteen feet long, just room enough for a row of ill-smelling closets at the base of the triangle and a hydrant at the apex. There was about as much light in this "yard" as in the average cellar. I gave up my self-imposed task in despair when I had counted one hundred and twenty-eight in forty families. Thirteen I had missed, or not found in. Applying the average for the forty to the whole fifty-three, the house contained one hundred and seventy children. It is not the only time I have had to give up such census work. I have in mind an alley—an inlet rather to a row of rear tenements—that is either two or four feet wide according as the wall of the crazy old building that gives on it bulges out or in. I tried to count the children that swarmed there, but could not. Sometimes I have doubted that anybody knows just how many there are about. Bodies of drowned children turn up in the rivers right along in summer whom no one seems to know anything about. When last spring some workmen, while moving a pile of lumber on a North River pier, found under the last plank the body of a little lad crushed to death, no one had missed a boy, though his parents afterward turned up. The truant officer assuredly does not know, though he spends his life trying to find out, somewhat illogically, perhaps, since the department that employs him admits that thousands of poor children are crowded out of the schools year by year for want of room. There was a big tenement in the Sixth Ward, now happily appropriated by the beneficent spirit of business that blots out so many foul spots in New York—it figured not long ago in the official reports as "an out-and-out hog pen"—that had a record of one hundred and two arrests in four years among its four hundred and seventy-eight tenants, fifty-seven of them for drunken and disorderly conduct. I do not know how many children there were in it, but the inspector reported that he found only seven in the whole house who owned that they went to school. The rest gathered all the instruction they received running for beer for their elders. Some of them claimed the "flat" as their home as a mere matter of form. They slept in the streets at night. The official came upon a little party of four drinking beer out of the cover of a milk can in the hallway. They were of the seven good boys and proved their claim to the title by offering him some.

The old question, what to do with the boy, assumes a new and serious phase in the tenements. Under the best conditions found there, it is not easily answered. In nine cases out of ten he would make an excellent mechanic, if trained early to work at a trade, for he is neither dull nor slow, but the short-sighted despotism of the trades unions has practically closed that avenue to him. Trade schools, however excellent, cannot supply the opportunity thus denied him, and at the outset the boy stands condemned by his own to low and ill-paid drudgery, held down by the hand that of all should labor to raise him. Home, the greatest factor of all in the training of the young, means nothing to him but a pigeonhole in a coop along with so many other human animals. Its influence is scarcely of the elevating kind, if it have any. The very games at which he takes a hand in the street become polluting in its atmosphere. With no steady hand to guide him, the boy takes naturally to idle ways. Caught in the street by the truant officer, or by the agents of the Children's Societies, peddling, perhaps, or begging, to help out the family resources, he runs the risk of being sent to a reformatory, where contacts with vicious boys older than himself soon develop the latent possibilities for evil that lie hidden in him. The city has no Truant Home in which to keep him, and all efforts of the children's friends to enforce school attendance are paralyzed by this want. The risk of the reformatory is too great. What is done in the end is to let him take chances—with the chances all against him. The result is the rough young savage, familiar from the street. Rough as he is, if anyone doubt that this child of common clay have in him the instinct of beauty, of love for the ideal of which his life has no embodiment, let him put the matter to the test. Let him take into a tenement block a handful of flowers from the fields and watch the brightened faces, the sudden abandonment of play and fight that go ever hand in hand where there is no elbowroom, the wild entreaty for "posies," the eager love with which the little messengers of peace are shielded, once possessed; then let him change his mind. I have seen an armful of daisies keep the peace of a block better than a policeman and his club, seen instincts awaken under their gentle appeal, whose very existence the soil in which they grew made seem a mockery. I have not forgotten the deputation of ragamuffins from a Mulberry Street alley that knocked at my office door one morning on a mysterious expedition for flowers, not for themselves, but for "a lady," and having obtained what they wanted, trooped off to bestow them, a ragged and dirty little band, with a solemnity that was quite unusual. It was not until an old man called the next day to thank me for the flowers that I found out they had decked the bier of a pauper, in the dark rear room where she lay waiting in her pine board coffin for the city's hearse. Yet, as I knew, that dismal alley with its bare brick walls, between which no sun ever rose or set, was the world of those children. It filled their young lives. Probably not one of them had ever been out of the sight of it. They were too dirty, too ragged, and too generally disreputable, too well hidden in their slum besides, to come into line with the Fresh Air summer boarders.

With such human instincts and cravings, forever unsatisfied, turned into a haunting curse; with appetite ground to keenest edge by a hunger that is never fed, the children of the poor grow up in joyless homes to lives of wearisome toil that claims them at an age when the play of their happier fellows has but just begun. Has a yard of turf been laid and a vine been coaxed to grow within their reach, they are banished and barred out from it as from a heaven that is not for such as they. I came upon a couple of youngsters in a Mulberry Street yard a while ago that were chalking on the fence their first lesson in "writin'." And this is what they wrote: "Keeb of te Grass." They had it by heart, for there was not, I verily believe, a green sod within a quarter of a mile. Home to them is an empty name. Pleasure? A gentleman once catechized a ragged class in a downtown public school on this point, and recorded the result: Out of forty-eight boys twenty had never seen the Brooklyn Bridge that was scarcely five minutes' walk away, three only had been in Central Park, fifteen had known the joy of a ride in a horsecar. The street, with its ash barrels and its dirt, the river that runs foul with mud, are their domain. What training they receive is picked up there. And they are apt pupils. If the mud and the dirt are easily reflected in their lives, what wonder? Scarce half-grown, such lads as these confront the world with the challenge to give them their due, too long withheld, or——. Our jails supply the answer to the alternative.

A little fellow who seemed clad in but a single rag was among the flotsam and jetsam stranded at Police Headquarters one day last summer. No one knew where he came from or where he belonged. The boy himself knew as little about it as anybody, and was the least anxious to have light shed on the subject after he had spent a night in the matron's nursery. The discovery that beds were provided for boys to sleep in there, and that he could have "a whole egg" and three slices of bread for breakfast put him on the best of terms with the world in general, and he decided that Headquarters was "a bully place." He sang "McGinty" all through, with Tenth Avenue variations, for the police, and then settled down to the serious business of giving an account of himself. The examination went on after this fashion:

"Where do you go to church, my boy?"

"We don't have no clothes to go to church." And indeed his appearance, as he was, in the door of any New York church would have caused a sensation.

"Well, where do you go to school, then?"

"I don't go to school," with a snort of contempt.

"Where do you buy your bread?"

"We don't buy no bread; we buy beer," said the boy, and it was eventually the saloon that led the police as a landmark to his "home." It was worthy of the boy. As he had said, his only bed was a heap of dirty straw on the floor, his daily diet a crust in the morning, nothing else.

Into the rooms of the Children's Aid Society were led two little girls whose father had "busted up the house" and put them on the street after their mother died. Another, who was turned out by her step-mother "because she had five of her own and could not afford to keep her," could not remember ever having been in church or Sunday school, and only knew the name of Jesus through hearing people swear by it. She had no idea what they meant. These were specimens of the overflow from the tenements of our home heathen that are growing up in New York's streets today, while tenderhearted men and women are busying themselves with the socks and the hereafter of well-fed little Hottentots thousands of miles away. According to Canon Taylor, of York, one hundred and nine missionaries in the four fields of Persia, Palestine, Arabia, and Egypt spent one year and sixty thousand dollars in converting one little heathen girl. If there is nothing the matter with those missionaries, they might come to New York with a good deal better prospect of success.

By those who lay flattering unction to their souls in the knowledge that today New York has, at all events, no brood of the gutters of tender years that can be homeless long unheeded, let it be remembered well through what effort this judgment has been averted. In thirty-seven years the Children's Aid Society, that came into existence as an emphatic protest against the tenement corruption of the young, has sheltered quite three hundred thousand outcast, homeless, and orphaned children in its lodging houses, and has found homes in the West for seventy thousand that had none.[1] Doubtless, as a mere stroke of finance, the five millions and a half thus spent were a wiser investment than to have let them grow up thieves and thugs. In the last fifteen years of this tireless battle for the safety of the state the intervention of the Society for the Prevention of Cruelty to Children has been invoked for 138,891 little ones; it has thrown its protection around more than twenty-five thousand helpless children, and has convicted nearly sixteen thousand wretches of child beating and abuse.[2] Add to this the standing army of fifteen thousand dependent children in New York's asylums and institutions, and some idea is gained of the crop that is garnered day by day in the tenements, of the enormous force employed to check their inroads on our social life, and of the cause for apprehension that would exist did their efforts flag for ever so brief a time.

Nothing is now better understood than that the rescue of the children is the key to the problem of city poverty, as presented for our solution today; that character may be formed where to reform it would be a hopeless task. The concurrent testimony of all who have to undertake it at a later stage: that the young are naturally neither vicious nor hardened, simply weak and undeveloped, except by the bad influences of the street, makes this duty all the more urgent as well as hopeful. Helping hands are held out on every side. To private charity the municipality leaves the entire care of its proletariat of tender years, lulling its conscience to sleep with liberal appropriations of money to foot the bills. Indeed, it is held by those whose opinions are entitled to weight that it is far too liberal a paymaster for its own best interests and those of its wards. It deals with the evil in the seed to a limited extent in gathering in the outcast babies from the streets. To the ripe fruit the gates of its prisons, its reformatories, and its workhouses are opened wide the year round. What the showing would be at this end of the line were it not for the barriers wise charity has thrown across the broad highway to ruin—is building day by day— may be measured by such results as those quoted above in the span of a single life.

of Johnny, for God's sake. I cannot." But even that is the rarest of all happenings.

The city divides with the Sisters of Charity the task of gathering them in. The real foundlings, the children of the gutter that are picked up by the police, are the city's wards. In midwinter, when the poor shiver in their homes, and in the dog days when the fierce heat and foul air of the tenements smother their babies by thousands, they are found, sometimes three and four in a night, in hallways, in areas and on the doorsteps of the rich, with whose comfort in luxurious homes the wretched mother somehow connects her own misery. Perhaps, as the drowning man clutches at a straw, she hopes that these happier hearts may have love to spare even for her little one. In this she is mistaken. Unauthorized babies especially are not popular in the abodes of the wealthy. It never happens outside of the storybooks that a baby so deserted finds home and friends at once. Its career, though rather more official, is less romantic, and generally brief. After a night spent at Police Headquarters it travels up to the Infants' Hospital on Randall's Island in the morning, fitted out with a number and a bottle, that seldom see much wear before they are laid aside for a fresh recruit. Few outcast babies survive their desertion long. Murder is the true name of the mother's crime in eight cases out of ten. Of 508 babies received at the Randall's Hospital last year 333 died, 65.55 percent. But of the 508 only 170 were picked up in the streets, and among these the mortality was much greater, probably nearer ninety percent, if the truth were told. The rest were born in the hospitals. The high mortality among the foundlings is not to be marvelled at. The wonder is, rather, that any survive. The stormier the night, the more certain is the police nursery to echo with the feeble cries of abandoned babes. Often they come half dead from exposure. One live baby came in a little pine coffin which a policeman found an inhuman wretch trying to bury in an uptown lot. But many do not live to be officially registered as a charge upon the county. Seventy-two dead babies were picked up in the streets last year. Some of them were doubtless put out by very poor parents to save funeral expenses. In hard times the number of dead and live foundlings always increases very noticeably. But whether travelling by way of the Morgue or the Infants' Hospital, the little army of waifs meets, reunited soon, in the trench in the Potter's Field where, if no medical student is in need of a subject, they are laid in squads of a dozen.

Most of the foundlings come from the East Side, where they are left by young mothers without wedding rings or other name than their own to bestow upon the baby, returning from the island hospital to face an unpitying world with the evidence of their shame. Not infrequently they wear the bedtick regimentals of the Public Charities, and thus their origin is easily enough traced. Oftener no ray of light penetrates the gloom, and no effort is made to probe the mystery of sin and sorrow. This also is the policy pursued in the great Foundling Asylum of the Sisters of Charity in Sixty-eighth Street, known all over the world as Sister Irene's Asylum. Years ago the crib that now stands just inside the street door, under the great main portal, was placed outside at night; but it filled up too rapidly. The babies took to coming in little squads instead of in single file, and in self-defense the sisters were forced to take the cradle in. Now the mother must bring her child inside and put it in the crib where she is seen by the sister on guard. No effort is made to question her, or discover the child's antecedents, but she is asked to stay and nurse her own and another baby. If she refuses, she is allowed to depart unhindered. If willing, she enters at once into the great family of the good Sister who in twenty-one years has gathered as many thousand homeless babies into her fold. One was brought in when I was last in the asylum, in the middle of July, that received in its crib the number 20715. The death rate is of course lowered a good deal where exposure of the child is prevented. Among the eleven hundred infants in the asylum it was something over nineteen percent last year; but among those actually received in the twelvemonth nearer twice that figure. Even the nineteen percent, remarkably low for a Foundling Asylum, was equal to the startling death rate of Gotham Court in the cholera scourge.

Four hundred and sixty mothers, who could not or would not keep their own babies, did voluntary penance for their sin in the asylum last year by nursing a strange waif besides their own until both should be strong enough to take their chances in life's battle. An even larger number than the eleven hundred were "pay babies," put out to be nursed by "mothers" outside the asylum. The money thus earned pays the rent of hundreds of poor families. It is no trifle, quite half of the quarter of a million dollars contributed annually by the city for the support of the asylum. The procession of these nursemothers, when they come to the asylum on the first Wednesday of each month to receive their pay and have the babies inspected by the sisters, is one of the sights of the city. The nurses, who are under strict supervision, grow to love their little charges and part from them with tears when, at the age of four or five, they are sent to western homes to be adopted. The sisters carefully encourage the home feeling in the child as their strongest ally in seeking its mental and moral elevation, and the toddlers depart happy to join their "papas and mammas" in the faraway, unknown home.

An infinitely more fiendish, if to surface appearances less deliberate, plan of child murder than desertion has flourished in New York for years under the title of baby farming. The name, put into plain English, means starving babies to death. The law has fought this most heinous of crimes by compelling the registry of all baby farms. As well might it require all persons intending murder to register their purpose with time and place of the deed under the penalty of exemplary fines. Murderers do not hang out a shingle. "Baby farms," said once Mr. Elbridge T. Gerry, the President of the Society charged with the execution of the law that was passed through his efforts, "are concerns by means of which persons, usually of disreputable character, eke out a living by taking two, or three, or four babies to board. They are the charges of outcasts, or illegitimate children. They feed them on sour milk, and give them paregoric to keep them quiet, until they die, when they get some young medical man without experience to sign a certificate to the Board of Health that the child died of inanition, and so the matter ends. The baby is dead, and there is no one to complain."[1] A handful of baby farms have been registered and licensed by the Board of Health with the approval of the Society for the Prevention of Cruelty to Children in the last five years, but none of this kind. The devil keeps the only complete register to be found anywhere. Their trace is found oftenest by the coroner or the police; sometimes they may be discovered hiding in the advertising columns of certain newspapers, under the guise of the scarcely less heartless traffic in helpless children that is dignified with the pretence of adoption—for cash. An idea of how this scheme works was obtained through the disclosures in a celebrated divorce case, a year or two ago. The society has among its records a very recent case* of a baby a week old (Baby "Blue Eyes") that was offered for sale—adoption, the dealer called it—in a newspaper. The agent bought it after some haggling for a dollar, and arrested the woman slave trader; but the law was powerless to punish her for her crime. Twelve unfortunate women awaiting dishonored motherhood were found in her house.

One gets a glimpse of the frightful depths to which human nature, perverted by avarice bred of ignorance and rasping poverty, can descend, in the mere suggestion of systematic insurance *for profit* of children's lives. A woman was put on trial in this city last year for in-

---

* Society for the Prevention of Cruelty to Children, Case 42,028, May 16, 1889.

credible cruelty in her treatment of a stepchild. The evidence aroused a strong suspicion that a pitifully small amount of insurance on the child's life was one of the motives for the woman's savagery. A little investigation brought out the fact that three companies that were in the business of insuring children's lives, for sums varying from $17 up, had issued not less than a million such policies! The premiums ranged from five to twenty-five cents a week. What untold horrors this business may conceal was suggested by a formal agreement entered into by some of the companies, "for the purpose of preventing speculation in the insurance of children's lives." By the terms of this compact, "no higher premium than ten cents could be accepted on children under six years old." Barbarism forsooth! Did ever heathen cruelty invent a more fiendish plot than the one written down between the lines of this legal paper?

It is with a sense of glad relief that one turns from this misery to the brighter page of the helping hands stretched forth on every side to save the young and the helpless. New York is, I firmly believe, the most charitable city in the world. Nowhere is there so eager a readiness to help, when it is known that help is worthily wanted; nowhere are such armies of devoted workers, nowhere such abundance of means ready to the hand of those who know the need and how rightly to supply it. Its poverty, its slums, and its suffering are the result of unprecedented growth with the consequent disorder and crowding, and the common penalty of metropolitan greatness. If the structure shows signs of being top heavy, evidences are not wanting —they are multiplying day by day—that patient toilers are at work among the underpinnings. The Day Nurseries, the numberless Kindergartens and charitable schools in the poor quarters, the Fresh Air Funds, the thousand and one charities that in one way or another reach the homes and the lives of the poor with sweetening touch, are proof that if much is yet to be done, if the need only grows with the

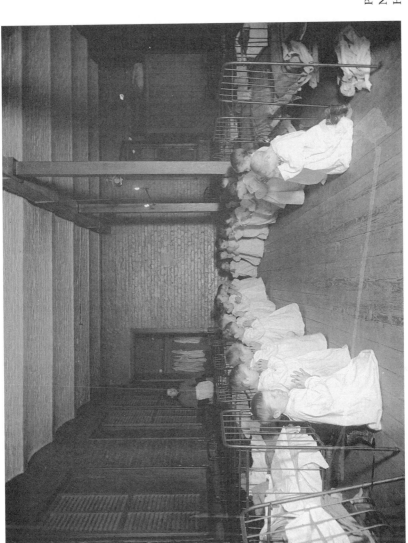

Prayer-Time in the Nursery—Five Points House of Industry

effort, hearts and hands will be found to do it in ever increasing measure. Black as the cloud is it has a silver lining, bright with promise. New York is today a hundredfold cleaner, better, purer, city than it was even ten years ago.

Two powerful agents that were among the pioneers in this work of moral and physical regeneration stand in Paradise Park today as milestones on the rocky, uphill road. The handful of noble women, who braved the foul depravity of the Old Brewery to rescue its child victims, rolled away the first and heaviest boulder, which legislatures and city councils had tackled in vain. The Five Points Mission[2] and the Five Points House of Industry[3] have accomplished what no machinery of government availed to do. Sixty thousand children have been rescued by them from the streets and had their little feet set in the better way. Their work still goes on, increasing and gathering in the waifs, instructing and feeding them, and helping their parents with advice and more substantial aid. Their charity knows not creed or nationality. The House of Industry is an enormous nursery school with an average of more than four hundred day scholars and constant boarders—"outsiders" and "insiders." Its influence is felt for many blocks around in that crowded part of the city. It is one of the most touching sights in the world to see a score of babies, rescued from homes of brutality and desolation, where no other blessing than a drunken curse was ever heard, saying their prayers in the nursery at bedtime. Too often their white nightgowns hide tortured little bodies and limbs cruelly bruised by inhuman hands. In the shelter of this fold they are safe, and a happier little group one may seek long and far in vain.

XVII

The Street Arab

NOT ALL THE BARRIERS erected by society against its nether life, not the labor of unnumbered societies for the rescue and relief of its outcast waifs, can dam the stream of homelessness that issues from a source where the very name of home is a mockery. The Street Arab is as much of an institution in New York as Newspaper Row, to which he gravitates naturally, following his Bohemian instinct. Crowded out of the tenements to shift for himself, and quite ready to do it, he meets there the host of adventurous runaways from every state in the Union and from across the sea, whom New York attracts with a queer fascination, as it attracts the older emigrants from all parts of the world. A census of the population in the Newsboys' Lodging House on any night will show such an odd mixture of small humanity as could hardly be got together in any other spot. It is a mistake to think that they are helpless little creatures, to be pitied and cried over because they are alone in the world. The unmerciful "guying" the good man would receive, who went to them with such a programme, would soon convince him that that sort of pity was wasted, and would very likely give him the idea that they were a set of hardened little scoundrels, quite beyond the reach of missionary effort.

But that would only be his second mistake. The Street Arab has all the faults and all the virtues of the lawless life he leads. Vagabond that he is, acknowledging no authority and owing no allegiance to anybody or anything, with his grimy fist raised against society whenever it tries to coerce him, he is as bright and sharp as the weasel, which, among all the predatory beasts, he most resembles. His sturdy independence, love of freedom and absolute self-reliance, together with his rude sense of justice that enables him to govern his little community, not always in accordance with municipal law or city ordinances, but often a good deal closer to the saving line of "doing to others as one would be done by"—these are strong handles by which those who know how can catch the boy and make him useful. Successful bankers, clergymen, and lawyers all over the country, statesmen in some instances of national repute, bear evidence in their lives to the potency of such missionary efforts. There is scarcely a learned profession, or branch of honorable business, that has not in the last twenty years borrowed some of its brightest light from the poverty and gloom of New York's streets.

Anyone, whom business or curiosity has taken through Park Row or across Printing House Square in the midnight hour, when the air is filled with the roar of great presses spinning with printers' ink on endless rolls of white paper the history of the world in the twenty-four hours that have just passed away, has seen little groups of these boys hanging about the newspaper offices; in winter, when snow is on the streets, fighting for warm spots around the grated vent holes that let out the heat and steam from the underground pressrooms with their noise and clatter, and in summer playing craps and 7–11 on the curb for their hard-earned pennies, with all the absorbing concern of hardened gamblers. This is their beat. Here the agent of the Society for the Prevention of Cruelty to Children finds those he thinks too young for "business," but does not always capture them. Like rabbits in their burrows, the little ragamuffins sleep with at least one eye open, and every sense alert to the approach of danger: of their enemy, the policeman, whose chief business in life is to move them on, and of the agent bent on robbing them of their cherished freedom. At the first warning shout they scatter and are off. To pursue them would be like chasing the fleet-footed mountain goat in his rocky fastnesses. There is not an open door, a hidden turn or runway which they do not know, with lots of secret passages and short cuts no one else ever found. To steal a march on them is the only way. There is a coal chute from the sidewalk to the boiler room in the sub-cellar of the Post Office which the Society's officer found the boys had made into a sort of toboggan slide to a snug berth in wintry weather. They used to slyly raise the cover in the street, slide down in single file, and snuggle up to the warm boiler out of harm's way, as they thought. It proved a trap, however. The agent slid down himself one cold night—there was no other way of getting there—and, landing right in the midst of the sleeping colony, had it at his mercy. After repeated raids upon their headquarters, the boys forsook it last summer, and were next found herding under the shore end of one of the East River banana docks, where they had fitted up a regular clubroom that was shared by thirty or forty homeless boys and about a million rats.

Newspaper Row is merely their headquarters. They are to be found all over the city, these Street Arabs, where the neighborhood offers a chance of picking up a living in the daytime and of "turning in" at night with a promise of security from surprise. In warm weather a truck in the street, a convenient outhouse, or a dugout in a hay barge at the wharf make good bunks. Two were found making their nest once in the end of a big iron pipe up by the Harlem Bridge, and an old boiler at the East River served as an elegant flat for another couple, who kept house there with a thief the police had long sought, little suspecting that he was hiding under their very noses for months together. When the Children's Aid Society first opened its lodging houses, and with some difficulty persuaded the boys that their charity was no "pious dodge" to trap them into a treasonable "Sunday school racket," its managers overheard a laughable discussion among the boys in their unwontedly comfortable beds—perhaps the first some of them had ever slept in—as to the relative merits of the different styles of their everyday berths. Preferences were divided between the steam grating and a sandbox; but the weight of the evidence was decided to be in favor of the sandbox, because, as its advocate put it, "you could curl all up in it." The new "find" was voted a good way ahead of any previous experience, however. "My eyes, ain't it nice!" said one of the lads, tucked in under his blanket up to the chin, and the roomful of boys echoed the sentiment. The compact silently made that night between the Street Arabs and their hosts has never been broken. They have been fast friends ever since.

Whence this army of homeless boys? is a question often asked. The answer is supplied by the procession of mothers that go out and in at Police Headquarters the year round, inquiring for missing boys, often not until they have been gone for weeks and months, and then sometimes rather as a matter of decent form than from any real interest in the lad's fate. The stereotyped promise of the clerks who fail to find his name on the books among the arrests, that he "will come back when he gets hungry," does not always come true. More likely he went away because he was hungry. Some are orphans, actually or in effect, thrown upon the world when their parents were "sent up" to the island or to Sing Sing, and somehow overlooked by the "Society," which thenceforth became the enemy to be shunned until growth and dirt

"Didn't Live Nowhere"

and the hardships of the street, that make old early, offer some hope of successfully floating the lie that they are "sixteen." A drunken father explains the matter in other cases, as in that of John and Willie, aged ten and eight, picked up by the police. They "didn't live nowhere," never went to school, could neither read nor write. Their twelve-year-old sister kept house for the father, who turned the boys out to beg, or steal, or starve. Grinding poverty and hard work beyond the years of the lad; blows and curses for breakfast, dinner, and supper; all these are recruiting agents for the homeless army. Sickness in the house, too many mouths to feed:

"We wuz six," said an urchin of twelve or thirteen I came across in the Newsboys' Lodging House, "and we ain't got no father. Some on us had to go." And so he went, to make a living by blacking boots. The going is easy enough. There is very little to hold the boy who has never known anything but a home in a tenement. Very soon the wild life in the streets holds him fast, and thenceforward by his own effort there is no escape. Left alone to himself, he soon enough finds a place in the police books, and there would be no other answer to the second question: "what becomes of the boy?" than that given by the criminal courts every day in the week.

But he is not left alone. Society in our day has no such suicidal intention. Right here, at the parting of the ways, it has thrown up the strongest of all its defences for itself and for the boy. What the Society for the Prevention of Cruelty to Children is to the baby waif, the Children's Aid Society is to the homeless boy at this real turning point in his career. The good it has done cannot easily be overestimated. Its lodging houses, its schools and its homes block every avenue of escape with their offer of shelter upon terms which the boy soon accepts, as on the whole cheap and fair. In the great Duane Street lodging house for newsboys, they are succinctly stated in a "notice" over the door that reads thus: "Boys who swear and chew tobacco cannot sleep here." There is another unwritten condition, viz.: that the boy shall be really without a home; but upon this the managers wisely do not insist too obstinately, accepting without too close inquiry his account of himself where that seems advisable, well knowing that many a home that sends forth such lads far less deserves the name than the one they are able to give them.

With these simple preliminaries the outcast boy may enter. Rags do not count; to ignorance the door is only opened wider. Dirt does not survive long, once within the walls of the lodging house. It is the settled belief of the men who conduct them that soap and water are as powerful moral agents in their particular field as preaching, and they have experience to back them. The boy may come and go as he pleases, so long as he behaves himself. No restraint of any sort is put on his independence. He is as free as any other guest at a hotel, and, like him, he is expected to pay for what he gets. How wisely the men planned who laid the foundation of this great rescue work and yet carry it on, is shown by no single feature of it better than by this. No pauper was ever bred within these houses. Nothing would have been easier with such material, or more fatal. But charity of the kind that pauperizes is furthest from their scheme. Self-help is its very keynote, and it strikes a response in the boy's sturdiest trait that raises him at once to a level with the effort made in his behalf. Recognized as an independent trader, capable of and bound to take care of himself, he is in a position to ask trust if trade has gone against him and he cannot pay cash for his "grub" and his bed, and to get it without question. He can even have the loan of the small capital required to start him in business with a boot-black's kit, or an armful of papers, if he is known or vouched for; but every cent is charged to him as carefully as though the transaction involved as many hundreds of dollars, and he is expected to pay back the money as soon as he has made enough to keep him going without it. He very rarely betrays the trust reposed in him. Quite on the contrary, around this sound core of self-help, thus encouraged, habits of thrift and ambitious industry are seen to grow up in a majority of instances. The boy is "growing" a character, and he

goes out to the man's work in life with that which for him is better than if he had found a fortune.

Six cents for his bed, six for his breakfast of bread and coffee, and six for his supper of pork and beans, as much as he can eat, are the rates of the boys' "hotel" for those who bunk together in the great dormitories that sometimes hold more than a hundred berths, two tiers high, made of iron, clean and neat. For the "upper ten," the young financiers who early take the lead among their fellows, hire them to work for wages and add a share of their profits to their own, and for the lads who are learning a trade and getting paid by the week, there are ten cent beds with a locker and with curtains hung about. Night schools and Sunday night meetings are held in the building and are always well attended, in winter especially, when the lodging houses are crowded. In summer the towpath and the country attract their share of the bigger boys. The "Sunday school racket" has ceased to have terror for them. They follow the proceedings with the liveliest interest, quick to detect cant of any sort, should any stray in. No one has any just conception of what congregational singing is until he has witnessed a roomful of these boys roll up their sleeves and start in on "I am a lily of the valley." The swinging trapeze in the gymnasium on the top floor is scarcely more popular with the boys than this tremendously vocal worship. The Street Arab puts his whole little soul into what interests him for the moment, whether it be pulverizing a rival who has done a mean trick to a smaller boy, or attending at the "gospel shop" on Sundays. This characteristic made necessary some extra supervision when recently the lads in the Duane Street Lodging House "chipped in" and bought a set of boxing gloves. The trapeze suffered a temporary eclipse until this new toy had been tested to the extent of several miniature black eyes upon which soap had no effect, and sundry little scores had been settled that evened things up, as it were, for a fresh start.

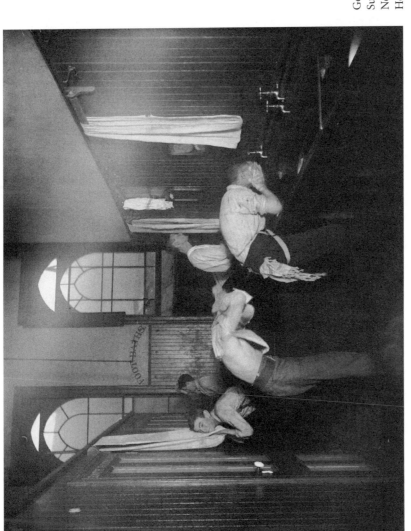

Getting Ready for Supper in the Newsboys' Lodging House

I tried one night, not with the best of success I confess, to photograph the boys in their washroom, while they were cleaning up for
supper. They were quite turbulent, to the disgust of one of their number who assumed, unasked, the office of general manager of the show,
and expressed his mortification to me in very polite language. "If they
would only behave, sir!" he complained, "you could make a good picture."

"Yes," I said, "but it isn't in them, I suppose."

"No, b'gosh!" said he, lapsing suddenly from grace under the provocation, "them kids ain't got no sense, nohow!"

The Society maintains five of these boys' lodging houses, and one
for girls, in the city. The Duane Street Lodging House alone has sheltered since its foundation in 1855 nearly a quarter of a million different boys, at a total expense of a good deal less than half a million dollars. Of this amount, up to the beginning of the present year, the
boys and the earnings of the house had contributed no less than
$172,776.38. In all of the lodging houses together, 12,153 boys and girls
were sheltered and taught last year. The boys saved up no inconsider-
able amount of money in the savings banks provided for them in the
houses, a simple system of lock boxes that are emptied for their benefit once a month. Besides these, the Society has established and oper-
ates in the tenement districts twenty-one industrial schools, coordi-
nate with the public schools in authority, for the children of the poor
who cannot find room in the city's schoolhouses, or are too ragged
to go there; two free reading rooms, a dressmaking and typewriting
school and a laundry for the instruction of girls; a sick children's mission in the city and two on the seashore, where poor mothers may
take their babies; a cottage by the sea for crippled girls, and a brush
factory for crippled boys in Forty-fourth Street. The Italian school in
Leonard Street, alone, had an average attendance of over six hundred
pupils last year. The daily average attendance at all of them was 4,105,

while 11,331 children were registered and taught. When the fact that there were among these 1,132 children of drunken parents, and 416 that had been found begging in the street, is contrasted with the showing of $1,337.21 deposited in the school savings banks by 1,745 pupils, something like an adequate idea is gained of the scope of the Society's work in the city.

A large share of it, in a sense the largest, certainly that productive of the happiest results, lies outside of the city, however. From the lodging houses and the schools are drawn the battalions of young emigrants that go every year to homes in the far west, to grow up self-supporting men and women safe from the temptations and the vice of the city. Their number runs far up in the thousands. The Society never loses sight of them. The records show that the great mass, with this start given them, become useful citizens, an honor to the communities in which their lot is cast. Not a few achieve place and prominence in their new surroundings. Rarely bad reports come of them. Occasionally one comes back, lured by homesickness even for the slums; but the briefest stay generally cures the disease for good. I helped once to see a party off for Michigan, the last sent out by that great friend of the homeless children, Mrs. Astor, before she died.[1] In the party was a boy who had been an "Insider" at the Five Points House of Industry, and brought along as his only baggage a padlocked and iron-bound box that contained all his wealth, two little white mice of the friendliest disposition. They were going with him out to live on the fat of the land in the fertile west, where they would never be wanting for a crust. Alas! for the best-laid plans of mice and men. The western diet did not agree with either. I saw their owner some months later in the old home at the Five Points. He had come back, walking part of the way, and was now pleading to be sent out once more. He had at last had enough of the city. His face fell when I asked him about the mice. It was a sad story, indeed. "They had so much corn to eat," he said, "and they couldn't stand it. They burned all up inside, and then they busted."

Mrs. Astor set an example during her noble and useful life in gathering every year a company of homeless boys from the streets and sending them to good homes, with decent clothes on their backs—she had sent out no less than thirteen hundred when she died, and left funds to carry on her work—that has been followed by many who, like her, had the means and the heart for such a labor of love. Most of the lodging houses and school buildings of the society were built by some one rich man or woman who paid all the bills, and often objected to have even the name of the giver made known to the world. It is one of the pleasant experiences of life that give one hope and courage in the midst of all this misery to find names, that stand to the unthinking mass only for money-getting and grasping, associated with such unheralded benefactions that carry their blessings down to generations yet unborn. It is not so long since I found the carriage of a woman, whose name is synonymous with millions, standing in front of the boys' lodging house in Thirty-fifth Street. Its owner was at that moment busy with a surgeon making a census of the crippled lads in the brush shop, the most miserable of all the Society's charges, as a preliminary to fitting them out with artificial limbs.

Farther uptown than any reared by the Children's Aid Society, in Sixty-seventh Street, stands a lodging house intended for boys of a somewhat larger growth than most of those whom the Society shelters. Unlike the others, too, it was built by the actual labor of the young men it was designed to benefit. In the day when more of the boys from our streets shall find their way to it and to the New York Trade Schools,[2] of which it is a kind of home annex, we shall be in a fair way of solving in the most natural of all ways the question what to do with this boy, in spite of the ignorant opposition of the men whose tyrannical policy is now to blame for the showing that, out of twenty-three millions of dollars paid annually to mechanics in the building trades in this city, less than six millions go to the workman born in New York, while his boy roams the streets with every chance of growing up a vagabond and next to none of becoming an honest artisan. Colonel Auchmuty is a practical philanthropist to whom the growing youth of New York will one day owe a debt of gratitude not easily paid. The progress of the system of trade schools established by him, at which a young man may acquire the theory as well as the practice of a trade in a few months at a merely nominal outlay, has not been nearly as rapid as was to be desired, though the fact that other cities are copying the model, with their master mechanics as the prime movers in the enterprise, testifies to its excellence. But it has at last taken a real start, and with union men and even the officers of unions now sending their sons to the trade schools to be taught,* one may perhaps be permitted to hope that an era of better sense is dawning that shall witness a rescue work upon lines which, when the leaven has fairly had time to work, will put an end to the existence of the New York Street Arab, of the native breed at least.

* Colonel Auchmuty's own statement.

XVIII

The Reign of Rum

WHERE GOD BUILDS A CHURCH the devil builds next
door—a saloon, is an old saying that has lost its point in New
York. Either the devil was on the ground first, or he has been doing a
good deal more in the way of building. I tried once to find out how
the account stood, and counted to 111 Protestant churches, chapels,
and places of worship of every kind below Fourteenth Street, 4,065
saloons. The worst half of the tenement population lives down there,
and it has to this day the worst half of the saloons. Uptown the account stands a little better, but there are easily ten saloons to every
church today. I am afraid, too, that the congregations are larger by a
good deal; certainly the attendance is steadier and the contributions
more liberal the week round, Sunday included. Turn and twist it as
we may, over against every bulwark for decency and morality which
society erects, the saloon projects its colossal shadow, omen of evil
wherever it falls into the lives of the poor.

Nowhere is its mark so broad or so black. To their misery it sticketh closer than a brother, persuading them that within its doors only is refuge, relief. It has the best of the argument, too, for it is true, worse pity, that in many a tenement house block the saloon is the one bright and cheery and humanly decent spot to be found. It is a sorry admission to make, that to bring the rest of the neighborhood up to the level of the saloon would be one way of squelching it; but it is so. Wherever the tenements thicken, it multiplies. Upon the direst poverty of their crowds it grows fat and prosperous, levying upon it a tax heavier than all the rest of its grievous burdens combined. It is not yet two years since the Excise Board made the rule that no three corners of any street crossing, not already so occupied, should thenceforward be licensed for rum selling. And the tardy prohibition was intended for the tenement districts. Nowhere else is there need of it. One may walk many miles through the homes of the poor searching vainly for an open reading room, a cheerful coffeehouse, a decent club that is not a cloak for the traffic in rum. The dramshop yawns at every step, the poor man's club, his forum and his haven of rest when weary and disgusted with the crowding, the quarrelling, and the wretchedness at home. With the poison dealt out there he takes his politics, in quality not far apart. As the source, so the stream. The rumshop turns the political crank in New York. The natural yield is rum politics. Of what that means, successive Boards of Aldermen, composed in a measure, if not of a majority, of dive keepers, have given New York a taste. The disgrace of the infamous "Boodle Board"[1] will be remembered until some corruption even fouler crops out and throws it into the shade.

What relation the saloon bears to the crowds, let me illustrate by a comparison. Below Fourteenth Street were, when the Health Department took its first accurate census of the tenements a year and a half ago, 13,220 of the 32,390 buildings classed as such in the whole city. Of the eleven hundred thousand tenants, not quite half a mil lion, embracing a host of more than sixty-three thousand children under five years of age, lived below that line. Below it, also, were 234 of the cheap lodging houses accounted for by the police last year, with a total of four millions and a half of lodgers for the twelvemonth, 59 of the city's 110 pawnshops, and 4,065 of its 7,884 saloons. The four most densely peopled precincts, the Fourth, Sixth, Tenth, and Eleventh, supported together in round numbers twelve hundred saloons, and their returns showed twenty-seven percent of the whole number of arrests for the year. The Eleventh Precinct, that has the greatest and the poorest crowds of all—it is the Tenth Ward—and harbored one-third of the army of homeless lodgers and fourteen percent of all the prisoners of the year, kept 485 saloons going in 1889. It is not on record that one of them all failed for want of support. A number of them, on the contrary, had brought their owners wealth and prominence. From their bars these eminent citizens stepped proudly into the councils of the city and the State. The very floor of one of the barrooms, in a neighborhood that lately resounded with the cry for bread of starving workmen, is paved with silver dollars!

East Side poverty is not alone in thus rewarding the tyrants that sweeten its cup of bitterness with their treacherous poison. The Fourth Ward points with pride to the honorable record of the conductors of its "Tub of Blood," and a dozen barrooms with less startling titles; the West Side to the wealth and "social" standing of the owners of such resorts as the "Witches' Broth" and the "Plug Hat" in the region of Hell's Kitchen three-cent whiskey, names ominous of the concoctions brewed there and of their fatally generous measure. Another ward, that boasts some of the best residences and the bluest blood on Manhattan Island, honors with political leadership in the ruling party the proprietor of one of the most disreputable Black-and-Tan dives and dancing-hells to be found anywhere. Criminals and policemen alike do him homage. The list might be strung out to make texts for sermons with a stronger home flavor than many that are preached in our pulpits on Sunday. But I have not set out to write the political history of New York. Besides, the list would not be complete. Secret dives are skulking in the slums and out of them, that are not labelled respectable by a Board of Excise and support no "family entrance." Their business, like that of the stale-beer dives, is done through a side door the week through. No one knows the number of unlicensed saloons in the city. Those who have made the matter a study estimate it at a thousand, more or less. The police make occasional schedules of a few and report them to headquarters. Perhaps there is a farce in the police court, and there the matter ends. Rum and "influence" are synonymous terms. The interests of the one rarely suffer for the want of attention from the other.

With the exception of these free lances that treat the law openly with contempt, the saloons all hang out a sign announcing in fat type that no beer or liquor is sold to children. In the downtown "morgues" that make the lowest degradation of tramp humanity pan out a paying interest, as in the "reputable resorts" uptown where Inspector Byrnes's men spot their worthier quarry elbowing citizens whom the idea of associating with a burglar would give a shock they would not get over for a week, this sign is seen conspicuously displayed. Though apparently it means submission to a beneficent law, in reality the sign is a heartless, cruel joke. I doubt if one child in a thousand, who brings his growler to be filled at the average New York bar, is sent away empty-handed, if able to pay for what he wants. I once followed a little boy, who shivered in bare feet on a cold November night so that he seemed in danger of smashing his pitcher on the icy pavement, into a Mulberry Street saloon where just such a sign hung on the wall, and forbade the barkeeper to serve the boy. The man was as astonished at my interference as if I had told him to shut up his shop and go home, which in fact I might have done with as good a right, for it

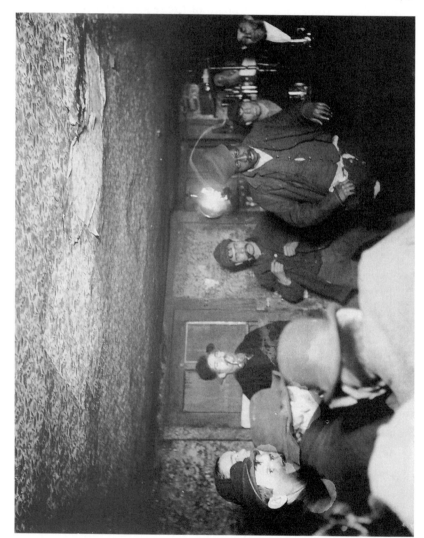

A Downtown "Morgue"

was after 1 A.M., the legal closing hour. He was mighty indignant too, and told me roughly to go away and mind my business, while he filled the pitcher. The law prohibiting the selling of beer to minors is about as much respected in the tenement house districts as the ordinance against swearing. Newspaper readers will recall the story, told little more than a year ago, of a boy who after carrying beer a whole day for a shopful of men over on the East Side, where his father worked, crept into the cellar to sleep off the effects of his own share in the rioting. It was Saturday evening. Sunday his parents sought him high and low; but it was not until Monday morning, when the shop was opened, that he was found, killed and half-eaten by the rats that overran the place.

All the evil the saloon does in breeding poverty and in corrupting politics; all the suffering it brings into the lives of its thousands of innocent victims, the wives and children of drunkards it sends forth to curse the community; its fostering of crime and its shielding of criminals—it is all as nothing to this, its worst offence. In its affinity for the thief there is at least this compensation that, as it makes, it also unmakes him. It starts him on his career only to trip him up and betray him into the hands of the law, when the rum he exchanged for his honesty has stolen his brains as well. For the corruption of the child there is no restitution. None is possible. It saps the very vitals of society; undermines its strongest defences, and delivers them over to the enemy. Fostered and filled by the saloon, the "growler" looms up in the New York street boy's life, baffling the most persistent efforts to reclaim him. There is no escape from it; no hope for the boy, once its blighting grip is upon him. Thenceforward the logic of the slums, that the world which gave him poverty and ignorance for his portion "owes him a living," is his creed, and the career of the "tough" lies open before him, a beaten track to be blindly followed to a bad end in the wake of the growler.

XIX

The Harvest of Tares

T HE "GROWLER" STOOD AT the cradle of the tough. It bosses him through his boyhood apprenticeship in the "gang," and leaves him, for a time only, at the door of the jail that receives him to finish his training and turn him loose upon the world a thief, to collect by stealth or by force the living his philosophy tells him that it owes him, and will not voluntarily surrender without an equivalent in the work which he hates. From the moment he, almost a baby, for the first time carries the growler for beer, he is never out of its reach, and the two soon form a partnership that lasts through life. It has at least the merit, such as it is, of being loyal. The saloon is the only thing that takes kindly to the lad. Honest play is interdicted in the streets. The policeman arrests the ball tossers, and there is no room in the backyard. In one of these, between two enormous tenements that swarmed with children, I read this ominous notice: *"All boys caught in this yard will be delt with accorden to law."*

more relentless, or less discriminating, than this nemesis of New York. The difference is of intent. Murder with that was the serious purpose; with ours it is the careless incident, the wanton brutality of the moment. Bravado and robbery are the real purposes of the gangs; the former prompts the attack upon the policeman, the latter that upon the citizen. Within a single week last spring, the newspapers recorded six murderous assaults on unoffending people, committed by young highwaymen in the public streets. How many more were suppressed by the police, who always do their utmost to hush up such outrages "in the interests of justice," I shall not say. There has been no lack of such occurrences since, as the records of the criminal courts show. In fact, the past summer has seen, after a period of comparative quiescence of the gangs, a reawakening to renewed turbulence of the East Side tribes, and over and over again the reserve forces of a precinct have been called out to club them into submission. It is a peculiarity of the gangs that they usually break out in spots, as it were. When the West Side is in a state of eruption, the East Side gangs "lie low," and when the toughs along the North River are nursing broken heads at home, or their revenge in Sing Sing, fresh trouble breaks out in the tenements east of Third Avenue. This result is brought about by the very efforts made by the police to put down the gangs. In spite of local feuds, there is between them a species of ruffianly Freemasonry that readily admits to full fellowship a hunted rival in the face of the common enemy. The gangs belt the city like a huge chain from the Battery to Harlem—the collective name of the "chain gang" has been given to their scattered groups in the belief that a much closer connection exists between them than commonly supposed—and the ruffian for whom the East Side has become too hot, has only to step across town and change his name, a matter usually much easier for him than to change his shirt, to find a sanctuary in which to plot fresh outrages. The more notorious he is, the warmer the welcome, and if he has "done" his man he is by common consent accorded the leadership in his new field.

From all this it might be inferred that the New York tough is a very fierce individual, of indomitable courage and naturally as bloodthirsty as a tiger. On the contrary he is an arrant coward. His instincts of ferocity are those of the wolf rather than the tiger. It is only when he hunts with the pack that he is dangerous. Then his inordinate vanity makes him forget all fear or caution in the desire to distinguish himself before his fellows, a result of his swallowing all the flash literature and penny-dreadfuls he can beg, borrow, or steal—and there is never any lack of them—and the strongly dramatic element in his nature that is nursed by such a diet into rank and morbid growth. He is a queer bundle of contradictions at all times. Drunk and foulmouthed, ready to cut the throat of a defenceless stranger at the toss of a cent, fresh from beating his decent mother black and blue to get money for rum,* he will resent as an intolerable insult the imputation that he is "no gentleman." Fighting his battles with the coward's weapons, the brass knuckles and the deadly sandbag, or with brickbats from the housetops, he is still in all seriousness a lover of fair play, and as likely as not, when his gang has downed a policeman in a battle that has cost a dozen heads, to be found next saving a drowning child or woman at the peril of his own life. It depends on the angle at which he is seen, whether he is a cowardly ruffian, or a possible hero with different training and under different social conditions. Ready wit he has at all times, and there is less meanness in his makeup than

---

* This very mother will implore the court with tears, the next morning, to let her renegade son off. A poor woman, who claimed to be the widow of a soldier, applied to the Tenement House Relief Committee of the King's Daughters last summer, to be sent to some home, as she had neither kith nor kin to care for her. Upon investigation it was found she had four big sons, all toughs, who beat her regularly and took from her all the money she could earn or beg; she was "a respectable woman, of good habits," the inquiry developed, and lied only to shield her rascally sons.

in that of the bully of the London slums; but an intense love of show and applause, that carries him to any length of bravado, which his twin brother across the sea entirely lacks. I have a very vivid recollection of seeing one of his tribe, a robber and murderer before he was nineteen, go to the gallows unmoved, all fear of the rope overcome, as it seemed, by the secret, exultant pride of being the center of a first-class show, shortly to be followed by that acme of tenement life bliss, a big funeral. He had his reward. His name is to this day a talisman among West Side ruffians, and is proudly borne by the gang of which, up till the night when he "knocked out his man," he was an obscure though aspiring member.

The crime that made McGloin famous was the cowardly murder of an unarmed saloonkeeper who came upon the gang while it was sacking his barroom at the dead of night. McGloin might easily have fled, but disdained to "run for a Dutchman." His act was a fair measure of the standard of heroism set up by his class in its conflicts with society. The finish is worthy of the start. The first long step in crime taken by the half-grown boy, fired with ambition to earn a standing in his gang, is usually to rob a "lush," *i.e.*, a drunken man who has strayed his way, likely enough is lying asleep in a hallway. He has served an apprenticeship on copper-bottom washboilers and like articles found lying around loose, and capable of being converted into cash enough to give the growler a trip or two; but his first venture at robbery moves him up into full fellowship at once. He is no longer a "kid," though his years may be few, but a tough with the rest. He may even in time—he is reasonably certain of it—get his name in the papers as a murderous scoundrel, and have his cup of glory filled to the brim. I came once upon a gang of such young rascals passing the growler after a successful raid of some sort, down at the West Thirty-seventh Street dock, and, having my camera along, offered to "take" them. They were not old and wary enough to be shy of the photographer, whose acquaintance they usually first make in handcuffs and the grip of a policeman; or their vanity overcame their caution. It is entirely in keeping with the tough's character that he should love of all things to pose before a photographer, and the ambition is usually the stronger the more repulsive the tough. These were of that sort, and accepted the offer with great readiness, dragging into their group a disreputable-looking sheep that roamed about with them (the slaughterhouses were close at hand) as one of the band. The homeliest ruffian of the lot, who insisted on being taken with the growler to his "mug," took the opportunity to pour what was left in it down his throat and this caused a brief unpleasantness, but otherwise the performance was a success. While I was getting the camera ready, I threw out a vague suggestion of cigarette-pictures, and it took root at once. Nothing would do then but that I must take the boldest spirits of the company "in character." One of them tumbled over against a shed, as if asleep, while two of the others bent over him, searching his pockets with a deftness that was highly suggestive. This, they explained for my benefit, was to show how they "did the trick." The rest of the band were so impressed with the importance of this exhibition that they insisted on crowding into the picture by climbing upon the shed, sitting on the roof with their feet dangling over the edge, and disposing themselves in every imaginable manner within view, as they thought. Lest any reader be led into the error of supposing them to have been harmless young fellows enjoying themselves in peace, let me say that within half an hour after our meeting, when I called at the police station three blocks away, I found there two of my friends of the "Montgomery Guards" under arrest for robbing a Jewish pedlar who had passed that way after I left them, and trying to saw his head off, as they put it, "just for fun. The sheeny cum along an' the saw was there, an' we socked it to him." The prisoners were described to me by the police as Dennis, "the Bum," and "Mud" Foley.

A Growler Gang in Session

It is not always that their little diversions end as harmlessly as did this, even from the standpoint of the Jew, who was pretty badly hurt. Not far from the preserves of the Montgomery Guards, in Poverty Gap, directly opposite the scene of the murder to which I have referred in a note explaining the picture of the Cunningham family (p. 160), a young lad, who was the only support of his aged parents, was beaten to death within a few months by the "Alley Gang," for the same offence that drew down the displeasure of its neighbors upon the pedlar: that of being at work trying to earn an honest living. I found a part of the gang asleep the next morning, before young Healey's death was known, in a heap of straw on the floor of an unoccupied room in the same row of rear tenements in which the murdered boy's home was. One of the tenants, who secretly directed me to their lair, assuring me that no worse scoundrels went unhung, ten minutes later gave the gang, to its face, an official character for sobriety and inoffensiveness that very nearly startled me into an unguarded rebuke of his duplicity. I caught his eye in time and held my peace. The man was simply trying to protect his own home, while giving such aid as he safely could toward bringing the murderous ruffians to justice. The incident shows to what extent a neighborhood may be terrorized by a determined gang of these reckless toughs.

In Poverty Gap there were still a few decent people left. When it comes to Hell's Kitchen, or to its compeers at the other end of Thirty-ninth Street over by the East River, and further down First Avenue in "the Village," the Rag Gang and its allies have no need of fearing treachery in their periodical battles with the police. The entire neighborhood takes a hand on these occasions, the women in the front rank, partly from sheer love of the "fun," but chiefly because husbands, brothers, and sweethearts are in the fight to a man and need their help. Chimney tops form the staple of ammunition then, and stacks of loose brick and paving stones, carefully hoarded in upper rooms as a prudent provision against emergencies. Regular patrol posts are established by the police on the housetops in times of trouble in these localities, but even then they do not escape whole-skinned, if, indeed, with their lives; neither does the gang. The policeman knows of but one cure for the tough, the club, and he lays it on without stint whenever and wherever he has the chance, knowing right well that, if caught at a disadvantage, he will get his outlay back with interest. Words are worse than wasted in the gang districts. It is a blow at sight, and the tough thus accosted never stops to ask questions. Unless he is "wanted" for some signal outrage, the policeman rarely bothers with arresting him. He can point out half a dozen at sight against whom indictments are pending by the basketful, but whom no jail ever held many hours. They only serve to make him more reckless, for he knows that the political backing that has saved him in the past can do it again. It is a commodity that is only exchangeable "for value received," and it is not hard to imagine what sort of value is in demand. The saloon, in ninety-nine cases out of a hundred, stands behind the bargain.

For these reasons, as well as because he knows from frequent experience his own way to be the best, the policeman lets the gangs alone except when they come within reach of his long nightstick. They have their "club-rooms" where they meet, generally in a tenement, sometimes under a pier or a dump, to carouse, play cards, and plan their raids; their "fences," who dispose of the stolen property. When the necessity presents itself for a descent upon the gang after some particularly flagrant outrage, the police have a task on hand that is not of the easiest. The gangs, like foxes, have more than one hole to their dens. In some localities, where the interior of a block is filled with rear tenements, often set at all sorts of odd angles, surprise alone is practicable. Pursuit through the winding ways and passages is impossible. The young thieves know them all by heart. They have their runways over roofs and fences which no one else could find. Their lair is generally selected with special reference to its possibilities of escape. Once pitched upon, its occupation by the gang, with its earmark of nightly symposiums, "can-rackets" in the slang of the street, is the signal for a rapid deterioration of the tenement, if that is possible. Relief is only to be had by ousting the intruders. An instance came under my notice in which valuable property had been well-nigh ruined by being made the thoroughfare of thieves by night and by day. They had chosen it because of a passage that led through the block by way of several connecting halls and yards. The place came soon to be known as "Murderers Alley." Complaint was made to the Board of Health, as a last resort, of the condition of the property. The practical inspector who was sent to report upon it suggested to the owner that he build a brick wall in a place where it would shut off communication between the streets, and he took the advice. Within the brief space of a few months the house changed character entirely, and became as decent as it had been before the convenient runway was discovered.

This was in the Sixth Ward, where the infamous Whyo Gang until a few years ago absorbed the worst depravity of the Bend and what is left of the Five Points. The gang was finally broken up when its leader was hanged for murder after a life of uninterrupted and unavenged crimes, the recital of which made his father confessor turn pale, listening in the shadow of the scaffold, though many years of labor as chaplain of the Tombs had hardened him to such rehearsals. The great Whyo had been a "power in the ward," handy at carrying elections for the party or faction that happened to stand in need of his services and was willing to pay for them in money or in kind. Other gangs have sprung up since with as high ambition and a fair prospect of outdoing their predecessor. The conditions that bred it still exist, practically unchanged. Inspector Byrnes is authority for the state-

Typical Toughs (from the Rogues' Gallery)

ment that throughout the city the young tough has more "ability" and "nerve" than the thief whose examples he successfully emulates. He begins earlier, too. Speaking of the increase of the native element among criminal prisoners exhibited in the census returns of the last thirty years,* the Rev. Frederick H. Wines says, "their youth is a very striking fact."[1] Had he confined his observations to the police courts of New York, he might have emphasized that remark and found an explanation of the discovery that "the ratio of prisoners in cities is two and one-quarter times as great as in the country at large," a com-

---

* "The percentage of foreign-born prisoners in 1850, as compared with that of natives, was more than five times that of native prisoners, now (1880) it is less than double." American Prisons in the Tenth Census.

putation that takes no account of the reformatories for juvenile delinquents, or the exhibit would have been still more striking. Of the 82,200 persons arrested by the police in 1889, 10,505 were under twenty years old. The last report of the Society for the Prevention of Cruelty to Children enumerates, as "a few typical cases," eighteen "professional cracksmen," between nine and fifteen years old, who had been caught with burglars' tools, or in the act of robbery. Four of them, hardly yet in long trousers, had "held up" a wayfarer in the public street and robbed him of $73. One, aged sixteen, "was the leader of a noted gang of young robbers in Forty-ninth Street. He committed murder, for which he is now serving a term of nineteen years in State's Prison." Four of the eighteen were girls and quite as bad as the worst. In a few years they would have been living with the toughs of their choice without the ceremony of a marriage, egging them on by their pride in their lawless achievements, and fighting side by side with them in their encounters with the "cops."

The exploits of the Paradise Park Gang in the way of highway robbery showed last summer that the embers of the scattered Whyo Gang, upon the wreck of which it grew, were smouldering still. The hanging of Driscoll broke up the Whyos because they were a comparatively small band, and, with the incomparable master spirit gone, were unable to resist the angry rush of public indignation that followed the crowning outrage. This is the history of the passing away of famous gangs from time to time. The passing is more apparent than real, however. Some other daring leader gathers the scattered elements about him soon, and the war on society is resumed. A bare enumeration of the names of the best-known gangs would occupy pages of this book. The Rock Gang, the Rag Gang, the Stable Gang, and the Short Tail Gang down about the "Hook"[2] have all achieved bad eminence, along with scores of others that have not paraded so frequently in the newspapers. By day they loaf in the corner groggeries on their beat, at night they plunder the stores along the avenues, or lie in wait at the river for unsteady feet straying their way. The man who is sober and minds his own business they seldom molest, unless he be a stranger inquiring his way, or a policeman and the gang twenty against the one. The tipsy wayfarer is their chosen victim, and they seldom have to look for him long. One has not far to go to the river from any point in New York. The man who does not know where he is going is sure to reach it sooner or later. Should he foolishly resist or make an outcry—dead men tell no tales. "Floaters" come ashore every now and then with pockets turned inside out, not always evidence of a postmortem inspection by dock rats. Police patrol the rivers as well as the shore on constant lookout for these, but seldom catch up with them. If overtaken after a race during which shots are often exchanged from the boats, the thieves have an easy way of escaping and at the same time destroying the evidence against them; they simply upset the boat. They swim, one and all, like real rats; the lost plunder can be recovered at leisure the next day by diving or grappling. The loss of the boat counts for little. Another is stolen, and the gang is ready for business again.

The fiction of a social "club," which most of the gangs keep up, helps them to a pretext for blackmailing the politicians and the storekeepers in their bailiwick at the annual seasons of their picnic, or ball. The "thieves' ball" is as well known and recognized an institution on the East Side as the Charity Ball in a different social stratum, although it does not go by that name, in print at least. Indeed, the last thing a New York tough will admit is that he is a thief. He dignifies his calling with the pretence of gambling. He does not steal: he "wins" your money or your watch, and on the police returns he is a "speculator." If, when he passes around the hat for "voluntary" contributions, any storekeeper should have the temerity to refuse to chip in, he may look for a visit from the gang on the first dark night, and account himself

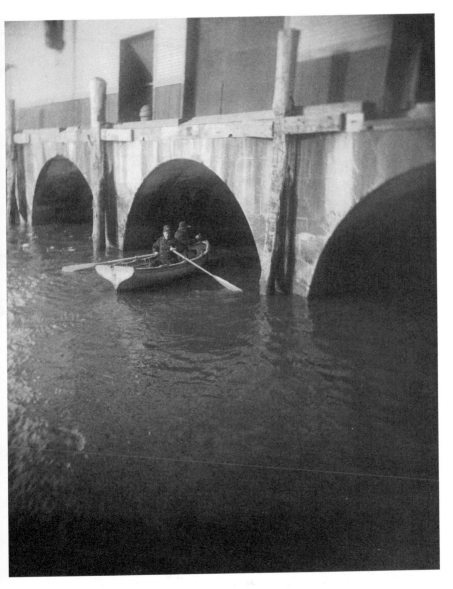

Hunting River Thieves

lucky if his place escapes being altogether wrecked. The Hell's Kitchen Gang and the Rag Gang have both distinguished themselves within recent times by blowing up objectionable stores with stolen gunpowder. But if no such episode mar the celebration, the excursion comes off and is the occasion for a series of drunken fights that as likely as not end in murder. No season has passed within my memory that has not seen the police reserves called out to receive some howling pandemonium returning from a picnic grove on the Hudson or on the Sound. At least one peaceful community up the river, that had borne with this nuisance until patience had ceased to be a virtue, received a boatload of such picnickers in a style befitting the occasion and the cargo. The outraged citizens planted a howitzer on the dock, and bade the party land at their peril. With the loaded gun pointed dead at them, the furious toughs gave up and the peace was not broken on the Hudson that day, at least not ashore. It is good cause for congratulation that the worst of all forms of recreation popular among the city's toughs, the moonlight picnic, has been effectually discouraged. Its opportunities for disgraceful revelry and immorality were unrivalled anywhere.

In spite of influence and protection, the tough reaches eventually the end of his rope. Occasionally—not too often—there is a noose on it. If not, the world that owes him a living, according to his creed, will insist on his earning it on the safe side of a prison wall. A few, a very few, have been clubbed into an approach to righteousness from the police standpoint. The condemned tough goes up to serve his "bit" or couple of "stretches," followed by the applause of his gang. In the prison he meets older thieves than himself, and sits at their feet listening with respectful admiration to their accounts of the great doings that sent them before. He returns with the brand of the jail upon him, to encounter the hero worship of his old associates as an offset to the cold shoulder given him by all the rest of the world. Even if he is willing to work, disgusted with the restraint and hard labor of prison life, and in a majority of cases that thought is probably uppermost in his mind, no one will have him around. If, with the assistance of Inspector Byrnes, who is a philanthropist in his own practical way, he secures a job, he is discharged on the slightest provocation, and for the most trifling fault. Very soon he sinks back into his old surroundings, to rise no more until he is lost to view in the queer, mysterious way in which thieves and fallen women disappear. No one can tell how. In the ranks of criminals he never rises above that of the "laborer," the small thief or burglar, or general crook, who blindly does the work planned for him by others, and runs the biggest risk for the poorest pay. It cannot be said that the "growler" brought him luck, or its friendship fortune. And yet, if his misdeeds have helped to make manifest that all effort to reclaim his kind must begin with the conditions of life against which his very existence is a protest, even the tough has not lived in vain. This measure of credit at least should be accorded him, that, with or without his goodwill, he has been a factor in urging on the battle against the slums that bred him. It is a fight in which eternal vigilance is truly the price of liberty and the preservation of society.

XX

The Working Girls of New York

O F THE HARVEST OF TARES, sown in iniquity and reaped in wrath, the police returns tell the story. The pen that wrote the "Song of the Shirt" is needed to tell of the sad and toil-worn lives of New York's working women. The cry echoes by night and by day through its tenements:

> Oh, God! that bread should be so dear,
> And flesh and blood so cheap![1]

Six months have not passed since at a great public meeting in this city, the Working Women's Society reported: "It is a known fact that men's wages cannot fall below a limit upon which they can exist, but woman's wages have no limit, since the paths of shame are always open to her. It is simply impossible for any woman to live without assistance on the low salary a saleswoman earns, without depriving herself of real necessities . . . It is inevitable that they must in many instances resort to evil." It was only a few brief weeks before that verdict was uttered, that the community was shocked by the story of a gentle and refined woman who, left in direst poverty to earn her own living alone among strangers, threw herself from her attic window, preferring death to dishonor. "I would have done any honest work, even to scrubbing," she wrote, drenched and starving, after a vain search for work in a driving storm. She had tramped the streets for weeks on her weary errand, and the only living wages that were offered her were the wages of sin. The ink was not dry upon her letter before a woman in an East Side tenement wrote down her reason for self-murder: "Weakness, sleeplessness, and yet obliged to work. My strength fails me. Sing at my coffin: 'Where does the soul find a home and rest?'" Her story may be found as one of two typical "cases of despair" in one little church community, in the *City Mission Society's Monthly* for last February. It is a story that has many parallels in the experience of every missionary, every police reporter and every family doctor whose practice is among the poor.

It is estimated that at least one hundred and fifty thousand women and girls earn their own living in New York; but there is reason to believe that this estimate falls far short of the truth when sufficient account is taken of the large number who are not wholly dependent upon their own labor, while contributing by it to the family's earnings. These alone constitute a large class of the women wage earners, and it is characteristic of the situation that the very fact that some need not starve on their wages condemns the rest to that fate. The pay they are willing to accept all have to take. What the "everlasting law of supply and demand," that serves as such a convenient gag for public indignation, has to do with it, one learns from observation all along the road of inquiry into these real woman's wrongs. To take the case of the saleswomen for illustration: The investigation of the Working Women's Society disclosed the fact that wages averaging from $2 to

$4.50 a week were reduced by excessive fines, the employers placing a value upon time lost that is not given to services rendered."[2] A little girl, who received two dollars a week, made cash sales amounting to $167 in a single day, while the receipts of a fifteen-dollar male clerk in the same department footed up only $125; yet for some trivial mistake the girl was fined sixty cents out of her two dollars. The practice prevailed in some stores of dividing the fines between the superintendent and the time keeper at the end of the year. In one instance they amounted to $3,000, and "the superintendent was heard to charge the timekeeper with not being strict enough in his duties." One of the causes for fine in a certain large store was sitting down. The law requiring seats for saleswomen, generally ignored, was obeyed faithfully in this establishment. The seats were there, but the girls were fined when found using them.

Cashgirls receiving $1.75 a week for work that at certain seasons lengthened their day to sixteen hours were sometimes required to pay for their aprons. A common cause for discharge from stores in which, on account of the oppressive heat and lack of ventilation, "girls fainted day after day and came out looking like corpses," was too long service. No other fault was found with the discharged saleswomen than that they had been long enough in the employ of the firm to justly expect an increase of salary. The reason was even given with brutal frankness, in some instances.

These facts give a slight idea of the hardships and the poor pay of a business that notoriously absorbs child labor. The girls are sent to the store before they have fairly entered their teens, because the money they can earn there is needed for the support of the family. If the boys will not work, if the street tempts them from home, among the girls at least there must be no drones. To keep their places they are told to lie about their age and to say that they are over fourteen. The precaution is usually superfluous. The Women's Investigating Committee found the majority of the children employed in the stores to be under age, but heard only in a single instance of the truant officers calling. In that case they came once a year and sent the youngest children home; but in a month's time they were all back in their places, and were not again disturbed. When it comes to the factories, where hard bodily labor is added to long hours, stifling rooms, and starvation wages, matters are even worse. The legislature has passed laws to prevent the employment of children, as it has forbidden saloon-keepers to sell them beer, and it has provided means of enforcing its mandate, so efficient, that the very number of factories in New York is *guessed* at as in the neighborhood of twelve thousand. Up till this summer, a single inspector was charged with the duty of keeping the run of them all, and of seeing to it that the law was respected by the owners.

Sixty cents is put as the average day's earnings of the 150,000, but into this computation enters the stylish "cashier's" two dollars a day, as well as the thirty cents of the poor little girl who pulls threads in an East Side factory, and, if anything, the average is probably too high. Such as it is, however, it represents board, rent, clothing, and "pleasure" to this army of workers. Here is the case of a woman employed in the manufacturing department of a Broadway house. It stands for a hundred like her own. She averages three dollars a week. Pays $1.50 for her room; for breakfast she has a cup of coffee; lunch she cannot afford. One meal a day is her allowance. This woman is young, she is pretty. She has "the world before her." Is it anything less than a miracle if she is guilty of nothing worse than the "early and improvident marriage," against which moralists exclaim as one of the prolific causes of the distress of the poor? Almost any door might seem to offer welcome escape from such slavery as this. "I feel so much healthier since I got three square meals a day," said a lodger in one of the Girls' Homes.[3] Two young sewing girls came in seeking domestic service, so that they might get enough to eat. They had been only half-fed for some time, and starvation had driven them to the one door at which the pride of the American-born girl will not permit her to knock, though poverty be the price of her independence.

The tenement and the competition of public institutions and farmers' wives and daughters, have done the tyrant shirt to death, but they have not bettered the lot of the needlewomen. The sweater of the East Side has appropriated the flannel shirt. He turns them out today at forty-five cents a dozen, paying his Jewish workers from twenty to thirty-five cents. One of these testified before the State Board of Arbitration, during the shirtmakers' strike, that she worked eleven hours in the shop and four at home, and had never in the best of times made over six dollars a week. Another stated that she worked from 4 o'clock in the morning to 11 at night.[4] These girls had to find their own thread and pay for their own machines out of their wages. The white shirt has gone to the public and private institutions that shelter large numbers of young girls, and to the country. There are not half as many shirtmakers in New York today as only a few years ago, and some of the largest firms have closed their city shops. The same is true of the manufacturers of underwear. One large Broadway firm has nearly all its work done by farmers' girls in Maine, who think themselves well off if they can earn two or three dollars a week to pay for a Sunday silk, or the wedding outfit, little dreaming of the part they are playing in starving their city sisters. Literally, they sew "with double thread, a shroud as well as a shirt."[5] Their pin money sets the rate of wages for thousands of poor sewing girls in New York. The average earnings of the worker on underwear today do not exceed the three dollars which her competitor among the Eastern hills is willing to accept as the price of her play. The shirtmaker's pay is better only because the very finest custom work is all there is left for her to do.

Calico wrappers at a dollar and a half a dozen—the very expert

Sewing and Starving in an Elizabeth Street Attic

sewers able to make from eight to ten, the common run five or six—neckties at from 25 to 75 cents a dozen, with a dozen as a good day's work, are specimens of women's wages. And yet people persist in wondering at the poor quality of work done in the tenements! Italian cheap labor has come of late also to possess this poor field, with the sweater in its train. There is scarce a branch of woman's work outside of the home in which wages, long since at low-water mark, have not fallen to the point of actual starvation. A case was brought to my notice recently by a woman doctor, whose heart as well as her lifework is with the poor, of a widow with two little children she found at work in an East Side attic, making paper bags. Her father, she told the doctor, had made good wages at it; but she received only five cents for six hundred of the little three-cornered bags, and her fingers had to be very swift and handle the paste brush very deftly to bring her earnings up to twenty-five and thirty cents a day. She paid four dollars a month for her room. The rest went to buy food for herself and the children. The physician's purse, rather than her skill, had healing for their complaint.

I have aimed to set down a few dry facts merely. They carry their own comment. Back of the shop with its weary, grinding toil—the home in the tenement, of which it was said in a report of the State Labor Bureau: "Decency and womanly reserve cannot be maintained there—what wonder so many fall away from virtue?" Of the outlook, what? Last Christmas Eve my business took me to an obscure street among the West Side tenements. An old woman had just fallen on the doorstep, stricken with paralysis. The doctor said she would never again move her right hand or foot. The whole side was dead. By her bedside, in their cheerless room, sat the patient's aged sister, a hopeless cripple, in dumb despair. Forty years ago the sisters had come, five in number then, with their mother, from the North of Ireland to make their home and earn a living among strangers. They were lace embroiderers and found work easily at good wages. All the rest had died as the years went by. The two remained and, firmly resolved to lead an honest life, worked on though wages fell and fell as age and toil stiffened their once nimble fingers and dimmed their sight. Then one of them dropped out, her hands palsied and her courage gone. Still the other toiled on, resting neither by night nor by day, that the sister might not want. Now that she too had been stricken, as she was going to the store for the work that was to keep them through the holidays, the battle was over at last. There was before them starvation, or the poorhouse. And the proud spirits of the sisters, helpless now, quailed at the outlook.

These were old, with life behind them. For them nothing was left but to sit in the shadow and wait. But of the thousands, who are travelling the road they trod to the end, with the hot blood of youth in their veins, with the love of life and of the beautiful world to which not even sixty cents a day can shut their eyes—who is to blame if their feet find the paths of shame that are "always open to them"? The very paths that have effaced the saving "limit," and to which it is declared to be "inevitable that they must in many instances resort." Let the moralist answer. Let the wise economist apply his rule of supply and demand, and let the answer be heard in this city of a thousand charities where justice goes begging.

To the everlasting credit of New York's working girl let it be said that, rough though her road be, all but hopeless her battle with life, only in the rarest instances does she go astray. As a class she is brave, virtuous, and true. New York's army of profligate women is not, as in some foreign cities, recruited from her ranks. She is as plucky as she is proud. That "American girls never whimper" became a proverb long ago, and she accepts her lot uncomplainingly, doing the best she can and holding her cherished independence cheap at the cost of a meal, or of half her daily ration, if need be. The home in the tenement and the traditions of her childhood have neither trained her to luxury nor predisposed her in favor of domestic labor in preference to the shop. So, to the world she presents a cheerful, uncomplaining front that sometimes deceives it. Her courage will not be without its reward. Slowly, as the conviction is thrust upon society that woman's work must enter more and more into its planning, a better day is dawning. The organization of working girls' clubs, unions, and societies with a community of interests, despite the obstacles to such a movement, bears testimony to it, as to the devotion of the unselfish women who have made their poorer sisters' cause their own, and will yet wring from an unfair world the justice too long denied her.

of calculations which deal with New York's population as a whole. They estimate upon the basis of their everyday experience that, allowing for those who have died, moved away, or become for the time being at least self-supporting, eighty-five percent of the registry are still within, or lingering upon, the borders of dependence. Precisely how the case stands with this great horde of the indigent is shown by a classification of 5,169 cases that were investigated by the Society in one year. This was the way it turned out: 327 worthy of continuous relief, or 6.4 percent; 1,269 worthy of temporary relief, or 24.4 percent; 2,698 in need of work, rather than relief, or 52.2 percent; 875 unworthy of relief, or 17 percent.

That is, nearly six and a half percent of all were utterly helpless—orphans, cripples, or the very aged; nearly one-fourth needed just a lift to start them on the road of independence, or of permanent pauperism, according to the wisdom with which the lever was applied. More than half were destitute because they had no work and were unable to find any, and one-sixth were frauds, professional beggars, training their children to follow in their footsteps—a veritable "tribe of Ishmael," tightening its grip on society as the years pass, until society shall summon up pluck to say with Paul, "if any man will not work neither shall he eat,"[2] and stick to it. It is worthy of note that almost precisely the same results followed a similar investigation in Boston. There were a few more helpless cases of the sort true charity accounts it a gain to care for, but the proportion of a given lot that was crippled for want of work, or unworthy, was exactly the same as in this city. The bankrupt in hope, in courage, in purse, and in purpose, are not peculiar to New York. They are found the world over, but we have our full share. If further proof were wanted, it is found in the prevalence of pauper burials. The Potter's Field stands ever for utter, hopeless surrender. The last the poor will let go, however miserable their lot in life, is the hope of a decent burial. But for the five years

A Flat in the Pauper Barracks, West Thirty-eighth Street, with All Its Furniture ending with 1888 the average of burials in the Potter's Field has been 10.03 percent of all. In 1889 it was 9.64. In that year the proportion to the total mortality of those who died in hospitals, institutions, and in the Almshouse was as 1 in 5.

The 135,595 families inhabited no fewer than 31,000 different tenements. I say tenements advisedly, though the society calls them buildings, because at least ninety-nine percent were found in the big barracks, the rest in shanties scattered here and there, and now and then a fraud or an exceptional case of distress in a dwelling house of better class. Here, undoubtedly, allowance must be made for the constant moving about of those who live on charity, which enables one active beggar to blacklist a dozen houses in the year. Still the great mass of the tenements are shown to be harboring alms seekers. They might almost as safely harbor the smallpox. That scourge is not more contagious than the alms seeker's complaint. There are houses that have been corrupted through and through by this pestilence, until their very atmosphere breathes beggary. More than a hundred and twenty pauper families have been reported from time to time as living in one such tenement.

The truth is that pauperism grows in the tenements as naturally as weeds in a garden lot. A moral distemper, like crime, it finds there its more fertile soil. All the surroundings of tenement house life favor its growth, and where once it has taken root it is harder to dislodge than the most virulent of physical diseases. The thief is infinitely easier to deal with than the pauper, because the very fact of his being a thief presupposes some bottom to the man. Granted that it is bad, there is still something, a possible handle by which to catch him. To the pauper there is none. He is as hopeless as his own poverty. I speak of the *pauper*, not of the honestly poor. There is a sharp line between the two; but athwart it stands the tenement, all the time blurring and blotting it out. "It all comes down to character in the end," was the rested an Italian woman who was begging along Madison Avenue with a poor little wreck of a girl, whose rags and pinched face were calculated to tug hard at the purse strings of a miser. Over five dollars in nickles and pennies were taken from the woman's pockets, and when her story of poverty and hunger was investigated at the family's home in a Baxter Street tenement, bankbooks turned up that showed the Masonis to be regular pauper capitalists, able to draw their check for three thousand dollars, had they been so disposed. The woman was fined $250, a worse punishment undoubtedly than to have sent her to prison for the rest of her natural life. Her class has, unhappily, representatives in New York that have not yet been brought to grief.

Nothing short of making street begging a crime has availed to clear our city of this pest to an appreciable extent. By how much of an effort this result has been accomplished may be gleaned from the fact that the Charity Organization Society alone, in five years, caused the taking up of 2,594 street beggars, and the arrest and conviction of 1,474 persistent offenders. Last year it dealt with 612 perambulating mendicants. The police report only 19 arrests for begging during the year 1889, but the real facts of the case are found under the heading "vagrancy." In all, 2,633 persons were charged with this offence, 947 of them women. A goodly proportion of these latter came from the low groggeries of the Tenth Ward, where a peculiar variety of the female tramp-beggar is at home, the "scrub." The scrub is one degree perhaps above the average pauper in this, that she is willing to work at least one day in the week, generally the Jewish Sabbath. The orthodox Jew can do no work of any sort from Friday evening till sunset on Saturday, and this interim the scrub fills out in Ludlow Street. The pittance she receives for this vicarious sacrifice of herself upon the altar of the ancient faith buys her rum for at least two days of the week at one of the neighborhood "morgues." She lives through the other four by begging. There are distilleries in Jewtown, or just across its borders, that depend almost wholly on her custom. Recently, when one in Hester Street was raided because the neighbors had complained of the boisterous hilarity of the hags over their beer, thirty-two aged "scrubs" were marched off to the station house.

It is curious to find preconceived notions quite upset in a review of the nationalities that go to make up this squad of street beggars. The Irish head the list with fifteen percent, and the native American is only a little way behind with twelve percent, while the Italian, who in his own country turns beggary into a fine art, has less than two percent. Eight percent were Germans. The relative prevalence of the races in our population does not account for this showing. Various causes operate, no doubt, to produce it. Chief among them is, I think, the tenement itself. It has no power to corrupt the Italian, who comes here in almost every instance to work—no beggar would ever emigrate from anywhere unless forced to do so. He is distinctly on its lowest level from the start. With the Irishman the case is different. The tenement, especially its lowest type, appears to possess a peculiar affinity for the worse nature of the Celt, to whose best and strongest instincts it does violence, and soonest and most thoroughly corrupts him. The "native" twelve percent represent the result of this process, the hereditary beggar of the second or third generation in the slums.

The blind beggar alone is winked at in New York's streets, because the authorities do not know what else to do with him. There is no provision for him anywhere after he is old enough to strike out for himself. The annual pittance of thirty or forty dollars which he receives from the city serves to keep his landlord in good humor; for the rest his misfortune and his thin disguise of selling pencils on the street corners must provide. Until the city affords him some systematic way of earning his living by work (as Philadelphia has done, for instance) to banish him from the street would be tantamount to sentencing him to death by starvation. So he possesses it in peace, that is, if he is blind in good earnest, and begs without "encumbrance." Professional mendicancy does not hesitate to make use of the greatest of human afflictions as a pretence for enlisting the sympathy upon which it thrives. Many New Yorkers will remember the French schoolmaster who was "blinded by a shell at the siege of Paris," but miraculously recovered his sight when arrested and deprived of his children by the officers of Mr. Gerry's society.[3] When last heard of he kept a "museum" in Hartford, and acted the overseer with financial success. His sign with its pitiful tale, that was a familiar sight in our streets for years and earned for him the capital upon which he started his business, might have found a place among the curiosities exhibited there, had it not been kept in a different sort of museum here as a memento of his rascality. There was another of his tribe, a woman, who begged for years with a deformed child in her arms, which she was found to have hired at an almshouse in Genoa for fifteen francs a month. It was a good investment, for she proved to be possessed of a comfortable fortune. Some time before that, the Society for the Prevention of Cruelty to Children, that found her out, had broken up the dreadful padrone system, a real slave trade in Italian children, who were bought of poor parents across the sea and made to beg their way on foot through France to the port whence they were shipped to this city, to be beaten and starved here by their cruel masters and sent out to beg, often after merciless mutilation to make them "take" better with a pitying public.

But, after all, the tenement offers a better chance of fraud on impulsive but thoughtless charity, than all the wretchedness of the street, and with fewer risks. To the tenderhearted and unwary it is, in itself, the strongest plea for help. When such a cry goes up as was heard recently from a Mott Street den, where the family of a "sick" husband, a despairing mother, and half a dozen children in rags and dirt were destitute of the "first necessities of life," it is not to be wondered at that a stream of gold comes pouring in to relieve. It happens too often, as in that case, that a little critical inquiry or reference to the "black list" of the Charity Organization Society, justly dreaded only by the frauds, discovers the "sickness" to stand for laziness, and the destitution to be the family's stock in trade; and the community receives a shock that for once is downright wholesome, if it imposes a check on an undiscriminating charity that is worse than none at all.

The case referred to furnished an apt illustration of how thoroughly corrupting pauperism is in such a setting. The tenement woke up early to the gold mine that was being worked under its roof, and before the day was three hours old the stream of callers who responded to the newspaper appeal found the alley blocked by a couple of "toughs," who exacted toll of a silver quarter from each tearful sympathizer with the misery in the attic.

A volume might be written about the tricks of the professional beggar, and the uses to which he turns the tenement in his trade. The Boston "widow" whose husband turned up alive and well after she had buried him seventeen times with tears and lamentation, and made the public pay for the weekly funerals, is not without representatives in New York. The "gentleman tramp" is a familiar type from our streets, and the "once respectable Methodist" who patronized all the revivals in town with his profitable story of repentance, only to fall from grace into the saloon door nearest the church after the service was over, merely transferred the scene of his operations from the tenement to the church as the proper setting for his specialty. There is enough of real suffering in the homes of the poor to make one wish that there were some effective way of enforcing Paul's plan of starving the drones into the paths of self-support: no work, nothing to eat.

The message came from one of the Health Department's summer doctors, last July, to the King's Daughters' Tenement House Committee, that a family with a sick child was absolutely famishing in an uptown tenement. The address was not given. The doctor had forgotten to write it down, and before he could be found and a visitor sent

Coffee at One Cent

to the house the baby was dead, and the mother had gone mad. The nurse found the father, who was an honest laborer long out of work, packing the little corpse in an orange box partly filled with straw, that he might take it to the morgue for pauper burial. There was absolutely not a crust to eat in the house, and the other children were crying for food. The great immediate need in that case, as in more than half of all according to the record, was work and living wages. Alms do not meet the emergency at all. They frequently aggravate it, degrading and pauperizing where true help should aim at raising the sufferer to self-respect and self-dependence. The experience of the Charity Organization Society in raising, in eight years, 4,500 families out of the rut of pauperism into proud, if modest, independence, without alms, but by a system of "friendly visitation," and the work of the Society for Improving the Condition of the Poor and kindred organizations along the same line, shows what can be done by well-directed effort. It is estimated that New York spends in public and private charity every year a round $8,000,000. A small part of this sum intelligently invested in a great labor bureau, that would bring the seeker of work and the one with work to give together under auspices offering some degree of mutual security, would certainly repay the amount of the investment in the saving of much capital now worse than wasted, and would be prolific of the best results. The ultimate and greatest need, however, the real remedy, is to remove the cause—the tenement that was built for "a class of whom nothing was expected," and which has come fully up to the expectation. Tenement house reform holds the key to the problem of pauperism in the city. We can never get rid of either the tenement or the pauper. The two will always exist together in New York. But by reforming the one, we can do more toward exterminating the other than can be done by all other means together that have yet been invented, or ever will be.

XXII

The Wrecks and the Waste

PAUPERDOM IS TO BLAME FOR the unjust yoking of poverty with punishment, "charities" with "correction," in our municipal ministering to the needs of the Nether Half. The shadow of the work-house points like a scornful finger toward its neighbor, the almshouse, when the sun sets behind the teeming city across the East River, as if, could its stones speak, it would say before night drops its black curtain between them: "You and I are brothers. I am not more bankrupt in moral purpose than you. A common parent begat us. Twin breasts, the tenement and the saloon, nourished us. Vice and unthrift go hand in hand. Pauper, behold thy brother!" And the almshouse owns the bitter relationship in silence.

Over on the islands that lie strung along the river and far up the Sound the Nether Half hides its deformity, except on show days, when distinguished visitors have to be entertained and the sore is uncovered by the authorities with due municipal pride in the exhibit. I shall spare the reader the sight. The aim of these pages has been to lay bare its source. But a brief glance at our proscribed population is needed to give background and tone to the picture. The review begins with the Charity Hospital with its thousand helpless human wrecks; takes in the penitentiary, where the "tough" from Battle Row and Poverty Gap is made to earn behind stone walls the living the world owes him; a thoughtless, jolly convict band with opportunity at last "to think" behind the iron bars, but little desire to improve it; governed like unruly boys, which in fact most of them are. Three of them were taken from the dinner table while I was there one day, for sticking pins into each other, and were set with their faces to the wall in sight of six hundred of their comrades for punishment. Pleading incessantly for tobacco, when the keeper's back is turned, as the next best thing to the whiskey they cannot get, though they can plainly make out the saloon signs across the stream where they robbed or "slugged" their way to prison. Every once in a while the longing gets the best of some prisoner from the penitentiary or the workhouse, and he risks his life in the swift currents to reach the goal that tantalizes him with the promise of "just one more drunk." The chances are at least even of his being run down by some passing steamer and drowned, even if he is not overtaken by the armed guards who patrol the shore in boats, or his strength does not give out.

This workhouse comes next, with the broken-down hordes from the dives, the lodging houses, and the tramps' nests, the "hell-box"* rather than the repair shop of the city. In 1889 the registry at the workhouse footed up 22,477, of whom some had been there as many as twenty times before. It is the popular summer resort of the slums, but business is brisk at this stand the year round. Not a few of its patrons

---

* In printing offices the broken, worn-out, and useless type is thrown into the "hell-box," to be recast at the foundry.

drift back periodically without the formality of a commitment, to take their chances on the island when there is no escape from the alternative of work in the city. Work, but not too much work, is the motto of the establishment. The "workhouse step" is an institution that must be observed on the island, in order to draw any comparison between it and the snail's pace that shall do justice to the snail. Nature and man's art have made these islands beautiful; but weeds grow luxuriantly in their gardens, and spiders spin their cobwebs unmolested in the borders of sweet-smelling box. The work which two score of hired men could do well is too much for these thousands.

Rows of old women, some smoking stumpy, black clay pipes, others knitting or idling, all grumbling, sit or stand under the trees that hedge in the almshouse, or limp about in the sunshine, leaning on crutches or beanpole staffs. They are a "growler-gang" of another sort than may be seen in session on the rocks of the opposite shore at that very moment. They grumble and growl from sunrise to sunset, at the weather, the breakfast, the dinner, the supper; at pork and beans as at corned beef and cabbage; at their Thanksgiving dinner as at the half rations of the sick ward; at the past that had no joy, at the present whose comfort they deny, and at the future without promise. The crusty old men in the next building are not a circumstance to them. The warden, who was in charge of the almshouse for many years, had become so snappish and profane by constant association with a thousand cross old women that I approached him with some misgivings, to request his permission to "take" a group of a hundred or so who were within shot of my camera. He misunderstood me.

"Take them?" he yelled. "Take the thousand of them and be welcome. They will never be still, by ——, till they are sent up on Hart's Island in a box, and I'll be blamed if I don't think they will growl then at the style of the funeral."

And he threw his arms around me in an outburst of enthusiasm over the wondrous good luck that had sent a friend indeed to his door. I felt it to be a painful duty to undeceive him. When I told him that I simply wanted the old women's picture, he turned away in speechless disgust, and to his dying day, I have no doubt, remembered my call as the day of the champion fool's visit to the island.

When it is known that many of these old people have been sent to the almshouse to die by their heartless children, for whom they had worked faithfully as long as they were able, their growling and discontent is not hard to understand. Bitter poverty threw them all "on the county," often on the wrong county at that. Very many of them are old-country poor, sent, there is reason to believe, to America by the authorities to get rid of the obligation to support them. "The almshouse," wrote a good missionary, "affords a sad illustration of St. Paul's description of the 'last days.' The class from which comes our poorhouse population is to a large extent 'without natural affection.'" I was reminded by his words of what my friend, the doctor, had said to me a little while before: "Many a mother has told me at her child's deathbed, 'I cannot afford to lose it. It costs too much to bury it.' And when the little one did die there was no time for the mother's grief. The question crowded on at once, 'where shall the money come from?' Natural feelings and affections are smothered in the tenements." The doctor's experience furnished a sadly appropriate text for the priest's sermon.

Pitiful as these are, sights and sounds infinitely more saddening await us beyond the gate that shuts this world of woe off from one whence the light of hope and reason have gone out together. The shuffling of many feet on the macadamized roads heralds the approach of a host of women, hundreds upon hundreds—beyond the turn in the road they still keep coming, marching with the faltering step, the unseeing look and the incessant, senseless chatter that betrays the darkened mind. The lunatic women of the Blackwell's Island

Asylum are taking their afternoon walk. Beyond, on the wide lawn, moves another still stranger procession, a file of women in the asylum dress of dull gray, hitched to a queer little wagon that, with its gaudy adornments, suggests a cross between a baby carriage and a circus chariot. One crazy woman is strapped in the seat; forty tug at the rope to which they are securely bound. This is the "chain-gang," so called once in scoffing ignorance of the humane purpose the contrivance serves. These are the patients afflicted with suicidal mania, who cannot be trusted at large for a moment with the river in sight, yet must have their daily walk as a necessary part of their treatment. So this wagon was invented by a clever doctor to afford them at once exercise and amusement. A merry-go-round in the grounds suggests a variation of this scheme. Ghastly suggestion of mirth, with that stricken host advancing on its aimless journey! As we stop to see it pass, the plaintive strains of a familiar song float through a barred window in the gray stone building. The voice is sweet, but inexpressibly sad: "Oh, how my heart grows weary, far from——" The song breaks off suddenly in a low, troubled laugh. She has forgotten, forgotten——. A woman in the ranks, whose head has been turned toward the window, throws up her hands with a scream. The rest stir uneasily. The nurse is by her side in an instant with words half soothing, half stern. A messenger comes in haste from the asylum to ask us not to stop. Strangers may not linger where the patients pass. It is apt to excite them. As we go in with him the human file is passing yet, quiet restored. The troubled voice of the unseen singer still gropes vainly among the lost memories of the past for the missing key: "Oh! how my heart grows weary, far from——"

"Who is she, doctor?"

"Hopeless case. She will never see home again."

An average of seventeen hundred women this asylum harbors; the asylum for men up on Ward's Island even more. Altogether 1,419 pa-

tients were admitted to the city asylums for the insane in 1889, and at
the end of the year 4,913 remained in them. There is a constant ominous increase in this class of helpless unfortunates that are thrown on
the city's charity. Quite two hundred are added year by year, and the
asylums were long since so overcrowded that a great "farm" had to be
established on Long Island to receive the surplus. The strain of our
hurried, overworked life has something to do with this. Poverty has
more. For these are all of the poor. It is the harvest of sixty and a hundredfold, the "fearful rolling up and rolling down from generation
to generation, through all the ages, of the weakness, vice, and moral
darkness of the past."*[1] The curse of the island haunts all that come
once within its reach. "No man or woman," says Dr. Louis L. Seaman,
who speaks from many years' experience in a position that gave him
full opportunity to observe the facts, "who is 'sent up' to these colonies ever returns to the city scotfree. There is a lien, visible or hidden,
upon his or her present or future, which too often proves stronger
than the best purposes and fairest opportunities of social rehabilita-
tion. The underworld holds in rigorous bondage every unfortunate
or miscreant who has once 'served time.' There is often tragic interest in the struggles of the ensnared wretches to break away from the
meshes spun about them. But the maelstrom has no bowels of mercy;
and the would-be fugitives are flung back again and again into the
devouring whirlpool of crime and poverty, until the end is reached
on the dissecting table, or in the Potter's Field. What can the moralist
or scientist do by way of resuscitation? Very little at best. The flotsam and jetsam are mere shreds and fragments of wasted lives. Such a
ministry must begin at the sources—is necessarily prophylactic, nu-
tritive, educational. On these islands there are no flexible twigs, only

* Dr. Louis L. Seaman, late chief of staff of the Blackwell's Island hospitals: "Social
Waste of a Great City," read before the American Association for the Advancement of
Science, 1886.

XXIII

The Man with the Knife

A MAN STOOD AT THE corner of Fifth Avenue and Fourteenth Street the other day, looking gloomily at the carriages that rolled by, carrying the wealth and fashion of the avenues to and from the big stores downtown. He was poor, and hungry, and ragged. This thought was in his mind: "They behind their well-fed teams have no thought for the morrow; they know hunger only by name, and ride down to spend in an hour's shopping what would keep me and my little ones from want a whole year." There rose up before him the picture of those little ones crying for bread around the cold and cheerless hearth —then he sprang into the throng and slashed about him with a knife, blindly seeking to kill, to revenge.

The man was arrested, of course, and locked up. Today he is probably in a madhouse, forgotten. And the carriages roll by to and from the big stores with their gay throng of shoppers. The world forgets easily, too easily, what it does not like to remember.

Nevertheless the man and his knife had a mission. They spoke in their ignorant, impatient way the warning one of the most conservative, dispassionate of public bodies had sounded only a little while before: "Our only fear is that reform may come in a burst of public indignation destructive to property and to good morals."* They represented one solution of the problem of ignorant poverty *versus* ignorant wealth that has come down to us unsolved, the danger cry of which we have lately heard in the shout that never should have been raised on American soil—the shout of "the masses against the classes" —the solution of violence.

There is another solution, that of justice. The choice is between the two. Which shall it be?

"Well!" say some well-meaning people; "we don't see the need of putting it in that way. We have been down among the tenements, looked them over. There are a good many people there; they are not comfortable, perhaps. What would you have? They are poor. And their houses are not such hovels as we have seen and read of in the slums of the Old World. They are decent in comparison. Why, some of them have brownstone fronts. You will own at least that they make a decent show."

Yes! that is true. The worst tenements in New York do not, as a rule, *look bad*. Neither Hell's Kitchen, nor Murderers' Row bears its true character stamped on the front. They are not quite old enough, perhaps. The same is true of their tenants. The New York tough may be ready to kill where his London brother would do little more than scowl; yet, as a general thing he is less repulsively brutal in looks. Here again the reason may be the same: the breed is not so old. A few generations more in the slums, and all that will be changed. To get at the pregnant facts of tenement house life one must look beneath the sur-

* Forty-fourth Annual Report of the Association for Improving the Condition of the Poor. 1887.

face. Many an apple has a fair skin and a rotten core. There is a much better argument for the tenements in the assurance of the Registrar of Vital Statistics that the death rate of these houses has of late been brought below the general death rate of the city, and that it is lowest in the biggest houses. This means two things: one, that the almost exclusive attention given to the tenements by the sanitary authorities in twenty years has borne some fruit, and that the newer tenements are better than the old—there is some hope in that; the other, that the whole strain of tenement house dwellers has been bred down to the conditions under which it exists, that the struggle with corruption has begotten the power to resist it. This is a familiar law of nature, necessary to its first and strongest impulse of self-preservation. To a certain extent, we are all creatures of the conditions that surround us, physically and morally. But is the knowledge reassuring? In the light of what we have seen, does not the question arise: what sort of creature, then, this of the tenement? I tried to draw his likeness from observation in telling the story of the "tough." Has it nothing to suggest the man with the knife?

I will go further. I am not willing even to admit it to be an unqualified advantage that our New York tenements have less of the slum look than those of older cities. It helps to delay the recognition of their true character on the part of the well-meaning, but uninstructed, who are always in the majority.

The "dangerous classes"[1] of New York long ago compelled recognition. They are dangerous less because of their own crimes than because of the criminal ignorance of those who are not of their kind. The danger to society comes not from the poverty of the tenements, but from the ill-spent wealth that reared them, that it might earn a usurious interest from a class from which "nothing else was expected." That was the broad foundation laid down, and the edifice built upon it corresponds to the groundwork. That this is well understood on the "unsafe" side of the line that separates the rich from the poor, much better than by those who have all the advantages of discriminating education, is good cause for disquietude. In it a keen foresight may again dimly discern the shadow of the man with the knife.

Two years ago a great meeting was held at Chickering Hall—I have spoken of it before—a meeting that discussed for days and nights the question how to banish this specter; how to lay hold with good influences of this enormous mass of more than a million people, who were drifting away faster and faster from the safe moorings of the old faith. Clergymen and laymen from all the Protestant denominations took part in the discussion; nor was a good word forgotten for the brethren of the other great Christian fold who labor among the poor. Much was said that was good and true, and ways were found of reaching the spiritual needs of the tenement population that promise success. But at no time throughout the conference was the real keynote of the situation so boldly struck as has been done by a few far-seeing business men, who had listened to the cry of that Christian builder: "How shall the love of God be understood by those who have been nurtured in sight only of the greed of man?"[2] Their practical program of "Philanthropy and five percent" has set examples in tenement building that show, though they are yet few and scattered, what may in time be accomplished even with such poor opportunities as New York offers today of undoing the old wrong. This is the gospel of justice, the solution that must be sought as the one alternative to the man with the knife.

"Are you not looking too much to the material condition of these people," said a good minister to me after a lecture in a Harlem church last winter, "and forgetting the inner man?" I told him, "No! for you cannot expect to find an inner man to appeal to in the worst tenement house surroundings. You must first put the man where he can respect himself. To reverse the argument of the apple: you cannot expect to find a sound core in a rotten fruit."

of the poor has been taken by the throat, and something has unquestionably been done, where that was possible, to lift those lives out of the rut where they were equally beyond the reach of hope and of ambition. It is no longer lawful to construct barracks to cover the whole of a lot. Air and sunlight have a legal claim, and the day of rear tenements is past. Two years ago a hundred thousand people burrowed in these inhuman dens; but some have been torn down since. Their number will decrease steadily until they shall have become a bad tradition of a heedless past. The dark, unventilated bedroom is going with them, and the open sewer. The day is at hand when the greatest of all evils that now curse life in the tenements—the dearth of water in the hot summer days—will also have been remedied, and a long step taken toward the moral and physical redemption of their tenants.

Public sentiment has done something also, but very far from enough. As a rule, it has slumbered peacefully until some flagrant outrage on decency and the health of the community aroused it to noisy but ephemeral indignation, or until a dreaded epidemic knocked at our door. It is this unsteadiness of purpose that has been to a large extent responsible for the apparent lagging of the authorities in cases not involving immediate danger to the general health. The law needs a much stronger and readier backing of a thoroughly enlightened public sentiment to make it as effective as it might be made. It is to be remembered that the health officers, in dealing with this subject of dangerous houses, are constantly trenching upon what each landlord considers his private rights, for which he is ready and bound to fight to the last. Nothing short of the strongest pressure will avail to convince him that these individual rights are to be surrendered for the clear benefit of the whole. It is easy enough to convince a man that he ought not to harbor the thief who steals people's property; but to make him see that he has no right to slowly kill his neighbors, or his

Evolution of the Tenement in Twenty Years.
Left: Old Style Tenement. *Right:* Single Lot Tenement of Today.

tenants, by making a deathtrap of his house, seems to be the hardest
of all tasks. It is apparently the slowness of the process that obscures
his mental sight. The man who will fight an order to repair the plumbing in his house through every court he can reach, would suffer tor-
tures rather than shed the blood of a fellow-man by actual violence.
Clearly, it is a matter of education on the part of the landlord no less
than the tenant.

In spite of this, the landlord has done his share; chiefly perhaps by yielding—not always gracefully—when it was no longer of any use to fight. There have been exceptions, however: men and women who have mended and built with an eye to the real welfare of their tenants as well as to their own pockets. Let it be well understood that the two are inseparable, if any good is to come of it. The business of housing the poor, if it is to amount to anything, must be business, as it was business with our fathers to put them where they are. As charity, pastime, or fad, it will miserably fail, always and everywhere. This is an inexorable rule, now thoroughly well understood in England and continental Europe, and by all who have given the matter serious thought here. Call it poetic justice, or divine justice, or anything else, it is a hard fact, not to be gotten over. Upon any other plan than the assumption that the workman has a just claim to a decent home, and the right to demand it, any scheme for his relief fails. It must be a fair exchange of the man's money for what he can afford to buy at a reasonable price. Any charity scheme merely turns him into a pauper, however it may be disguised, and drowns him hopelessly in the mire out of which it proposed to pull him. And this principle must pervade the whole plan. Expert management of model tenements succeeds where amateur management, with the best intentions, gives up the task, discouraged, as a flat failure. Some of the best-conceived enterprises, backed by abundant capital and goodwill, have been wrecked on this rock. Sentiment, having prompted the effort, forgot to stand aside and let business make it.

Business, in a wider sense, has done more than all other agencies together to wipe out the worst tenements. It has been New York's real Napoleon III, from whose decree there was no appeal. In ten years I have seen plague spots disappear before its onward march, with which health officers, police, and sanitary science had struggled vainly since such struggling began as a serious business. And the process goes on still. Unfortunately, the crowding in some of the most densely packed quarters down town has made the property there so valuable, that relief from this source is less confidently to be expected, at all events in the near future. Still, their time may come also. It comes so quickly sometimes as to fairly take one's breath away. More than once I have returned, after a few brief weeks, to some specimen rookery in which I was interested, to find it gone and an army of workmen delving twenty feet underground to lay the foundation of a mighty warehouse. That was the case with the "Big Flat" in Mott Street.[1] I had not had occasion to visit it for several months last winter, and when I went there, entirely unprepared for a change, I could not find it. It had always been conspicuous enough in the landscape before, and I marvelled much at my own stupidity until, by examining the number of the house, I found out that I had gone right. It was the "flat" that had disappeared. In its place towered a six-story carriage factory with business going on on every floor, as if it had been there for years and years.

This same "Big Flat" furnished a good illustration of why some well-meant efforts in tenement building have failed. Like Gotham Court,[2] it was originally built as a model tenement, but speedily came to rival the Court in foulness. It became a regular hotbed of thieves and peacebreakers, and made no end of trouble for the police. The immediate reason, outside of the lack of proper supervision, was that it had open access to two streets in a neighborhood where thieves and "toughs" abounded. These took advantage of an arrangement that had been supposed by the builders to be a real advantage as a means of ventilation, and their occupancy drove honest folk away. Murderers' Alley, of which I have spoken elsewhere, and the sanitary inspector's experiment with building a brick wall athwart it to shut off travel through the block, is a parallel case.

The causes that operate to obstruct efforts to better the lot of the tenement population are, in our day, largely found among the tenants themselves. This is true particularly of the poorest. They are shiftless, destructive, and stupid; in a word, they are what the tenements have made them. It is a dreary old truth that those who would fight for the poor must fight the poor to do it. It must be confessed that there is little enough in their past experience to inspire confidence in the sincerity of the effort to help them. I recall the discomfiture of a certain well-known philanthropist, since deceased, whose heart beat responsive to other suffering than that of human kind. He was a large owner of tenement property, and once undertook to fit out his houses with stationary tubs, sanitary plumbing, wood-closets, and all the latest improvements. He introduced his rough tenants to all this magnificence without taking the precaution of providing a competent housekeeper, to see that the new acquaintances got on together. He felt that his tenants ought to be grateful for the interest he took in them. They were. They found the boards in the wood closets fine kindling wood, while the pipes and faucets were as good as cash at the junk shop. In three months the owner had to remove what was left of his improvements. The pipes were cut and the houses running full of water, the stationary tubs were put to all sorts of uses except washing, and of the wood closets not a trace was left. The philanthropist was ever after a firm believer in the total depravity of tenement house people. Others have been led to like reasoning by as plausible arguments, without discovering that the shiftlessness and ignorance that offended them were the consistent crop of the tenement they were trying to reform, and had to be included in the effort. The owners of a block of model tenements uptown had got their tenants comfortably settled, and were indulging in high hopes of their redemption under proper management, when a contractor ran up a row of "skin" tenements, shaky but fair to look at, with brownstone trimmings and gewgaws. The result was to tempt a lot of the well-housed tenants away. It was a very astonishing instance of perversity to the planners of the benevolent scheme; but, after all, there was nothing strange in it. It is all a matter of education, as I said about the landlord.

That the education comes slowly need excite no surprise. The forces on the other side are ever active. The faculty of the tenement for appropriating to itself every foul thing that comes within its reach, and piling up and intensifying its corruption until out of all proportion to the beginning, is something marvellous. Drop a case of scarlet fever, of measles, or of diphtheria into one of these barracks, and, unless it is caught at the very start and stamped out, the contagion of the one case will sweep block after block, and half people a graveyard. Let the police break up a vile dive, goaded by the angry protests of the neighborhood—forthwith the outcasts set in circulation by the raid betake themselves to the tenements, where in their hired rooms, safe from interference, they set up as many independent centers of contagion, infinitely more destructive, each and every one, than was the known dive before. I am not willing to affirm that this is the police reason for letting so many of the dives alone; but it might well be. They are perfectly familiar with the process, and entirely helpless to prevent it.

This faculty, as inherent in the problem itself—the prodigious increase of the tenement house population that goes on without cessation, and its consequent greater crowding—is the chief obstacle to its solution. In 1869 there were 14,872 tenements in New York, with a population of 468,492 persons. In 1879 the number of the tenements was estimated at 21,000, and their tenants had passed the half-million mark. At the end of the year 1888, when a regular census was made for the first time since 1869, the showing was: 32,390 tenements, with a population of 1,093,701 souls. Today we have 37,316 tenements, including 2,630 rear houses, and their population is over 1,250,000.[3] A large share of this added population, especially of that which came to

us from abroad, crowds in below Fourteenth Street, where the population is already packed beyond reason, and confounds all attempts to
make matters better there. At the same time new slums are constantly
growing up uptown, and have to be kept down with a firm hand. This
drift of the population to the great cities has to be taken into account
as a steady factor. It will probably increase rather than decrease for
many years to come. At the beginning of the century the percentage of our population that lived in cities was as one in twenty-five. In
1880 it was one in four and one-half, and in 1890 the census will in all
probability show it to be one in four. Against such tendencies, in the
absence of suburban outlets for the crowding masses, all remedial
measures must prove more or less ineffective. The "confident belief"
expressed by the Board of Health in 1874, that rapid transit would
solve the problem, is now known to have been a vain hope.[4]

Workingmen, in New York at all events, will live near their work,
no matter at what sacrifice of comfort—one might almost say at
whatever cost, and the city will never be less crowded than it is. To
distribute the crowds as evenly as possible is the effort of the authorities, where nothing better can be done. In the first six months of the
present year 1,068 persons were turned out of not quite two hundred
tenements below Houston Street by the sanitary police on their midnight inspections, and this covered only a very small part of that field.
The uptown tenements were practically left to take care of themselves
in this respect.

The quick change of economic conditions in the city that often
outpaces all plans of relief, rendering useless today what met the demands of the situation well enough yesterday, is another cause of per-
plexity. A common obstacle also—I am inclined to think quite as
common as in Ireland, though we hear less of it in the newspapers—
is the absentee landlord. The home article, who fights for his rights, as
he chooses to consider them, is bad enough; but the absentee land-

lord is responsible for no end of trouble. He was one of the first obstructions the sanitary reformers stumbled over, when the Health Department took hold. It reported in 1869 that many of the tenants were entirely uncared for, and that the only answer to their requests to have the houses put in order was an invitation to pay their rent or get out. "Inquiry often disclosed the fact that the owner of the property was a wealthy gentleman or lady, either living in an aristocratic part of the city, or in a neighboring city, or, as was occasionally found to be the case, in Europe. The property is usually managed entirely by an agent, whose instructions are simple but emphatic: collect the rent in advance, or, failing, eject the occupants." The Committee having the matter in charge proposed to compel owners of tenements with ten families or more to put a housekeeper in the house, who should be held responsible to the Health Department. Unluckily the powers of the Board gave out at that point, and the proposition was never acted upon. Could it have been, much trouble would have been spared the Health Board, and untold suffering the tenants in many houses. The tribe of absentee landlords is by no means extinct in New York. Not a few who fled from across the sea to avoid being crushed by his heel there have groaned under it here, scarcely profiting by the exchange. Sometimes—it can hardly be said in extenuation—the heel that crunches is applied in saddening ignorance. I recall the angry indignation of one of these absentee landlords, a worthy man who, living far away in the country, had inherited city property, when he saw the condition of his slum tenements. The man was shocked beyond expression, all the more because he did not know whom to blame except himself for the state of things that had aroused his wrath, and yet, conscious of the integrity of his intentions, felt that he should not justly be held responsible.

The experience of this landlord points directly to the remedy which the law failed to supply to the early reformers. It has since been fully demonstrated that a competent agent on the premises, a man of the best and the highest stamp, who knows how to instruct and guide with a firm hand, is a prerequisite to the success of any reform tenement scheme. This is a plain business proposition, that has been proved entirely sound in some notable instances of tenement building, of which more hereafter. Even among the poorer tenements, those are always the best in which the owner himself lives. It is a hopeful sign in any case. The difficulty of procuring such assistance without having to pay a ruinous price, is one of the obstructions that have vexed in this city efforts to solve the problem of housing the poor properly, because it presupposes that the effort must be made on a larger scale than has often been attempted.

The readiness with which the tenants respond to intelligent efforts in their behalf, when made under fair conditions, is as surprising as it is gratifying, and fully proves the claim that tenants are only satisfied in filthy and unwholesome surroundings because nothing better is offered. The moral effect is as great as the improvement of their physical health. It is clearly discernible in the better class of tenement dwellers today. The change in the character of the colored population in the few years since it began to move out of the wicked rookeries of the old "Africa" to the decent tenements in Yorkville, furnishes a notable illustration, and a still better one is found in the contrast between the model tenement in the Mulberry Street Bend and the barracks across the way, of which I spoke in the chapter devoted to the Italian. The Italian himself is the strongest argument of all. With his fatal contentment in the filthiest surroundings, he gives undoubted evidence of having in him the instinct of cleanliness that, properly cultivated, would work his rescue in a very little while. It is a queer contradiction, but the fact is patent to anyone who has observed the man in his home life. And he is not alone in this. I came across an instance, this past summer, of how a refined, benevolent personality works like a leaven in even the roughest tenement house crowd. This was no model tenement; far from it. It was a towering barrack in the Tenth Ward, sheltering more than twenty families. All the light and air that entered its interior came through an air shaft two feet square, upon which two bedrooms and the hall gave in every story. In three years I had known of two domestic tragedies, prompted by poverty and justifiable disgust with life, occurring in the house, and had come to look upon it as a typically bad tenement, quite beyond the pale of possible improvement. What was my surprise, when chance led me to it once more after a while, to find the character of the occupants entirely changed. Some of the old ones were there still, but they did not seem to be the same people. I discovered the secret to be the new housekeeper, a tidy, mild-mannered, but exceedingly strict little body, who had a natural faculty of drawing her depraved surroundings within the beneficent sphere of her strong sympathy, and withal of exacting respect for her orders. The worst elements had been banished from the house in short order under her management, and for the rest a new era of self-respect had dawned. They were, as a body, as vastly superior to the general run of their class as they had before seemed below it. And this had been effected in the short space of a single year.

My observations on this point are more than confirmed by those of nearly all the practical tenement reformers I have known, who have patiently held to the course they had laid down. One of these, whose experience exceeds that of all of the rest together, and whose influence for good has been very great, said to me recently: "I hold that not ten percent of the people now living in tenements would refuse to avail themselves of the best improved conditions offered, and come fully up to the use of them, properly instructed; but they cannot get them. They are up to them now, fully, if the chances were only offered. They don't have to come up. It is all a gigantic mistake on the part of the public, of which these poor people are the victims. I have built homes for more than five hundred families in fourteen years, and I have been getting daily more faith in human nature from my work among the poor tenants, though approaching that nature on a plane and under conditions that could scarcely promise better for disappointment." It is true that my friend has built his houses in Brooklyn; but human nature does not differ greatly on the two shores of the East River. For those who think it does, it may be well to remember that only five years ago the Tenement House Commission summed up the situation in this city in the declaration that, "the condition of the tenants is in advance of the houses which they occupy," quite the severest arraignment of the tenement that had yet been uttered.[5]

The many philanthropic efforts that have been made in the last few years to render less intolerable the lot of the tenants in the homes where many of them must continue to live, have undoubtedly had their effect in creating a disposition to accept better things, that will make plainer sailing for future builders of model tenements. In many ways, as in the "College Settlement" of courageous girls, the Neighborhood Guilds, through the efforts of the King's Daughters, and numerous other schemes of practical mission work, the poor and the well-to-do have been brought closer together, in an everyday companionship that cannot but be productive of the best results, to the one who gives no less than to the one who receives.[6] And thus, as a good lady wrote to me once, though the problem stands yet unsolved, more perplexing than ever; though the bright spots in the dreary picture be too often bright only by comparison, and many of the expedients hit upon for relief sad makeshifts, we can dimly discern behind it all that good is somehow working out of even this slough of despond the while it is deepening and widening in our sight, and in His own good season, if we labor on with courage and patience, will bear fruit sixty and a hundred fold.

XXV

How the Case Stands

WHAT, THEN, are the bald facts with which we have to deal in New York?

I. That we have a tremendous, ever swelling crowd of wage earners which it is our business to house decently.

II. That it is not housed decently.

III. That it must be so housed *here* for the present, and for a long time to come, all schemes of suburban relief being as yet utopian, impracticable.

IV. That it pays high enough rents to entitle it to be so housed, as a right.

V. That nothing but our own slothfulness is in the way of so housing it, since "the condition of the tenants is in advance of the condition of the houses which they occupy" (Report of Tenement House Commission).

VI. That the security of the one no less than of the other half
   demands, on sanitary, moral, and economic grounds, that it be
   decently housed.
VII. That it will pay to do it. As an investment, I mean, and in hard
   cash. This I shall immediately proceed to prove.
VIII. That the tenement has come to stay, and must itself be the
   solution of the problem with which it confronts us.

This is the fact from which we cannot get away, however we may
deplore it. Doubtless the best would be to get rid of it altogether; but
as we cannot, all argument on that score may at this time be dismissed
as idle. The practical question is what to do with the tenement. I
watched a Mott Street landlord, the owner of a row of barracks that
have made no end of trouble for the health authorities for twenty
years, solve that question for himself the other day. His way was to
give the wretched pile a coat of paint, and put a gorgeous tin cornice
on with the year 1890 in letters a yard long. From where I stood watching the operation, I looked down upon the same dirty crowds camping on the roof, foremost among them an Italian mother with two
stark-naked children who had apparently never made the acquaintance of a washtub. That was a landlord's way, and will not get us out
of the mire.

The "flat" is another way that does not solve the problem. Rather, it
extends it. The flat is not a model, though it is a modern, tenement. It
gets rid of some of the nuisances of the low tenement, and of the
worst of them, the overcrowding—if it gets rid of them at all—at a
cost that takes it at once out of the catalogue of "homes for the poor,"
while imposing some of the evils from which they suffer upon those
who ought to escape from them.

There are three effective ways of dealing with the tenements in
New York:

I. By law.

II. By remodelling and making the most out of the old houses.

III. By building new, model tenements.

Private enterprise—conscience, to put it in the category of duties, where it belongs—must do the lion's share under these last two heads. Of what the law has effected I have spoken already. The drastic measures adopted in Paris, in Glasgow, and in London are not practicable here on anything like as large a scale.[1] Still it can, under strong pressure of public opinion, rid us of the worst plague spots. The Mulberry Street Bend will go the way of the Five Points when all the red tape that binds the hands of municipal effort has been unwound. Prizes were offered in public competition, some years ago, for the best plans of modern tenement houses. It may be that we shall see the day when the building of model tenements will be encouraged by subsidies in the way of a rebate of taxes. Meanwhile the arrest and summary punishment of landlords, or their agents, who persistently violate law and decency, will have a salutary effect. If a few of the wealthy absentee landlords, who are the worst offenders, could be got within the jurisdiction of the city, and by arrest be compelled to employ proper overseers, it would be a proud day for New York. To remedy the overcrowding, with which the night inspections of the sanitary police cannot keep step, tenements may eventually have to be licensed, as now the lodging houses, to hold so many tenants, and no more; or the state may have to bring down the rents that cause the crowding, by assuming the right to regulate them as it regulates the fares on the elevated roads. I throw out the suggestion, knowing quite well that it is open to attack. It emanated originally from one of the brightest minds that have had to struggle officially with this tenement house question in the last ten years. In any event, to succeed, reform by law must aim at making it unprofitable to own a bad tenement. At best, it is apt to travel at a snail's pace, while the enemy it pursues is putting the best foot foremost.

In this matter of profit the law ought to have its strongest ally in the landlord himself, though the reverse is the case. This condition of things I believe to rest on a monstrous error. It cannot be that tenement property that is worth preserving at all can continue to yield larger returns, if allowed to run down, than if properly cared for and kept in good repair. The point must be reached, and soon, where the cost of repairs, necessary with a house full of the lowest, most ignorant tenants, must overbalance the saving of the first few years of neglect; for this class is everywhere the most destructive, as well as the poorest paying. I have the experience of owners, who have found this out to their cost, to back me up in the assertion, even if it were not the statement of a plain business fact that proves itself. I do not include tenement property that is deliberately allowed to fall into decay because at some future time the ground will be valuable for business or other purposes. There is unfortunately enough of that kind in New York, often leasehold property owned by wealthy estates or soulless corporations that oppose all their great influence to the efforts of the law in behalf of their tenants.

There is abundant evidence, on the other hand, that it can be made to pay to improve and make the most of the worst tenement property, even in the most wretched locality. The example set by Miss Ellen Collins in her Water Street houses will always stand as a decisive answer to all doubts on this point.[2] It is quite ten years since she bought three old tenements at the corner of Water and Roosevelt Streets, then as now one of the lowest localities in the city. Since then she has leased three more adjoining her purchase, and so much of Water Street has at all events been purified. Her first effort was to let in the light in the hallways, and with the darkness disappeared, as if by magic, the heaps of refuse that used to be piled up beside the sinks. A few of the most refractory tenants disappeared with them, but a very considerable proportion stayed, conforming readily to the new rules, and are there yet. It should here be stated that Miss Collins's tenants are distinctly of the poorest. Her purpose was to experiment with this class, and her experiment has been more than satisfactory. Her plan was, as she puts it herself, fair play between tenant and landlord. To this end the rents were put as low as consistent with the idea of a business investment that must return a reasonable interest to be successful. The houses were thoroughly refitted with proper plumbing. A competent janitor was put in charge to see that the rules were observed by the tenants, when Miss Collins herself was not there. Of late years she has had to give very little time to personal superintendence, and the caretaker told me only the other day that very little was needed. The houses seemed to run themselves in the groove once laid down. Once the reputed haunt of thieves, they have become the most orderly in the neighborhood. Clothes are left hanging on the lines all night with impunity, and the pretty flower beds in the yard where the children not only from the six houses, but of the whole block, play, skip, and swing, are undisturbed. The tenants, by the way, provide the flowers themselves in the spring, and take all the more pride in them because they are their own. The six houses contain forty-five families, and there "has never been any need of putting up a bill." As to the income from the property, Miss Collins said to me last August: "I have had six and even six and three-quarters percent on the capital invested; on the whole, you may safely say five and a half percent. This I regard as entirely satisfactory." It should be added that she has persistently refused to let the corner store, now occupied by a butcher, as a saloon; or her income from it might have been considerably increased.

Miss Collins's experience is of value chiefly as showing what can be accomplished with the worst possible material, by the sort of personal interest in the poor that alone will meet their real needs. All the charity in the world, scattered with the most lavish hand, will not take its place. "Fair play" between landlord and tenant is the key, too long mislaid, that unlocks the door to success everywhere as it did for Miss Collins. She has not lacked imitators whose experience has been akin to her own. The case of Gotham Court has been already cited. On the other hand, instances are not wanting of landlords who have undertaken the task, but have tired of it or sold their property before it had been fully redeemed, with the result that it relapsed into its former bad condition faster than it had improved, and the tenants with it. I am inclined to think that such houses are liable to fall even below the average level. Backsliding in brick and mortar does not greatly differ from similar performances in flesh and blood.

Backed by a strong and steady sentiment, such as these pioneers have evinced, that would make it the personal business of wealthy owners with time to spare to look after their tenants, the law would be able in a very short time to work a salutary transformation in the worst quarters, to the lasting advantage, I am well persuaded, of the landlord no less than the tenant. Unfortunately, it is in this quality of personal effort that the sentiment of interest in the poor, upon which we have to depend, is too often lacking. People who are willing to give money feel that that ought to be enough. It is not. The money thus given is too apt to be wasted along with the sentiment that prompted the gift.

Even when it comes to the third of the ways I spoke of as effective in dealing with the tenement house problem, the building of model structures, the personal interest in the matter must form a large share of the capital invested, if it is to yield full returns. Where that is the case, there is even less doubt about its paying, with ordinary business management, than in the case of reclaiming an old building, which is, like putting life into a defunct newspaper, pretty apt to be uphill work. Model tenement building has not been attempted in New York on anything like as large a scale as in many other great cities, and it is perhaps owing to this, in a measure, that a belief prevails that it cannot succeed here. This is a wrong notion entirely. The various undertakings of that sort that have been made here under intelligent management have, as far as I know, all been successful.

From the managers of the two best-known experiments in model tenement building in the city, the Improved Dwellings Association and the Tenement House Building Company,[3] I have letters dated last August, declaring their enterprises eminently successful. There is no reason why their experience should not be conclusive. That the Philadelphia plan is not practicable in New York is not a good reason why our own plan, which is precisely the reverse of our neighbor's, should not be. In fact it is an argument for its success. The very reason why we cannot house our working masses in cottages, as has been done in Philadelphia—viz., that they must live on Manhattan Island, where the land is too costly for small houses—is the best guarantee of the success of the model tenement house, properly located and managed. The drift in tenement building, as in everything else, is toward concentration, and helps smooth the way. Four families on the floor, twenty in the house, is the rule of today. As the crowds increase, the need of guiding this drift into safe channels becomes more urgent. The larger the scale upon which the model tenement is planned, the more certain the promise of success. The utmost ingenuity cannot build a house for sixteen or twenty families on a lot 25 × 100 feet in the middle of a block like it, that shall give them the amount of air and sunlight to be had by the erection of a dozen or twenty houses on a common plan around a central yard. This was the view of the committee that awarded the prizes for the best plan for the conventional tenement, ten years ago.[4] It coupled its verdict with the emphatic declaration that, in its view, it was "impossible to secure the requirements of physical and moral health within these narrow and arbitrary limits." Houses have been built since on better plans than any the committee saw, but its judgment stands unimpaired. A point, too, that is not to be overlooked, is the reduced cost of expert superintendence—the first condition of successful management—in the larger buildings.

The Improved Dwellings Association put up its block of thirteen houses in East Seventy-second Street nine years ago. Their cost, estimated at about $240,000 with the land, was increased to $285,000 by troubles with the contractor engaged to build them. Thus the Association's task did not begin under the happiest auspices. Unexpected expenses came to deplete its treasury. The neighborhood was new and not crowded at the start. No expense was spared, and the benefit of all the best and most recent experience in tenement building was given to the tenants. The families were provided with from two to four rooms, all "outer" rooms, of course, at rents ranging from $14 per month for the four on the ground floor, to $6.25 for two rooms on the top floor. Coal lifts, ash chutes, common laundries in the basement, and free baths, are features of these buildings that were then new enough to be looked upon with suspicion by the doubting Thomases who predicted disaster. There are rooms in the block for 218 families, and when I looked in recently all but nine of the apartments were let. One of the nine was rented while I was in the building. The superintendent told me that he had little trouble with disorderly tenants, though the buildings shelter all sorts of people. Mr. W. Bayard Cutting, the President of the Association, writes to me:

"By the terms of subscription to the stock before incorporation, dividends were limited to five percent on the stock of the Improved Dwellings Association. These dividends have been paid (two percent each six months) ever since the expiration of the first six months of the buildings operation. All surplus has been expended upon the buildings. New and expensive roofs have been put on for the comfort of such tenants as might choose to use them. The buildings have been completely painted inside and out in a manner not contemplated at the outset. An expensive set of fire escapes has been put on at the command of the Fire Department, and a considerable number of other improvements made. *I regard the experiment as eminently successful and satisfactory*, particularly when it is considered that the buildings were the first erected in this city upon anything like a large scale, where it was proposed to meet the architectural difficulties that present themselves in the tenement house problem. I have no doubt that the experiment could be tried today with the improved knowledge which has come with time, and a much larger return be shown upon the investment. The results referred to have been attained in spite of the provision which prevents the selling of liquor upon the Association's premises. You are aware, of course, how much larger rent can be obtained for a liquor saloon than for an ordinary store. An investment at five percent net upon real estate security worth more than the principal sum, ought to be considered desirable."

The Tenement House Building Company made its "experiment" in a much more difficult neighborhood, Cherry Street, some six years later. Its houses shelter many Russian Jews, and the difficulty of keeping them in order is correspondingly increased, particularly as there are no ash chutes in the houses. It has been necessary even to shut the children out of the yards upon which the kitchen windows give, lest they be struck by something thrown out by the tenants, and killed. It is the Cherry Street style, not easily got rid of. Nevertheless, the houses are well kept. Of the one hundred and six "apartments," only four were vacant in August. Professor Edwin R. A. Seligman, the secretary of the company, writes to me: "The tenements are now a decided success." In the three years since they were built, they have returned an interest of from five to five and a half percent on the capital invested. The original intention of making the tenants profit sharers on a plan of rent insurance, under which all earnings above four percent would be put to the credit of the tenants, has not yet been carried out.

A scheme of dividends to tenants on a somewhat similar plan has been carried out by a Brooklyn builder, Mr. A. T. White, who has devoted a life of beneficent activity to tenement building, and whose experience, though it has been altogether across the East River, I regard as justly applying to New York as well. He so regards it himself. Discussing the cost of building, he says: "There is not the slightest reason to doubt that the financial result of a similar undertaking in any tenement-house district of New York City would be equally good. . . . High cost of land is no detriment, provided the value is made by the pressure of people seeking residence there. Rents in New York City bear a higher ratio to Brooklyn rents than would the cost of land and building in the one city to that in the other." The assertion that Brooklyn furnishes a better class of tenants than the tenement districts in New York would not be worth discussing seriously, even if Mr. White did not meet it himself with the statement that the proportion of day laborers and sewing women in his houses is greater than in any of the London model tenements, showing that they reach the humblest classes.

Mr. White has built homes for five hundred poor families since he began his work, and has made it pay well enough to allow good tenants a share in the profits, averaging nearly one month's rent out of the twelve, as a premium upon promptness and order. The plan of his last tenements, reproduced on p. 275, may be justly regarded as the *beau ideal* of the model tenement for a great city like New York.[5] It embodies all the good features of Sir Sydney Waterlow's London plan, with improvements suggested by the builder's own experience.[6] Its chief merit is that it gathers three hundred real homes, not simply three hundred families, under one roof. Three tenants, it will be seen,

General Plan of the Riverside Buildings (A. T. White's) in Brooklyn

Floor Plan of One Division in the Riverside Buildings, Showing Six "Apartments"

everywhere live together. Of the rest of the three hundred they may never know, rarely see, one. Each has his private front door. The common hall, with all that it stands for, has disappeared. The fireproof stairs are outside the house, a perfect fire escape. Each tenant has his own scullery and ash flue. There are no air shafts, for they are not needed. Every room, under the admirable arrangement of the plan, looks out either upon the street or the yard, that is nothing less than a great park with a playground set apart for the children, where they may dig in the sand to their hearts' content. Weekly concerts are given in the park by a brass band. The drying of clothes is done on the roof, where racks are fitted up for the purpose. The outside stairways end in turrets that give the buildings a very smart appearance. Mr. White never has any trouble with his tenants, though he gathers in the poorest; nor do his tenements have anything of the "institution character" that occasionally attaches to ventures of this sort, to their damage. They are like a big village of contented people, who live in peace with one another because they have elbowroom even under one big roof.

Enough has been said to show that model tenements can be built successfully and made to pay in New York, if the owner will be content with the five or six percent he does not even dream of when investing his funds in "governments" at three or four. It is true that in the latter case he has only to cut off his coupons and cash them. But the extra trouble of looking after his tenement property, that is the condition of his highest and lasting success, is the penalty exacted for the sins of our fathers that "shall be visited upon the children, unto the third and fourth generation." We shall indeed be well off, if it stop there. I fear there is too much reason to believe that our own iniquities must be added to transmit the curse still further. And yet, such is the leavening influence of a good deed in that dreary desert of sin and suffering, that the erection of a single good tenement has the power to change, gradually but surely, the character of a whole bad block. It sets up a standard to which the neighborhood must rise, if it cannot succeed in dragging it down to its own low level.

And so this task, too, has come to an end. Whatsoever a man soweth, that shall he also reap. I have aimed to tell the truth as I saw it. If this book shall have borne ever so feeble a hand in garnering a harvest of justice, it has served its purpose. While I was writing these lines I went down to the sea, where thousands from the city were enjoying their summer rest. The ocean slumbered under a cloudless sky. Gentle waves washed lazily over the white sand, where children fled before them with screams of laughter. Standing there and watching their play, I was told that during the fierce storms of winter it happened that this sea, now so calm, rose in rage and beat down, broke over the bluff, sweeping all before it. No barrier built by human hands had power to stay it then. The sea of a mighty population, held in galling fetters, heaves uneasily in the tenements. Once already our city, to which have come the duties and responsibilities of metropolitan greatness before it was able to fairly measure its task, has felt the swell of its resistless flood. If it rise once more, no human power may avail to check it. The gap between the classes in which it surges, unseen, unsuspected by the thoughtless, is widening day by day. No tardy enactment of law, no political expedient, can close it. Against all other dangers our system of government may offer defence and shelter; against this not. I know of but one bridge that will carry us over safe, a bridge founded upon justice and built of human hearts. I believe that the danger of such conditions as are fast growing up around us is greater for the very freedom which they mock. The words of the poet, with whose lines I prefaced this book, are truer today, have far deeper meaning to us, than when they were penned forty years ago:

Think ye that building shall endure
Which shelters the noble and crushes the poor?

APPENDIX:
Statistics Bearing on the Tenement Problem

Statistics of population were left out of the text in the hope that the results of this year's census would be available as a basis for calculation before the book went to press. They are now at hand, but their correctness is disputed. The statisticians of the Health Department claim that New York's population has been underestimated a hundred thousand at least, and they appear to have the best of the argument. A recount is called for, and the printer will not wait. Such statistics as follow have been based on the Health Department estimates, except where the census source is given. The extent of the quarrel of official figures may be judged from this one fact, that the ordinarily conservative and careful calculations of the Sanitary Bureau make the death rate of New York, in 1889, 25.19 for the thousand of a population of 1,575,073, while the census would make it 26.76 in a population of 1,482,273.

Population of New York, 1880 (census)	1,206,299
" London, 1881 "	3,816,483
" Philadelphia, 1880 "	846,980
" Brooklyn, 1880 "	566,689
" Boston, 1880 "	362,535
" New York, 1889 (estimated)	1,575,073
" London, 1889 "	4,351,738
" Philadelphia, 1889 "	1,040,245
" Brooklyn, " "	814,505
" Boston, " "	420,000
" New York under five years of age, in 1880	140,327
" " " " " 1889 (estimated)	182,770

Population of tenements in New York in 1869* (census)	468,492
" " " " 1888† "	1,093,701
" " " " " under five years of age	143,243

Population of New York in 1880 (census)	1,206,299
" Manhattan Island in 1880 (census)	1,164,673
" Tenth Ward in 1880 (census)	47,554
" Eleventh Ward " "	68,778
" Thirteenth Ward in 1880 (census)	37,797
" New York in 1890 (census)	1,513,501
" Manhattan Island in 1890 (census)	1,440,101
" Tenth Ward in 1890 (census)	57,514
" Eleventh Ward " "	75,708
" Thirteenth Ward in 1890 (census)	45,882

* In 1869 a tenement was a house occupied by four families or more.
† In 1888, a tenement was a house occupied by three families or more.

Number of acres in New York City			24,890
"	"	Manhattan Island	12,673
"	"	Tenth Ward	110
"	"	Eleventh Ward	196
"	"	Thirteenth Ward	107

Density of population per acre in 1880, New York City	48.4
Density of population per acre in 1880, Manhattan Island	92.6
Density of population per acre in 1880, Tenth Ward	432.3
Density of population per acre in 1880, Eleventh Ward	350.9
Density of population per acre in 1880, Thirteenth Ward	353.2
Density of population per acre in 1890, New York City (census)	60.08
Density of population per acre in 1890, Manhattan Island (census)	114.53
Density of population per acre in 1890, Tenth Ward (census)	522.00
Density of population per acre in 1890, Eleventh Ward (census)	386.00
Density of population per acre in 1890, Thirteenth Ward (census)	428.8
Density of population to the square mile in 1880, New York City (census)	30,976
Density of population to the square mile in 1880, Manhattan Island (census)	41,264
Density of population to the square mile in 1880, Tenth Ward (census)	276,672
Density of population to the square mile in 1880, Eleventh Ward (census)	224,576
Density of population to the square mile in 1880, Thirteenth Ward (census)	226,048

Density of population to the square mile in 1890, New York City (census)	38,451
Density of population to the square mile in 1890, Manhattan Island (census)	73,299
Density of population to the square mile in 1890, Tenth Ward (census)	334,080
Density of population to the square mile in 1890, Eleventh Ward (census)	246,040
Density of population to the square mile in 1890, Thirteenth Ward (census)	274,432

Number of persons to a dwelling in New York, 1880 (census)	16.37
Number of persons to a dwelling in London, 1881 (census)	7.9
Number of persons to a dwelling in Philadelphia, 1880 (census)	5.79
Number of persons to a dwelling in Brooklyn, 1880 (census)	9.11
Number of persons to a dwelling in Boston, 1880 (census)	8.26

Number of deaths in New York, 1880		31,937
"	" London, 1881	81,431
"	" Philadelphia, 1880	17,711
"	" Brooklyn, 1880	13,222
"	" Boston, 1880	8,612

Death rate of New York, 1880		26.47
"	London, 1881	21.3
"	Philadelphia, 1880	20.91
"	Brooklyn, 1880	23.33
"	Boston, 1880	23.75

Number of deaths in New York, 1889	39,679
" " London, 1889	75,683
" " Philadelphia, 1889	20,536
" " Brooklyn, 1889	18,288
" " Boston, 1889	10,259

Death rate of New York, 1889	25.19
" London, 1889	17.4
" Philadelphia, 1889	19.7
" Brooklyn, 1889	22.5
" Boston, 1889	24.42

For every person who dies there are always two disabled by illness, so that there was a regular average of 79,358 New Yorkers on the sick list at any moment last year. It is usual to count 28 cases of sickness the year round for every death, and this would give a total for the year 1889 of 1,111,082 of illness of all sorts.

Number of deaths in tenements in New York, 1869	13,285
" " " " " 1888	24,842

Death rate in tenements in New York, 1869	28.35
" " " " 1888	22.71

This is exclusive of deaths in institutions, properly referable to the tenements in most cases. The adult death rate is found to decrease in the larger tenements of newer construction. The child mortality increases, reaching 114.04 percent of 1,000 living in houses containing between 60 and 80 tenants. From this point it decreases with the adult death rate.

Number of deaths in prisons, New York, 1889	85
" " hospitals, New York, 1889	6,102

"	"	lunatic asylums, New York, 1889	448
"	"	institutions for children, New York, 1889	522
"	"	homes for aged, New York, 1889	238
"	"	almshouse, New York, 1889	424
"	"	other institutions, New York, 1889	162

Number of burials in city cemetery (paupers), New York, 1889	3,815
Percentage of such burials on total	9.64
Number of tenants weeded out of overcrowded tenements, New York, 1889	1,246
Number of tenants weeded out of overcrowded tenements, in first half of 1890*	1,068
Number of sick poor visited by summer corps of doctors, New York, 1890	16,501

Police Statistics

	Males	Females
Arrests made by the police in 1889	62,274	19,926
Number of arrests for drunkenness and disorderly conduct	20,253	8,981
Number of arrests for disorderly conduct	10,953	7,477
" " assault and battery	4,534	497
" " theft	4,399	721
" " robbery	247	10
" " vagrancy	1,686	947
Prisoners unable to read or write	2,399	1,281
Number of lost children found in the streets, 1889		2,968
" sick and destitute cared for, 1889		2,753
Found sick in the streets		1,211

* These figures represent less than two hundred of the worst tenements below Houston Street.

Number of pawnshops in city, 1889   110
    "   cheap lodging houses, 1889   270
    "   saloons, 1889   7,884

Tenements

Immigrants landed at Castle Garden in 20 years, ending   5,335,396
  with 1889
Immigrants landed at Castle Garden in 1889   349,233
Immigrants from England landed at Castle Garden in 1889   46,214
Immigrants from Scotland landed at Castle Garden in 1889   11,415
Immigrants from Ireland landed at Castle Garden in 1889   43,090
Immigrants from Germany landed at Castle Garden in 1889   75,458

	1883	1884	1885	1886	1887	1888	1889
Italy	25,485	14,076	16,033	29,312	44,274	43,927	28,810
Russia and Poland	7,577	12,432	16,578	23,987	33,203	33,052	31,329
Hungary	13,160	15,797	11,129	18,135	17,719	12,905	15,678
Bohemia	4,877	7,093	6,697	4,222	6,449	3,982	5,412

Tenements

Number of tenements in New York, December 1, 1888   32,390
Number built from June 1, 1888, to August 1, 1890   3,733
Rear tenements in existence, August 1, 1890   2,630
Total number of tenements, August 1, 1890   37,316
Estimated population of tenements, August 1, 1890   1,250,000
Estimated number of children under five years in   163,712
  tenements, 1890

Corner tenements may cover all of the lot, except 4 feet at the rear. Tenements in the block may only cover seventy-eight percent of the lot. They must have a rear yard 10 feet wide, and air shafts or open courts equal to twelve percent of the lot.

Tenements or apartment houses must not be built over 70 feet high in streets 60 feet wide.

Tenements or apartment houses must not be built over 80 feet high in streets wider than 60 feet.

Notes

Preface

1. "Doctor Roger Sherman Tracy, physician and sanitarian, joined the New York City Department of Health in 1870 as a sanitary inspector and later became registrar of records." Jacob A. Riis, *The Making of an American*, ed. Roy Lubove (New York, 1966), p. 99.

Epigraph

1. "A Parable." The poem was written in 1848.

Introduction

1. The quotation is commonly attributed to Rabelais: "There I began to think, that it is very true which is commonly said, that the one half of the world knoweth not how the other half liveth." This refers to a hitherto unreported land of cities, farms, and hills existing inside the giant Pantagruel's mouth, which the narrator explored for six months. François Rabelais, *Works*, trans. and ed. Albert J. Nock and Catherine R. Wilson (New York, 1931), book 2, chap. 32, p. 427.

The phrase which makes Riis's title seems to have been common to New York reform for many years prior to his employing it. John H. Griscom in his pioneering *The Sanitary Condition of the Laboring Population of New York* (New York, 1845), p. 5, uses the phrase in referring to the investigations of British and French sanitarians. Later it appeared in the title of some articles on slums and the need for lodging houses in "Our Homeless Poor; or 'How the Other Half of the World Lives,'" *Frank Leslie's Illustrated Newspaper,* March 2–23, 1872.

2. I was unable to locate the original text of the testimony of Dr. Elisha Harris, Corresponding Secretary of the Prison Association of New York, given before the legislative committee appointed to investigate the increase of crime in the state, but the selection used by Riis up to the elision was reprinted in New York Association for the Improvement of the Condition of the Poor [Hereafter cited as N.Y.A.I.C.P.], *Thirty-fifth Annual Report, 1878* (New York, 1878), pp. 33–34.

3. Citizens' Association of New York, *Report of the Council of Hygiene and Public Health upon the Sanitary Condition of the City* (New York, 1865), p. lxix, reported their survey of the city taken during December 1864, returned 15,309 "tenant houses" with an average of seven and one sixth persons per structure.

4. New York City, Board of Health, *Fifth and Sixth Annual Reports, 1874–1875* (New York, 1876), p. 7.

5. William Marcy Tweed (1823–1878), notorious boss of New York City, was born at 1 Cherry Street (formerly Cherry Hill) in what was then a middle-class neighborhood. His father was a successful manufacturer of chairs and had an interest in a brushmaking firm. Alexander B. Callow, Jr., *The Tweed Ring* (New York, 1966), pp. 12–13.

Citizens' Association of New York, *Report of the Council of Hygiene,* pp. 43–65, indicated that this neighborhood was very much a slum by the time of the Civil War. In 1872, however, Governor Alfred E. Smith was born at 174 South Street, just three blocks from Tweed's birthplace.

6. N.Y.A.I.C.P., *Forty-sixth Annual Report, 1889* (New York, 1889), p. 27.

7. "Each step made seemed to tread upon new fields of repulsive research, each startling fact of *misery* revealed was speedily paralleled by some close-following example of a kindred *vice* or *crime,* until the conclusion forced itself upon the reflection of all, that certain conditions and associations of human life and habitation are the prolific parents of corresponding habits and morals." *Report of the Select Committee Appointed*

to Examine into the Condition of Tenant Houses in New York and Brooklyn,
Assembly Document 205, March 9, 1857, p. 3.

8. The quotation comes from New York State, Metropolitan Board of
Health, *Fourth Annual Report, 1869* (New York, 1870), p. 24. I did not find in
the published testimony any evidence of 40 percent or 100 percent profits as
mentioned here by Riis in the text and notes. Witnesses testifying before the
senate commission mention net profits of 6–15 percent only. New York State,
Tenement House Commission, *Report*, Senate Document 36, February 17,
1885, pp. 96, 105–106. This senate commission was the one chaired by Riis's
friend Felix Adler, and Riis may be writing from memory of the hearings
which he attended.

9. Alfred T. White, *Improved Dwellings for the Working Classes: The
Need, and the Way to Meet It on Strict Commercial Principles, in New York
and Other Cities* (New York, 1879), p. 44.

I. Genesis of the Tenement

1. The Cherry Hill district, off Pearl Street in the Lower East Side, was
the site of a number of mansions in Revolutionary times. President
Washington occupied the home of the merchant Walter Franklin at the
intersection of Cherry, Pearl, and Dover Streets from April 30, 1789, to
February 23, 1790. John Hancock lived at 5 Cherry Street. One of the piers of
the Brooklyn Bridge now covers the site of the house Washington lived in.
Works Progress Administration, *New York City Guide* (New York, 1946),
pp. 114–115.

2. This quotation and those on the next few pages are taken from *Report
of the Select Committee Appointed to Examine into the Condition of Tenant
Houses in New York and Brooklyn*, Assembly Document 205, March 9, 1857,
pp. 11–13. Riis is freely adapting the text, taking his quotations out of
sequence, paraphrasing for his own purposes. He does not, however, distort
the report, which was written in a style of high moral indignation.

3. N.Y.A.I.C.P., *Fourteenth Annual Report, 1857* (New York, 1857), p. 18.

4. "New York was the most extravagant city in the known world as far as
charity was concerned. No other community ever had been so taxed with
providing for the destitute of all climes. They came bankrupt in character as
well as finances, wrecks of incapacity, miseducation, prodigality, and
crime—not only from across the ocean but from every part of our own
continent. The metropolis was a general asylum for vagrants. The brains of

political philosophers were vexed with the problem of how to provide most effectually for both poverty and vice, while humanity never faltered in the matter of dollars and cents." Martha J. Lamb and Mrs. Burton Harrison, *History of the City of New York: Its Origin, Rise, and Progress* (New York, 1877–1880), II, 728.

II. The Awakening

1. *Report of the Committee on Public Health, Medical Colleges and Societies, Relative to the Condition of Tenement Houses in the Cities of New York and Brooklyn,* Assembly Document 156, March 8, 1867, Laws of the State of New York, 90th sess., 1867 c. 908, sec. 17.

2. A citizen's committee formed from the active members of the State Charities Aid Association persuaded many of the clergy of New York to set aside February 23, 1879, as "Tenement House Sunday." Lawrence Veiller, *Tenement House Reform in New York, 1834–1900* (New York, 1900), pp. 22–23. The committee published a seven-page pamphlet for distribution to the cooperating ministers, State Charities Aid Association, Special Subcommittee, *The Tenement House System in New York* (New York, 1879).

3. Citizens' Association of New York, *Report of the Council of Hygiene and Public Health upon the Sanitary Condition of the City* (New York, 1865), p. lxxv.

4. This definition of a tenement was the one established by the 1867 New York statute.

III. The Mixed Crowd

1. Collect Pond was the largest pond on Manhattan Island. It covered an area between Baxter, Elm, Duane, and Canal Streets. A project to fill in the pond began in 1800, and when this was completed, the pond became the site of the famous Egyptian-style prison, "the Tombs," Citizens' Association of New York, *Report of the Council of Hygiene and Public Health upon the Sanitary Condition of the City* (New York, 1865), pp. 75–76.

IV. The Downtown Back Alleys

1. Gotham Court, a tenement barracks at 36–38 Cherry Street, was a classic object of housing reform and slum investigation. Riis used a photograph of it for the frontispiece of the 1890 edition of *How the Other Half Lives,* and it appeared in a number of other books and pamphlets over

the next twenty years. A full report by Dr. Ezra R. Pulling, Visiting Physician for the City of New York, made in 1859–1860, was reprinted in part and accompanied by plans and elevations in Citizens' Association of New York, *Report of the Council of Hygiene and Public Health upon the Sanitary Condition of the City* (New York, 1865), pp. 49–55.

2. The King's Daughters were a group of Brooklyn women who belonged to a Baptist service club which ran a day nursery for children of working mothers. They responded to Riis's call for flowers for the slums and in time became the sponsors of a Henry Street Settlement named after the author. See Jacob A. Riis Neighborhood Settlement, *Statement of Clubs and Work* (New York, 1900); *First Report of the King's Daughters Day Nursery,* 950 Atlantic Avenue, Brooklyn (New York, 1889); Louise Ware, *Jacob A. Riis, Police Reporter, Reformer, Useful Citizen* (New York, 1938), pp. 66, 111, 190, 252–253. (The first two items are pamphlets in the collection of the New York Public Library.)

3. There are so many slang uses of the word "can" in the American language that it is difficult to interpret the phrase "can racket" with precision. The context clearly suggests some sort of drunken brawl.

4. A "growler" was a can or pitcher used to carry beer from the saloon where it was sold by the measure. See p. 212.

5. Riis trimmed this quotation and slightly altered its ending thereby omitting some interesting material on the resources of New York's poor. After the word "consumption" the original text continues "and was earning a precarious living by gathering roots and flowers in the woods and selling them on the streets. But the inclement weather had kept him from going out, and a sick child claimed the mother's attention, so that these parents though willing were unable to provide either bread or fire for their little ones." The report goes on to say that the family was aided by the society, moved to better quarters, and that the father was better now owing to the help and care of his friends. The Board of Health was notified, and steps were taken to repair the tenement. N.Y.A.I.C.P., *Forty-fifth Annual Report, 1888* (New York, 1888), pp. 56–57.

V. The Italian in New York

1. The inquiries were probably made by Michigan Representative Melbourne H. Ford's Select Committee on Investigation of Foreign Immigration, which held hearings in New York and other cities during 1889

on violations of prohibitions against contracts for importation of workers. *House Report*, 50th Cong., 2d sess., no. 3792, 1889, vol. I.

VI. The Bend

1. The Five Points was the symbol of the New York slums in the pre-Civil War reform and sanitary literature. It consisted of a series of decayed houses and an old abandoned brewery immediately surrounding the intersection of five streets and alleys. The principal streets were Worth, Park, and Baxter (formerly Orange). One block east was "the Bend," which Riis gave several meanings in this chapter. In its narrowest sense it was that section of Mulberry Street which bent between Bayard and Park Streets. "The Bend Proper" was the entire area bounded by Bayard, Park, Mulberry, and Baxter Streets. Riis published the mortality statistics for these blocks in a table in this chapter, thereby repeating the study of New York State, Tenement House Commission, *Report*, Senate Document, February 17, 1885, Appendix E, pp. 232–235. Riis also uses the term "the Bend District" to refer to the entire area between Broadway and the Bowery, Canal and Chatham Streets.

2. Paradise Park was a small square formed by the pulling down of the old brewery and houses at the Five Points. It is now incorporated in the larger Columbia Park opposite the state office building at Baxter and Worth Streets. Works Progress Administration, *New York City Guide* (New York, 1946), p. 103.

3. Citizens' Association of New York, *Report of the Council of Hygiene and Public Health upon the Sanitary Condition of the City* (New York, 1865), p. 73.

4. Modern scholars do not give these "banks" such a sinister interpretation as Riis did. The Italian banks were, as Riis describes, multipurpose institutions which sprang up both in Italy and America to make a profit handling immigrants' currency. As an adjunct to this business they ran boardinghouses for immigrants, arranged for transportation, and served as hiring places. Charlotte Erikson, *American Industry and European Immigration* (Cambridge, 1967), pp. 84–85.

5. A special compilation of mortality statistics for one block in the Bend for the years 1880–1883 appeared in New York State, Tenement House Commission, *Report*, Senate Document 36, February 17, 1885, Appendix E, pp. 232–235.

6. The "island" is Blackwell's Island in the East River, where the city maintained in these years two almshouses, one for men and one for women, a correctional workhouse, a large charity hospital, a smallpox hospital, an asylum for the blind, a lunatic asylum, hospitals for paralytics and incurables, and a penitentiary. Martha J. Lamb and Mrs. Burton Harrison, *History of the City of New York: Its Origin, Rise, and Progress* (New York, 1877–1880), III, 737.

VII. A Raid on the Stale-Beer Dives

1. "Revolver" was a contemporary slang term for one who serves many sentences in the course of his life, a recidivist. The first date given for the term is 1888. See Eric Partridge, *A Dictionary of the Underworld, British and American* (London, 1949).

VIII. The Cheap Lodging Houses

1. Thomas Byrnes was Chief Inspector of Police in New York City when he wrote the article referred to in the text, "Nurseries of Crime," *North American Review,* 149 (September 1889), 355–362. He also wrote *Professional Criminals of America* (New York, 1886; reprint ed., Arthur M. Schlesinger, Jr., and S. J. Perelman, New York, 1969).

2. A picture of Edward Mulhearn and his burned arm appeared in Society for the Prevention of Cruelty to Children, New York, *Fifteenth Annual Report,* Case no. 41,287, April 6, 1889 (New York, 1890), pp. 27–29.

IX. Chinatown

1. "Joss" was a Javanese term for a Chinese idol or image of a deity; the "Joss House" of this chapter is thus a Chinese temple.

X. Jewtown

1. The term "Hebrew" in the late nineteenth century had significance as a term of gentility. More specifically, it was preferred by old American Jewish families to indicate their place as Americans of Hebrew faith. The term thus distinguished them from the new immigrant Jews just then arriving in large numbers from eastern Europe. Riis seems to observe this distinction by naming the Lower East Side immigrant quarter "Jewtown," the ghetto of the new immigrants, but sometimes he uses the terms

"Hebrew" and "Jew" as synonyms. See Moses Rischin, *The Promised City: New York's Jews 1870–1914* (Cambridge, Mass., 1962), p. 263.

XI. The Sweaters of Jewtown

1. Charles Booth, ed., *Labour and Life of the People* (London, 1889–1891), vol. III, contains a parallel study of Jewish garment trades and the "sweating system" written by Beatrice Potter (Mrs. Sidney Webb). The same high density, great energy, minute division of the work, and triumph of the small family workroom appeared in London. The big difference between the two cities seems to have been the relatively greater importance of provincial mechanized factories in the English clothing trade as opposed to the sweeping triumph of the small urban operators in the United States. Booth, *Labour and Life*, I, 209–240. Miss Potter concludes her discussion as follows: "The real 'sweater' therefore, has a threefold personality—an ignorant consumer, a grinding and fraudulent wholesale or retail slop trader, a rack-renting landlord; in some instances we might add a driving labor contractor. This is the body of the sweater; the soul is the spirit of the age, unrestrained competition." Booth, *Labour and Life*, I, 238.

In the same study the editor, Charles Booth, wrote a brief comparison of tailoring elsewhere in London as compared to the East End. *Labour and Life*, II, 305–321. High-priced work was controlled by small craft shops where work was only slightly subdivided and was still referred to as "bespoke work." Booth correctly identified the onrush of the sweating system as a return to the old "outwork" system of home manufacturing common during the eighteenth and preceding centuries.

2. The "battle between East Broadway and Broadway" was a battle between old established German tailoring shops on Broadway and the newer east European Jewish home workshops of the Lower East Side. The battle is chronicled in Abraham Cahan, *The Rise of David Levinsky* (New York, 1917).

3. Baron Maurice de Hirsch (1831–1896) was an Austrian investment banker and railway builder who devoted an enormous fortune to relief of eastern European Jews. With the enforcement of the May Laws of 1881 against Russian Jews Hirsch gave special attention to refugee and emigrant aid. In 1891 he regularized his American charity by establishing a New York corporation, the Baron de Hirsch Fund, with a capital of $2,400,000.

XIII. The Color Line in New York

1. In the original edition of *How the Other Half Lives*, Negro was spelled throughout with a small *n* according to the custom of Riis's day. It has been capitalized in this John Harvard Library edition as part of the modern custom which became general in the nineteen thirties. Richard B. Moore, *The Name "Negro": Its Origin and Evil Use* (New York, 1960).

2. Riis was writing at the opening of the decade of the migration of Negroes in New York City to Harlem, their first opportunity to occupy new housing. In 1889 the center of Negro settlement lay in the west fifties and sixties. Gilbert Osofsky, *Harlem: The Making of a Ghetto: Negro New York 1890–1930* (New York, 1963), pp. 11–16.

3. The material on Negro housing and the table on white and colored tenants in this chapter were taken from "Something About Our Colored Population: Do They Make Good Tenants?" *Real Estate Record and Builders' Guide*, 43 (January 26, 1889), 106–107.

XIV. The Common Herd

1. Hell's Kitchen covers roughly the area on the West Side of Manhattan from Ninth Avenue to the Hudson River, Thirtieth Street to Forty-first Street. "Its name, originally applied to a dive near Corlears Hook on the East Side, came from the Hell's Kitchen Gang, organized about 1868 by Dutch Heinrichs. The Gang specialized in raids on the Thirtieth Street yards of the Hudson River Railroad (now the Penn Central); its original repertoire included extortion, breaking and entering, professional mayhem, and highway robbery." Other gangs rose out of the original grouping and the district was terrorized until 1910, when New York Central Railroad police launched a violent counterwar of unremitting clubbing, shooting, and arresting the railroad's opponents. Works Progress Administration, *New York City Guide* (New York, 1946), pp. 155–156.

2. The list of causes of poverty in New York City went as follows: (1) intemperance the cause of distress or distress the cause of intemperance, 40 percent; (2) early and improvident marriages, 20 percent; (3) dependence and slothfulness, 20 percent; (4) worthy but in want fortuitously, 20 percent. N.Y.A.I.C.P., *Forty-sixth Annual Report, 1889* (New York, 1889), p. 27.

Charles Booth's contemporary analysis of the causes of poverty in the poorest classes of his 4,000 cases in east London listed the following categories and proportions of misfortune: loafers, 4 percent; problems of employment, 55 percent; intemperance, thriftlessness, and "questions of habit," 14 percent; illness, large families, "questions of circumstance," 27 percent. *Labour and Life,* I, 147.

3. All American cities during the nineteenth century suffered from dishonest elections, and Richard Croker, Democratic boss of New York from 1886 to 1901, stands accused of every irregularity. The particular fraud Riis is referring to in the text is the common practice of using paid repeaters who voted many times on election day. By first registering the names of dead persons on the election rolls politicians could later hire repeaters to go from poll to poll using such names. Morris R. Werner, *Tammany Hall* (New York, 1928), chap. 6.

XV. The Problem of the Children

1. The Children's Aid Society was founded in February 1853 to combat juvenile delinquency. Charles Loring Brace (1826–1890) was its first secretary and guiding spirit. Its early program consisted of a newsboy's lodging house and a few industrial schools which gave meals to the children, taught shoemaking to the boys, and straw-binding and sewing to the girls. By 1889 the Society had forty-four institutions scattered over Manhattan Island: twenty-one industrial schools, seven lodging houses, twelve night schools, and four summer homes. Children's Aid Society, *First Annual Report* (New York, 1854), pp. 7–13. Riis made extensive use of the Society's *Thirty-Seventh Annual Report* (New York, 1889).

2. To provide protection for foundlings and infants, an age group not reached by the Children's Aid Society, philanthropists formed a new society, the New York Society for the Prevention of Cruelty to Children, on April 24, 1875. Riis here quotes from its *Fifteenth Annual Report* (New York, 1890), p. 5.

XVI. Waifs of the City's Slums

1. Society for the Prevention of Cruelty to Children, New York, *Tenth Annual Report* (New York, 1885), p. 10.

2. In 1850 the New York Ladies' Methodist (Episcopal) Home Missionary Society established a mission at 61 Park Street at the Five Points under the management of Rev. Lewis M. Pease. Three years later the group purchased a farm in East Chester to be run as a school. *The Guide to the Charities of New York and Brooklyn* (New York, 1886), p. 85, reported that the

Society "educates and maintains missionaries to labor among the poor, and poor children receive education, clothes and food. Families accommodated last year seventeen. Three hundred and fifty children attended mission school during some time."

3. In 1854 Rev. Lewis M. Pease and a group of gentlemen associated with the Five Points Mission established the House of Industry; the building was completed at 155–159 Worth Street in the spring of 1856. The House contained a dormitory for the destitute, a common dining room, a chapel, and a school for children. The farm at East Chester supplied milk and vegetables, and the House sent its invalids to the farm. In the early years the House made a specialty of seeking country jobs for its residents. Five Points House of Industry, *Second Annual Report* (New York, 1856), pp. 1–9. According to *The Guide to the Charities* (1886), p. 85, the House "protects, instructs and provides for destitute people; supports neglected and abandoned children, and others incapable of self-support. 721 cases cared for last year." The institution is still alive and now manages a group of schools for homeless and for retarded children in Rockland County, New York.

XVII. The Street Arab

1. Mrs. John Jacob (Charlotte Gibbes) Astor (1825–1887) was the leading patron of the Children's Aid Society. *New York Times,* December 13, 16, 1887.

2. The architect Richard Tylden Auchmuty (1831–1893), former partner of James Renwick and colonel in the Civil War, founded the New York Trade Schools in 1881. The purpose of these schools was to supplant the apprentice system of the New York building trades with school training so that poor and immigrant boys could break into these crafts despite the policy of the unions to keep down the number of skilled artisans.

XVIII. The Reign of Rum

1. The corrupt New York Board of Aldermen during the Tweed Ring days, 1866–1871.

XIX. The Harvest of Tares

1. Rev. Frederick H. Wines (1838–1912) was a Presbyterian minister who served as secretary of the Illinois State Board of Public Charities from 1869 to 1892 and from 1896 to 1898. Over these years he became an expert penologist and was special adviser in the preparation of the U.S. Tenth

Census volume of the *Defective, Dependent and Delinquent Classes,* which Riis cites.

2. Corlears Hook on the East River, just south of the foot of Grand Street.

XX. The Working Girls of New York

1. "The Song of the Shirt" was written in 1843 by the popular English poet Thomas Hood (1799–1845).

2. The Working Women's Society of New York was organized in 1888 by a group of philanthropists to promote the unionization of women workers in manufacturing and retailing, to protect women and children from exploitation by employers, and to abolish tenement manufacturing shops. The report referred to here must be of an 1889 investigation, which led to the founding of the New York Consumers' League. This was a related organization which encouraged customers to shop only at stores where employees were treated according to the League's standards. Working Women's Society, *Annual Report, 1892* (New York, 1893). This report is in the collection of the New York Public Library.

3. These Girls' Homes were inexpensive room and board establishments run by churches and philanthropists. At the time Riis was writing, Manhattan had about a dozen such homes. U.S., Commissioner of Labor, *Working Women in Large Cities, Fourth Annual Report, 1888* (Washington, 1889), pp. 44–51.

4. In March 1890 the men of the Shirtmaker's Union and about 1,500 unorganized women workers in the trade went on strike for a ten-hour day and regular weekly wages. The strike and some of the testimony before the State Board of Arbitration was reported in the *New York Times,* March 13, 15, 19, 20, 1890.

5. Thomas Hood, "The Song of the Shirt":

O men with sisters dear!
  O men with mothers and wives!
It is not linen you're wearing out,
  But human creatures' lives!
  Stitch—stitch—stitch,
  In poverty, hunger and dirt,—
Sewing at once, with a double thread,
  A shroud as well as a shirt!

XXI. Pauperism in the Tenements

1. Riis appears to be drawing his statistics from the Central Council of the Charity Organization Society of the City of New York, *Eighth Annual Report* (New York, 1890), pp. 41, 89. His total number of cases and percentage distribution by categories of need are, however, not exactly the same as those in the report. I am at a loss to account for the discrepancy and can only guess that Riis perhaps had access to some unpublished totals. His interpretation in no way distorts their presentation.

2. 2 Thessalonians 3:10.

3. Elbridge T. Gerry had been President of the Society for the Prevention of Cruelty to Children since 1879, and his group took a particular interest in the exploitation of children for begging. For example, it secured the arrest and conviction of Antonio Giovanni Ancarola for importing seven children aged nine through thirteen, all of whom had been sold to him by their Italian parents. Society for the Prevention of Cruelty to Children, New York, *Fifth Annual Report* (New York, 1879), pp. 67–78; *idem, Sixth Annual Report* (New York, 1880), pp. 69–70.

XXII. The Wrecks and the Waste

1. The paper from which Riis quotes appeared in *Science, 7* (September 24, 1886), 283–290. In addition to the passage on the corruption of the political machine, which creates the destructive environment of the slum, Dr. Seaman makes a number of other statements that seem to have been appropriated by Riis indirectly. On the overwork of women and children: "When capital and commerce grow humane, and become as considerate of human hearts and lives as they are of machinery, vehicles, horses, and other useful appliances of machinery and honest increase, then, and not sooner, will this diabolical waste of womanhood be checked and stayed." On tramps, the insane, and criminals: "This discouraged, cowed, broken-down class is likely to increase under a civilization which develops millionaires and monopolies out of the feebleness and misfortunes of the masses. Strange illustrations of this soulless work of disintegration may be found any and every day in hospital, penitentiary, almshouse, insane asylum, or morgue."

2. Statistics from New York City, Department of Public Charities and Correction, *Thirtieth Annual Report, 1889* (New York, 1892).

XXIII. The Man with the Knife

1. Charles Loring Brace, *The Dangerous Classes of New York, and Twenty Years' Work Among Them* (New York, 1872).

2. Alfred T. White, *Improved Dwellings for the Working Classes: The Need, and the Way to Meet It on Strict Commercial Principles, in New York and Other Cities* (New York, 1879), p. 44.

XXIV. What Has Been Done

1. The "Big Flat" was one of the classic structures of New York charity literature. The long five-story barracks ran from 96–98 Mott Street to 47–49 Elizabeth Street. It was originally built in 1855 by Robert M. Hartley of the New York Association for Improving the Condition of the Poor as a model tenement. The building operated at a loss, decayed from ill-treatment, and was sold to the Five Points House of Industry, who remodeled it and managed it for a few years as a lodging house for women. Financial failure again forced sale, and from 1872 to 1889, when it was torn down, it was operated as slum property. New York Association for Improving the Condition of the Poor, *Forty-third Annual Report, 1886* (New York, 1886), pp. 43–58; Robert Bremner, "The Big Flat," *American Historical Review,* 64 (October 1958), 54–55.

2. Gotham Court was another classic slum structure of New York charity and reform literature. Located at 36–38 Cherry Street, it was well described in Citizens' Association of New York, *Report of the Council of Hygiene and Public Health upon the Sanitary Condition of the City* (New York, 1865), pp. 49–55; *Harper's Weekly,* 23 (March 29, 1879), 246.

3. I have been unable to find in the published reports the precise statistics Riis presents here. I did find similar magnitudes, however, and for that reason see no reason why the reader may not rely on Riis's figures, which were probably prepared by his friend Dr. Roger S. Tracy from unpublished tabulations of the Board of Health.

Approximations can be found in New York State, Metropolitan Board of Health, *Fourth Annual Report, 1869* (New York, 1870), pp. 9, 67–139, 329–353. The records of the New York Public Library indicate that during the years 1876–1880 the New York City Board of Health did not publish its annual report, only its *Vital Statistics,* which gives little information on tenements. New York City, Board of Health, *Vital Statistics, 1879* (New York, 1880), pp. 174–190. According to a new statute passed in 1887 the

Board of Health was to make a semiannual survey of all tenement houses in New York City, but the statistics of 1888–1890 were not published. New York City, Board of Health, *Annual Report, 1892* (New York, 1894), pp. 56–58.

4. The text of the report shows an excellent understanding of the constraints under which the New York housing market operated. "The enormous value of the tenement house property of this city—probably $200,000,000—the high taxes, and the depressed condition of business, compel the Board to make haste slowly in urging radical and expensive changes in the construction of the tenement houses, and it is doubtful whether the majority of the existing houses, built upon city lots, 25 feet by 100 feet, can be essentially modified to their plan. It is hoped that improved blocks of tenant houses will be constructed on new systems, affording more air and space to each occupant. The most important improvement in the condition of this population will result from dispersion over a wider area, which can, however, only come after rapid transit and cheap trains shall have been established in the upper wards beyond the Harlem River." New York City, Board of Health, *Fifth and Sixth Annual Reports, 1874–1875* (New York, 1876), p. 7.

5. The Tenement House Commission of 1884 hired a number of inspectors to survey about one thousand tenements in New York City, which they did during July 1884. In their canvass the inspectors rated the building, its plumbing, and its tenants. "It will be noticed that in the first of the above tables, the numbers in the 'tenant' column are higher than those under 'building' except for 'bad' cases, which the second table gives a difference of about 450 points in favor of the tenants. This seems to show that the condition of the tenants is slightly in advance of the buildings in which they live, and is against the statement frequently made that the dirty habits of the laboring classes made it impossible to give them decent accommodations and, therefore, reform must begin with them and not with the buildings." *Report of the Tenement House Commission of the State of New York,* Senate Document 36, February 17, 1885, pp. 33–34.

6. The Neighborhood Guild was the nation's first settlement house, founded in 1886 by Stanton Coit in rented rooms at 146 Forsyth Street. The College Settlement was founded and supported by graduates of Bryn Mawr, Smith, Vassar, and Wellesley Colleges. It opened in 1889 at 95 Rivington Street. Robert A. Woods and Albert J. Kennedy, *The Settlement Horizon: A National Estimate* (New York, 1922), pp. 40–52.

XXV. How the Case Stands

1. Riis, the New York Health Department officers, and the members of the many tenement house commissions appointed by the legislature were all aware of European, especially English, reforms. The "drastic measures" mentioned here probably referred to the sanitary legislation and condemnation powers of European municipalities, which far exceeded the slow and restricted common law nuisance powers of New York. The 1884 Tenement House Commission explicitly cited English sanitary legislation and concluded, "The commission alludes to this foreign legislation, not for the purpose of expressing an opinion as to the wisdom of the same, but to call the attention of the Legislature to the fact that there is much to be learned upon this subject from the experience of other countries, especially in regard to the problem of how to deal with rear tenements and other houses which are too closely crowded together in the poorer quarters of large cities. . . ." New York State, Tenement House Commission, *Report,* Senate Document 36, February 17, 1885, pp. 4–5. In 1890 British municipalities were authorized to start constructing public housing projects. U.S., Commissioner of Labor, *The Housing of the Working People, Eighth Special Report* (Washington, 1895), pp. 23–68.

2. In 1880 Miss Collins purchased two old tenement structures at 112½–114 Roosevelt Street at the corner of Water Street to carry out an experiment in renovation and tenement management according to the principles of the British reformer Octavia Hill. Miss Collins' project is described in N.Y.A.I.C.P., *Fortieth Annual Report, 1883* (New York, 1883), pp. 31–34.

3. The Improved Dwellings Association was New York's first limited-dividend, model tenement company in New York. It was organized in 1879 as a result of agitation by the State Charities Aid Association and opened its first building in 1882 on First Avenue between Seventy-first and Seventy-second Street. The Tenement House Building Company was a similar organization established in 1885. Its first building was erected in 1887 at 338–344 Cherry Street. James Ford, *Slums and Housing* (Cambridge, Mass., 1936), I, 175–178; II, 882–883.

4. *The Plumber and Sanitary Engineer,* 2 (March 1879), 90. This trade journal ran an architectural competition during the winter 1878–1879, hoping to improve the quality of cheap tenement design in New York City. All designs were constrained to use the standard lot of 25 × 100 feet, despite

the famous statement by the jury, which Riis quotes in the text, that such limits prevented decent multiple family housing. Despite the jury's recognition of the effect of narrow grid subdivision of lots upon housing it went on to award a prize for a cramped air shaft design, "the dumbell tenement," which later became the mass production tenement of New York until it was outlawed by 1901 legislation. The contest and the evolution of tenement design are well treated in Roy Lubove, *The Progressives and the Slums: Tenement Reform in New York City 1890–1917* (Pittsburgh, 1962), pp. 28–32; and in Ford, *Slums and Housing*, II, 872–873, 880–881, 907–911; Plates III, VI.

5. A convenient source for a full account of the management, plans, and occupancy of Alfred T. White's Riverside buildings is U.S., Commissioner of Labor, *Housing of the Working People*, pp. 177–186.

6. Sir Sydney H. Waterlow (1822–1906) was a wealthy printer in London who interested himself in philanthropic housing. He founded the Improved Dwellings Company in 1863, a limited-dividend housing corporation, which by the time of Riis's writing housed about 3,000 families in its various London buildings.

Selected Bibliography

Alland, Alexander, Sr. *Jacob A. Riis, Photographer & Citizen*. Millerton, N.Y.: Aperture Books, 1974.

———. "The Battle with the Slum, 1887–1897: The Early Documentary Photography of Jacob A. Riis." In *U.S. Camera*, 11–18, 345–346. New York: U.S. Camera Publishers, 1948.

Aubert, Didier. "The Graphic Sphere: Images and Civic Conscience in the Progressive Era." Paper presented at "Public Spheres and American Cultures" Conference, Brown University, Providence, R.I., June 4–6, 2004. http://unjobs.org/authors/didier-aubert.

Bodnar, John. *The Transplanted: A History of Immigrants in Urban America*. Bloomington: Indiana University Press, 1985.

Boyer, Paul. *Urban Masses and Moral Order in America, 1829–1920*. Cambridge, Mass.: Harvard University Press, 1978.

Brace, Charles Loring. *The Dangerous Classes of New York, and Twenty Years' Work among Them*. New York: Wyncoop & Hallenbeck, 1872.

Bremer, Robert. *The Discovery of Poverty in the United States*. New York: New York University Press, 1956.

Brown, Joshua. *Beyond the Lines: Pictorial Reporting, Everyday Life, and the*

Crisis of Gilded Age America. Berkeley: University of California Press, 2002.

Buk-Swienty, Tom. *The Other Half: The Life of Jacob Riis and the World of Immigrant America.* New York: W. W. Norton and Co., 2008.

Campbell, Helen. *Darkness and Daylight; or, Lights and Shadows of New York Life.* Hartford, Conn.: A.D. Worthington & Co., 1891.

Crane, Stephen. *Bowery Tales.* Charlottesville, Va.: University of Virginia Press, 1969.

Diner, Hasia R., Jeffrey Schandler, and Beth S. Wenger, eds. *Remembering the Lower East Side: American Jewish Reflections.* Bloomington: Indiana University Press, 2000.

Fried, Lewis. *Makers of the City.* Amherst, Mass.: University of Massachusetts Press, 1990.

Fried, Lewis, and John Fierst. *Jacob A. Riis: A Reference Guide.* Boston: G. K. Hall & Co., 1977.

Gandal, Keith. *The Virtues of the Vicious: Jacob Riis, Stephen Crane, and the Spectacle of the Slum.* New York: Oxford University Press, 1997.

Hales, Peter Bacon. *Silver Cities: The Photography of American Urbanization, 1839–1915.* Philadelphia: Temple University Press, 1984.

Hapgood, Hutchins. *The Spirit of the Ghetto.* Cambridge, Mass.: Harvard University Press, 1967.

Harris, Neil. "Iconography and Intellectual History: The Half-Tone Effect." In *New Directions in American Intellectual History,* edited by John Higham and Paul K. Conkin, 181–195. Baltimore: Johns Hopkins University Press, 1979.

Higham, John. "The Reorientation of American Culture in the 1890s." In *The Origins of Modern Consciousness,* edited by John Weiss, 25–48. Detroit: Wayne State University Press, 1965.

———. *Send These to Me: Immigrants in Urban America.* Baltimore: Johns Hopkins University Press, 1975.

———. *Strangers in the Land: Patterns of American Nativism, 1860–1925.* New York: Atheneum, 1977.

Jones, Gavin. *American Hungers: The Problem of Poverty in U.S. Literature, 1840–1945.* Princeton, N.J.: Princeton University Press, 2008.

Lane, James B. *Jacob A. Riis and the American City.* Port Washington, N.Y.: Kennikat Press, 1974.

Leviatin, David. "Framing the Poor: The Irresistibility of *How the Other Half*

Lives." In *How the Other Half Lives*, by Jacob Riis. Boston: Bedford/St. Martins, 1996.

Lubove, Roy. *The Progressives and the Slums*. Pittsburgh: University of Pittsburgh Press, 1962.

Meyer, Edith Patterson. *"Not Charity but Justice": The Story of Jacob Riis*. New York: Vanguard Press, 1974.

O'Donnell, Edward T. "Pictures vs. Words? Public History, Tolerance, and the Challenge of Jacob Riis." *The Public Historian* 26, no. 3 (Summer 2004): 7–26.

Park, Robert E. "The Natural History of the Newspaper." In *The City*, by Robert E. Park and Ernest W. Burgess, 80–98. Chicago: University of Chicago Press, 1967.

Riis, Jacob. *How the Other Half Lives: Studies Among the Tenements of New York*. New York: Charles Scribner's Sons, 1890.

———. *Children of the Poor*. New York: Charles Scribner's Sons, 1892.

———. *The Making of an American*. New York: The Macmillan Company, 1901.

———. *The Battle with the Slum*. New York: The Macmillan Company, 1902.

Rischin, Moses. *The Promised City: New York's Jews, 1870–1914*. Cambridge, Mass.: Harvard University Press, 1962.

Sante, Luc. Introduction to *How the Other Half Lives*, by Jacob Riis. East Rutherford, N.J.: Viking Penguin, 1997.

Schocket, Eric. "Undercover Explorations of the 'Other Half,' Or the Writer as Class Transvestite." *Representations* 64 (Fall 1998): 109–133.

Schoener, Allon. *Portal to America: The Lower East Side, 1870–1925*. New York: Holt, Rinehart and Winston, 1967.

Schudson, Michael. *Discovering the News: A Social History of American Newspapers*. New York: Basic Books, Inc., 1978.

Scobey, David M. *Empire City: The Making and Meaning of the New York City Landscape*. Philadelphia: Temple University Press, 2002.

Stange, Maren. *Symbols of Ideal Life: Social Documentary Photography in America, 1890–1950*. New York: Cambridge University Press, 1989.

Steffens, Lincoln. *The Autobiography of Lincoln Steffens*. New York: The Literary Guild, 1931.

Stein, Sally. "Making Connections with the Camera: Photography and Social Mobility in the Career of Jacob Riis." *Afterimage* 10, no. 10 (May 1983): 9–16.

Szasz, Ferenc M., and Ralph F. Bogardus. "The Camera and the American Social Conscience: The Documentary Photography of Jacob A. Riis." *New York History* 55, no. 4 (October 1974): 409–436.

Trachtenberg, Alan. *The Incorporation of America: Culture & Society in the Gilded Age.* New York: Hill & Wang, 1982.

———. *Reading American Photographs: Images as History, Mathew Brady to Walker Evans.* New York: Hill & Wang, 1989.

———. "Experiments in Another Country: Stephen Crane's City Sketches," *Southern Review* 10 (April 1974): 265–285.

Ware, Louise. *Jacob A. Riis: Police Reporter, Reformer, Useful Citizen.* New York: D. Appleton-Century Co., 1938.

Warner, Sam Bass, Jr. Editor's Introduction to *How the Other Half Lives,* by Jacob Riis. Cambridge, Mass.: Harvard University Press, 1970.

Woods, Robert A. *The Poor in the Great Cities: Their Problems and What Is Being Done to Solve Them.* New York: Charles Scribner's Sons, 1895.

Yochelson, Bonnie, and Daniel Czitrom. *Rediscovering Jacob Riis: Exposure Journalism and Photography in Turn-of-the-Century New York.* New York: The New Press, 2007.

Illustration Credits

Index